DATE DUE

FEB 21 '89	
MAY 1 7 1991	
JAN 2 1992	
MAR 2 8 1996	
FEB 22 1998	

BRODART, INC.   Cat. No. 23-221

WILDERNESS MANHUNT

The Spanish Search for La Salle

WILDERNESS MANHUNT

The Spanish Search for La Salle

ROBERT S. WEDDLE

UNIVERSITY OF TEXAS PRESS, AUSTIN & LONDON

Library of Congress Cataloging in Publication Data

Weddle, Robert S
  Wilderness manhunt.

  Bibliography: p.
  1. Mississippi Valley–Discovery and exploration.
2. La Salle, Robert Cavelier, sieur de, 1643-1687.
3. Spaniards in North America.   4. French in the
United States.   5. Texas–History–To 1846.
I.   Title.
F352.W42   973.1'6   72-1579
ISBN O-292-79000-7

For Nan Avis, with love

CONTENTS

ILLUSTRATIONS

PREFACE

In the sixteenth century the minions of Spain performed in the New World deeds of daring still unsurpassed in the history of the continent. From the keys of Florida to the Pacific shore Spain's stalwart soliders marched in exploration of the new land—which offered so many challenges, and so many hazards—seeking new soil in which to plant the seeds of Spanish civilization. From Cape Breton, Nova Scotia, to Cape Horn her navigators probed the shoreline of the two American continents.

As early as 1513 Juan Ponce de León coasted Florida with his three wooden vessels and on his way back to Española discovered the Bahama Channel, later to become the route of homeward-bound Spanish treasure ships. By 1519 the entire gulf coast between Florida and Yucatán had been explored and charted.

Chief among the explorers of the gulf coast was Alonso Alvarez de Pineda, who mapped the shoreline from Florida to Veracruz and gave the name Amichel to the portion between Apalachee Bay and Tampico—the precise region on which was focused the Spanish search for La Salle 165 years later. Pineda, on this voyage, discovered the mouth of the large river that emptied into the gulf—the Mississippi—and to it he gave the name Río del Espíritu Santo. It was a name that the Spaniards of a later year found confusing, because in the interim it had been applied to other rivers and bays. And the river it represented, in all her wiles, confounded these explorers no end, for they found her most elusive. The settlement that was supposed to be at her mouth was not there. In their perplexity they applied a different name to this river and assigned the name Espíritu Santo to still another.

From the coastline examined by Pineda, Spanish adelantados moved inland: Ponce de León, exploring "the island of Florida"; Alvar Núñez Cabeza de Vaca, a castaway of the ill-fated expedition of Pánfilo de Narváez, wandering through the wilderness from the Texas coast to the Pacific; Hernando de Soto and Luis de Moscoso, trudging through ten southern states in a stirring odyssey of suffering and death before finally reaching the mouth of the Río Pánuco. There were missionaries, too, like Fray Luis Cancér, martyred on the Florida shore in 1547; and settlers, like Tristán de Luna y Arellano, attempting to found a colony at Pensacola, and Pedro Menéndez de Avilés, mercilessly driving out the French to establish the first real European foothold on the North American continent outside Mexico, at St. Augustine.

But the fearless efforts of these frontrunners were voided when Spain, with the defeat of her armada by the English in 1588, lost her bid for mastery of the seas. The way was opened for the English to found colonies where Spain had failed. In fending off this encroachment, which came from the north, the Spanish settlers in Florida were forced to neglect the region to the west.

Despite the bold efforts of the adelantados, not a single Spanish settlement was to be found a century later in the area west of the Presidio of San Luis de Apalache (Tallahassee). Indeed the region was all but forgotten, the routes and maps of the early expeditions lost to memory. When in September, 1685, the Spaniards learned that a noted French explorer was forming a settlement at the mouth of a big river somewhere on the coast of Amichel, this long neglect jumped into sharp focus. The Spaniards theorized that the invaders had landed at the river referred to in earlier accounts as "Espíritu Santo," but no one could definitely fix its location. The only certain knowledge was that it lay somewhere between Apalache and Tampico, and that the colony must be found and extirpated.

So, after a lapse of well over a century, the Spaniards set out anew to "discover" the Río del Espíritu Santo and to reexplore the coastline and inland territory reconnoitered by Pineda, Cabeza de Vaca, De Soto, and Moscoso. The ensuing five maritime and six land expeditions in search of La Salle's Fort St. Louis were followed by other *entradas* to form lasting settlements.

Besides La Salle's decisive role in history otherwise, he proved a catalyst to Spanish activity in the New World. Because of his daring penetration to the coast of Spanish-claimed Texas, new expeditions examined the coastline from the top of Florida to

Tampico; land forces marched from Florida across Alabama, and from Mexico into Texas; new settlements were formed in Texas and Florida. Much of the southern area and nearly all the southwestern part of the United States were marked indelibly with the Spanish stamp.

While much attention has been devoted to La Salle's last expedition and its tragic outcome for the French colonists, the episode has seldom been approached from the viewpoint of the Spaniards. Largely overlooked also has been the part that survivors of the French colony played in later historic events in the New World, notably, the role of two of the Talon brothers in the famed St. Denis expedition of 1714. If this book suggests to some competent scholar further study of the interrelationship of such events as the thrusts of La Salle and Louis Juchereau de St. Denis, it will have fulfilled its purpose.

Robert S. Weddle
Austin, Texas

Abbreviations Used in the Notes

A.G.I., México: Archivo General de Indias,
Audiencia de México, 1685-1688, Dunn Transcripts,
University of Texas Archives, Austin
A.G.I., Guadalajara: Archivo General de Indias,
Audiencia de Guadalajara, 1683-1687, Dunn
Transcripts, University of Texas Archives,
Austin

ACKNOWLEDGMENTS

The idea for this book first came to me in 1967, during a conversation with Charles Ramsdell. It grew in discussions with Dr. Chester V. Kielman of the Barker Texas History Center, University of Texas Library, who has given moral support and tangible assistance throughout the project.

In contemplation of William Edward Dunn's *Spanish and French Rivalry in the Gulf Region of the United States, 1678-1702*, the idea almost died. The fact that it did not is due in part to correspondence with Dr. Dunn's widow, Mrs. Linda T. Dunn of Dallas, who provided material that served as further stimulus. My purpose has not been to redo *Spanish and French Rivalry*, which has a scope and emphasis all its own. Yet it proved an invaluable stepping stone, for which I am duely appreciative.

Of inestimable value in carrying out the project were the transcripts of Spanish documents (the Dunn Transcripts) that Dr. Dunn collected from the Archivo General de Indias for the University of Texas Library. It is a magnificent collection; without it this work would not have been possible.

Material, ideas, and encouragement for this study have come from many sources. For such support I am indebted to E. H. Swaim of Eden, Texas; Mrs. Robert Gilmore of Dallas; the Reverend Father Lino Gómez Canedo of the Academy of American Franciscan History, Washington, D.C.; Dr. Joseph W. McKnight of Dallas; Mrs. Aline H. Morris and Miss Rose Lambert of the Louisiana State Museum Library, New Orleans; John Barr Tomkins of the Bancroft Library, University of California, Berkeley; Miss Marsha Jackson of the Texas State Historical Survey Committee research staff, Austin; Mrs. J. B. Golden and Mrs. Linda McWhorter of the Texas State Library, Austin; Dr. Llerena B. Friend, Dr. Nettie Lee Benson, Kent Keeth, and J. C. Martin, all of the University of Texas Library, Austin; and Dr. Donald C. Cutter, professor of history, University of New Mexico, Albuquerque.

I am especially grateful for permission to use the maps from the J. P. Bryan Collection in the University of Texas Library (copies from originals in the Archivo General de Indias, Seville), and to John Keeran of Inez, Texas, for allowing me on his ranch to view the site of Fort St. Louis.

WILDERNESS MANHUNT

The Spanish Search for La Salle

1. THORN IN AMERICA'S HEART

Having made this discovery, the said Monsieur de Salaz returned to France, and his King granted him people. He came bringing ships and supplies for fortifying that place, with zeal for making new discoveries ... which news should not be ignored, it being so injurious to the communication of all the ports of America, and commerce of all galleons and fleets ...

—Pedro de la Bastida
"Repuesta del Señor Fiscal," p. 19

It was an ill wind that bore La Salle's small fleet from the port of La Rochelle on July 24, 1684. Aboard the 36-gun principal vessel, *Le Joly*, the air was charged with mutual mistrust and rancor between the noted explorer and the captain, Sieur de Beaujeu of the Royal French Navy. Each resented what he considered to be the excessive authority of the other. La Salle indulged in exasperating pettiness; Beaujeu responded in temper. The seeds of disaster were sown, even, before the four vessels were out of the harbor.

René Robert Cavelier, Sieur de la Salle, stood proudly on his record of achievement in the New World. He personally had traversed the length of the Mississippi, laying claim to its extensive valley for King Louis XIV. Now on his way to plant a colony at the great river's mouth—which could well prove to be the key to the conquest of a continent—he nurtured natural fears that word of his venture would leak to the Spaniards. He revealed his intended destination to Beaujeu only after they were well at sea. The captain, himself a prideful man, viewed darkly this evident lack of trust in his loyalty and judgment.

When the captain expressed the wish to put in at Madeira to

take on water, La Salle refused, lest loose talk in port betray the mission. They sailed on, the two leaders chafing constantly at each other, the *Joly* traveling twice the necessary distance as she took wide tacks to enable the other three vessels to keep pace. *L'Aimable*, *La Belle*, and the *St. François*, heavily laden with supplies, moved at reduced speed, a circumstance for which Beaujeu blamed La Salle.

As the fleet reached Santo Domingo, after a miserable two-month voyage, the problems multipled. Beaujeu, ignoring La Salle's wishes, sailed past Port-de-Paix in the night to anchor at Petit Goâve, on the opposite side of the island. In so doing he left the other three vessels behind. When the *Aimable* and the *Belle* arrived, they brought news that the *St. François* had been captured by Spanish privateers. Irreplaceable provisions and tools for building the colony were lost.

La Salle himself was desperately ill. He and fifty ailing men from the *Joly* were taken ashore to recuperate in more comfortable quarters. But the explorer's malady persisted, "as dangerous," in Beaujeu's words, "to the mind as to the body." While La Salle lay in feverish delirium, a party of Beaujeu's sailors spent the night in drunken revelry at a tavern adjacent to his quarters. Pleas of his attendants—including his brother, the Abbé Cavelier—only inspired the seafaring men to greater noise. "La Salle lost reason and well-nigh life, but at length his mind resumed its balance and the violence of the disease abated."[1] But then he had to be told of the loss of the *St. François*. His ailment returned full force.

While La Salle lay near insanity if not death, Beaujeu wrote complaining letters to France; Beaujeu's sailors and La Salle's soldiers consorted with buccaneers and bad women. From the latter many contracted diseases that eventually would kill them. Some deserted to the pirates, who painted such a sordid picture of the land for which the voyagers were bound that they completely lost heart for the enterprise. It was these deserters at Santo Domingo who eventually would take the news of La Salle's colonizing venture to those whom the leader feared most—the Spaniards, upon whose pretended realm he was about to encroach. The dread of these colonial rivals of the French sprang from the knowledge that

[1] Francis Parkman, *La Salle and the Discovery of the Great West*, p. 269.

they would view his project as did he himself: as a base from which he could strike by land at the northern provinces of Mexico, or by sea at the entire Mexican gulf coast and vital Spanish shipping.

At the end of November the voyage was resumed. At last the three French vessels passed through the Yucatán Channel and entered the Gulf of Mexico, a forbidden sea from which all foreigners were excluded by royal Spanish decree. "Not a man on board knew the secrets of its perilous navigation."[2] Land was sighted on the twenty-eighth of December. La Salle, now sailing on the *Aimable*, became separated from the *Joly*. When the ships were reunited days later, charge and countercharge passed between La Salle and Beaujeu, each attempting to place blame upon the other. Neither seemed aware that they had much more serious difficulties. La Salle, on his 1682 visit to the mouth of the Mississippi, had been unable to fix the longitude.[3] As a result of this gap in his knowledge, the expedition had sailed past its intended destination and now stood more than four hundred miles to the west.

After much deliberation, La Salle convinced himself that the Mississippi really discharged itself into the lagoons he now saw before him on the Texas coast. After considerable bickering with the naval commander, he put his colonists ashore at Matagorda Bay on February 20, 1685. While he treated with a party of Indians who offered signs of hostility, the *Aimable* entered the bay and shortly ran aground. A rising storm prevented extensive salvage, and for the second time almost a complete ship's cargo of provisions was lost. As sentries that night guarded what bales and boxes the sea yielded up—against curious savage and avaricious Frenchman—the courageous, visionary La Salle kept a dreary vigil, "encompassed with treachery, darkness, and the storm." There was grave suspicion that the wreck of the *Aimable* was intentional, for her captain, Sieur d'Aigron, had flagrantly disobeyed orders and disregarded signals. He had long been at odds with La Salle.

[2] Ibid., p. 271.
[3] Samuel Eliot Morison (*The European Discovery of America: The Northern Voyages, A.D. 500-1600*, pp. 136-137) observes that navigators had no accurate method of obtaining longitude until "lunar distances" and the chronometer were invented in the eighteenth century. La Salle, therefore, was at a tremendous disadvantage in trying to approach the mouth of the Mississippi from the Gulf of Mexico. Not only is his error understandable, but it also would have been little short of a miracle in that age for him to have been able to navigate accurately to the exact point he sought.

All ashore now at the inlet, La Salle's company was beset by dysentery, the result of brackish water and bad food, and by venereal disease, the fruit of the debauchery at Santo Domingo. Deaths occurred almost daily from the former ailment. From the latter, men wasted away gradually. Among the heaped-up salvage from the wrecked vessel, amidst the pens of fowls and swine, were gathered "the dejected men and homesick women who were to seize New Biscay and hold for France a region large as half of Europe. The Spaniards, whom they were to conquer, were they knew not where. They knew not where they were themselves; and for the fifteen thousand Indian allies who were to have joined them, they found two hundred squalid savages, more like enemies than friends."[4]

Relations between La Salle and Beaujeu finally were amicable. The ship's captain tendered an offer, pleading with La Salle to accept it, to set sail for Martinique to procure supplies for the colony. The great explorer steadfastly declined. At last, on the twelfth of March, Beaujeu put to sea. He reached France in July. La Salle, meanwhile, began to explore the countryside, seeking the Mississippi, which he was certain lay close at hand. Returning to his strife-torn colony, he brought sad news. No longer was it possible to believe that he had landed at the mouth of the river he sought.

The one remaining hope of the colonists was the frigate, *La Belle*, a gift to La Salle from the king. But, in the hands of an unskilled crew, she was caught in a sudden squall and driven upon a bar. Most of those aboard her were drowned in trying to reach shore. The ill-fated French colony was left irrevocably stranded in an uncharted wilderness where it had never meant to be.

Ironically, La Salle's fear of Spanish discovery still occupied a prominent place in his consciousness. Yet the plight of the misplaced French colony offered such formidable hazards as to make mockery of the invaders' dread of the jealous Spaniards.

La Salle's colonists, on a clear day in April, hardly six weeks after their landing, descried sails on the gulf horizon. Expecting

---

[4] Parkman, *La Salle and the Discovery of the Great West*, pp. 278-279. New Biscay (Nueva Vizcaya), during the colonial period, consisted of the present Mexican states of Chihuahua, Durango, Zacatecas, Sonora, Sinaloa, and the southern part of Coahuila.

the distant ship to be a Spanish search vessel, they made ready to defend the crude fort already erected at the site of their first settlement.[5] But the vessel passed them by, completely unaware of their presence.

While the French colonists groped about the harsh wilderness, officials of New Spain remained blissfully unaware of the encroachment upon their territory. The gulf breeze wafted rumors of evil intent on the part of Spain's chief colonial rival. Such idle talk was to be expected, in view of the fact that the two nations until recently had been at war with each other. Because of the avaricious designs of the French monarch, Louis XIV, the peace agreed to in the Treaty of Tregua—signed at Ratisbon (Regensburg) on August 15, 1684, three weeks after La Salle had put to sea—was scarcely less uneasy than the war.[6]

Spring and summer passed that year of 1685, and still the Spaniards had no definite news of French designs. Preoccupation with a host of more immediate colonial problems served even to dull the edge of suspicion. But then, toward summer's end, word of the French intrusion came crashing down upon Spanish ears with all the suddenness and violence of a gulf storm.

In April—a short time after the French colonists had stood tensely at arms while the unidentified ship passed—a Spanish salvage expedition put out from Cartagena, on the Colombian coast. In command was Admiral Gaspar de Palacios, seasoned veteran of the sea who served the Spanish crown as pilot major of the Indies. His mission was to recover cargos of silver bullion lost years before on the Caribbean banks south of Cuba, at La Serranilla and Isla Misteriosa. Nine days under sail brought Palacios's vessel to La Serranilla, where he found signs that the treasure had been removed. His men probed the area around the bank but produced nothing more than the bones of the men who had perished with the silver.[7]

[5] Henri Joutel, *Joutel's Journal of La Salle's Last Voyage, 1684-7*, p. 91.

[6] The aggressive policy of Louis XIV in Flanders had led to a declaration of war by King Charles II of Spain in October, 1683, following a period of Spanish apprehension that France was preparing an aggressive move against her colonies in America. The truce less than a year later was humiliating for Spain and failed to remove the tension between the two nations (William Edward Dunn, *Spanish and French Rivalry in the Gulf Region of the United States, 1678-1702*, p. 18).

[7] Gaspar de Palacios to Pedro de Oreytia y Vergara, November 17, 1685, A.G.I., México, 1685-1688 (61-6-20), p. 6.

From Serranilla, Palacios went in search of Isla Misteriosa. He failed to find it in twenty-nine days, as contrary winds blew with such force that the ship ran without sails and the current threatened to cast it upon the Yucatán Peninsula. Miraculously saved from grounding, the Spaniards gained the channel entrance to the Gulf of Mexico and sought refuge at Cabo Catoche. But as they approached the cape's sheltering arms, they ran fulltilt into a squadron of eight pirate ships. The buccaneers quickly put on sail and gave chase to the Spanish naval vessel.

Palacios ran westward across the top of the peninsula, the freebooters hard astern. Escaping at nightfall, he made the port of Campeche. The following day, June 24, he went ashore to report the pirate threat to the governor, then sailed on for Veracruz, where he arrived July 2 to dispatch the news hastily to the viceroy, Conde de Paredes. The high official ordered the arming of the coast and the dispatch of aid to Campeche.

The coastal town used the time it had (twelve days) to prepare for the onslaught, removing everything of value either to Mérida, a considerable distance up the coast, or to the inland wilds. On July 6 the pirates entered the port of Campeche; 750 freebooters led by the notorious French buccaneer Michel de Grammont and the Dutch pirate Laurens de Graff (Lorencillo) overran the town. Another 550 stood by on the twenty-three ships—fifteen piraguas and sloops in addition to the eight larger ships encountered by Admiral Palacios. Angry at finding no plunder, the pirates vented their wrath upon the villagers, destroying everything that lay in their path. They burned the fort at the harbor entrance and spiked its cannon. Of more than two hundred prisoners captured by the buccaneers during their fifty-seven day orgy, nine were hanged, and the pirates were bent on doing the same with the rest, who somehow "were freed by the grace of God."[8] Forces sent by the viceroy eventually reinforced the Campeche governor, who then marched up the coast with 350 men to lay an ambush for Grammont's cutthroats, killing many. The pirates, their mission a singular failure from the aspect of pecuniary gain, decided to withdraw.

As the orgy of almost two months came to its bloody climax,

[8] Ibid., p. 8.

De Graff sailed out of Campeche on September 3, steering to windward along the coast. Beyond the last point of land on the peninsula, his lookouts spotted sails on the horizon, and he soon realized that he was being pursued by the Spanish *armada de barlovento.* The windward squadron closed in with booming cannon, answered in kind by the guns of the pirate vessels. Don Andrés de Ochoa commanded the Spanish attack, sending missiles of destruction into De Graff's rigging. First the Spanish ships overhauled and boarded a pirate vessel called *Reglita*—later identified as a captured Spanish ship whose proper name was *Nuestra Señora de Regla.* A pirate sloop burst into flames, and Spanish ships gathered in her crew. Closing fast on De Graff, the armada's flagship suffered an accident that deprived the Spaniards of complete success. One of the cannon exploded, killing three men and maiming another five. During the ensuing confusion on the flagship, De Graff was able to right his vessel and slip beyond the Spanish grasp. Even so, the armada counted one ship captured and one destroyed, with 120 prisoners, including the captain of the *Regla,* Pedro Bart.

From interrogating the captured pirates the Spanish colonial officials learned the news that would dominate their thoughts and actions for years to come: La Salle had sailed from France more than a year previously with plans to establish a French colony on the shores of the Gulf of Mexico.

The key to the startling discovery was one of La Salle's own men, one of six who had deserted him at Santo Domingo and joined the pirate crew. He was Denis Thomas, a befuddled young fellow as uncertain of himself as of the circumstances that had propelled him into his present predicament. He was at a loss to understand the series of events that had placed him in the web from which, it now seemed, there was no escape. How the young Frenchman longed to be back in Longueville, three leagues from Dieppe, where he had been born into a peasant home twenty-two years before.

In his native France, young Thomas had served as a page for the Marquis de Greville, an adviser to the king. When word was whispered of a pending expedition to the New World, he jumped at the opportunity to enlist. He obtained leave for one year and sailed with Captain Beaujeu on the *Joly*. On the first stage of the voyage, to Santo Domingo, there was much talk, and Denis Thomas was a good listener. He turned his ear mostly to a servant of the Sieur de la Salle. This servant, whose name the Spaniards were to read as "La Esperanza," claimed to have been with the great explorer on his long voyage down the Mississippi to discover the river's mouth and to claim its valley for King Louis XIV. His knowledge also extended to plans and purposes for the proposed French settlement on the Gulf of Mexico, and many other facts related to it. These facts he freely communicated to young Denis, whom he swore to secrecy. Denis Thomas was hardly able to conceive of the set of circumstances that would force him to break his vow.

Occasionally the young page found opportunity to eavesdrop on La Salle himself. The result was that he gleaned more knowledge of the voyage, perhaps, than any of the voyagers outside La Salle's immediate circle. But with knowledge came a growing anxiety. Denis Thomas began to fear that he had let himself in for more than he had bargained. And then came Santo Domingo, with all its abortive happenings: the loss of the *St. François*; the illness of La Salle; the growing resentment between La Salle and Beaujeu; and the restlessness of the French sailors, abetted by strong drink, diseased women, and conniving pirates.

Thomas, like many another sailor from La Salle's vessels, consorted with and confided in the shadowy characters found on the island. In return he reaped a harrowing description of the hazards that lay ahead, in the desolate wilderness beyond the uncharted seas. His thirst for adventure suddenly was slaked; he no longer wished to be a part of the daring venture into the land of unknown savages, upon which the jealous Spaniards looked with marked cupidity. His new-found friends offered him an alternative.

Uppermost in Denis Thomas's mind was a desire to return to France, but he had no money, either for food or for passage. His new associates importuned him. The friendly strangers were careful not to impart too much information about their proposed voyage; Thomas, hungry and fearful, asked no questions. Unknown to him, the vessel he signed on was one the buccaneers of Petit Goâve had recently captured from the Spaniards, called

Nuestra Señora de Regla.[9] Captained by Pedro Bart, himself a deserter from La Salle, the vessel sailed under the French flag.

From Petit Goâve the *Regla* sailed to "Isla Baca"—Ile à Vache, off the south coast of Haiti—where it joined other vessels to set a southwestward course for Cartagena. Denis Thomas turned to— along with the motley crew of Spaniards, mulattoes, and Negroes, as well as Frenchmen—to make a deck hand.

As the corsairs approached Cartagena, three vessels sailed to meet them, opening fire with cannon. The *Regla* and the others of her group turned about and crowded on sail for Isla de Pinos, just off the southwest Cuban shore. Thomas now began to realize the nature of the ship he had signed on, for the Isle of Pinos was a veritable pirate hangout. Rum and talk flowed freely, as the free-booters swapped tales of their recent voyages. The pirate captains withdrew from the others to plan their next move.

Disagreement arose in the conference of the buccaneer chieftains. The majority favored striking the coast of Mexico at Vera-cruz and Lorenzo, and five large ships, including the *Regla*, agreed to join the venture. A number of the captains, under the influence of De Graff, declined because of scarce provisions and short crews. The five ships under Grammont's command weighed anchor to sail through the Yucatán Channel toward the Bay of Campeche. Within view of Veracruz they lay becalmed four days, the breeze too slight to carry them shoreward. Realizing their vulnerable position, the pirates at last turned back to sea, passing again through the channel to maneuver southward toward the Mosquito Coast of Honduras and Nicaragua. There the corsairs regrouped and deter-mined to make Campeche their target. At Cabo Catoche, on the tip of the Yucatán Peninsula, the ships—twelve, by Thomas's account—rendezvoused. It was while the vessels were gathering

[9] Denis Thomas, "Declaración de Dionicio Thomas," A.G.I., México, 1678-1686 (61-6-20), pp. 6-7. This ship may have been the one captained by Martín de Echagaray before her capture by the French pirates, for it had the same name. Echagaray served the Spanish king at St. Augustine in various capacities from 1671 to 1678, when he retired to take command of the vessel. Reentering the service in 1680, he served as pilot major of St. Augustine. He sailed for Spain in July, 1683, and early the next year presented a memorial to the king in which he warned of French designs on the gulf region and offered to explore the coast from Apalache to Tampico (Dunn, *Spanish and French Rivalry*, pp. 20-22).

that Admiral Palacios had happened upon them, thus being able to give notice of the disaster in store for the port of Campeche. The pirate fleet poured into the harbor on July 6, 1685, and emptied its hundreds of cutthroats upon the city to pillage and burn. They remained in Campeche more than six weeks, by Thomas's recollection, in one prolonged spree of plunder and debauchery.[10]

On the Isla de Pinos, over the question of attacking Veracruz, a rift had opened between the two main pirate leaders, Grammont and De Graff. The breach widened at Campeche. "Lorencillo," though never one to quail at bloodshed, saw no sense in the vengeful tactics of harassment. Obviously no plunder was to be had. De Graff, Pedro Bart, and some of the other captains, out of disgust with Grammont, sailed from Campeche before their leader called off the attack. They set a course for Petit Goâve, with plans to proceed to France. Then they ran afoul of Don Andrés de Ochoa, and the *Regla* was captured.

Soon after escorting the French privateer to Veracruz, Ochoa succumbed to illness, leaving interrogation of the prisoners to Antonio de Astina, senior admiral of the windward squadron. Testimony was taken from thirty-eight of Pedro Bart's buccaneers. Among the many statements, that of Denis Thomas was outstanding. The admiral summoned a royal notary and an interpreter who, having established that young Thomas was a Roman Catholic, administered the oath and transcribed his deposition, that it might be sent to the viceroy. In the testimony of the erstwhile page the Spaniards saw a grave threat to the security of Spain and all her colonial possessions.

With candor Thomas told of having left France more than a year before on a royal French vessel commanded by "Monsieur de Bonchiut" (Beaujeu), accompanied by one large gunboat, a small six-gun frigate, and a ketch that had been seized by pirates off Santo Domingo. The ships, bound for a place called "Micipipi," where the French planned to settle, carried 250 men, including the infantry soldiers, carpenters, and other tradesmen. There were four religious missionaries and three Capuchin friars on board, as well as four women: "They brought no more women, because

---

[10]Thomas, "Declaración," p. 11. Palacios (Palacios to Oreytia, p. 8) says the pirates remained at Campeche fifty-seven days.

they would have Indian women for this purpose." The lost ketch had been loaded with wine, biscuit, and wheat for sowing, the other vessels with all kinds of tools and merchandise, six campaign pieces, and six guns for the fortress the French settlers planned to build.[11] Of his personal knowledge, Thomas said, the big ship of the king—*Le Joly*—carried many kinds of seed, trunks of trinkets, jewel cases, knives, combs, and merchandise for trade with the Indians. The ships, he related, had stopped at Petit Goâve "to replenish their water supply and refresh the people" before continuing the voyage. He told of his impulsive decision to leave his ship in hope of returning to France, and of his unwitting association with the pirates, who had posed as honest merchant seamen.[12]

Under the sharp questioning of the Spaniards, Thomas revealed that the entire colonization scheme was the plan of one "Monsieur de Salaz." This persistent explorer, he had been told, had spent eighteen years in making the explorations that led to his journey down the Mississippi to the river's mouth.[13] During all that time the great leader had returned to France only twice. For his diligence the king had rewarded him with a chest full of gold and a title of nobility, and had made him viceroy of the "Land of Micipipi."

The Spaniards, however, were more interested in how this "Monsieur de Salaz" had achieved such a feat. Thomas, doubtless hoping to exonerate himself from the charge of piracy, told them what he had learned from La Salle's servant La Esperanza. From Canada, he related, La Salle had traveled by land, by rivers, and by lakes, which many times were covered with ice as deep as a man's waist. With him went religious missionaries—including the ex-

---

[11] Thomas, "Declaración," p. 6. Joutel (*Journal*, p. 61) says the ketch carried "Provisions, Ammunition, Utensils and proper Tools for the setling of our new Colonies." Thomas was mistaken concerning the number of women. While the exact number is not found, various sources indicate more than four. The figure he gives for the men agrees with other sources.

[12] Thomas, "Declaración," pp. 6-8. Roberto Gil Munilla ("Política española en el Golfo Mexicano: Expediciones motivados por la entrada del Caballero La Salle [1685-1707]," *Anuario de Estudios Americanos* 12 [1955]:515) says six of the pirates admitted having been a part of the La Salle expedition. He lists them as "Thomas, Pedro Bart[t], Julián de Jon, Francisco de Lion, Juan Antis, and Guillermo de Lima."

[13] Thomas, "Declaración," p. 8. Actually, only eighteen years had elapsed between La Salle's first journey to Canada in the spring of 1666 and his departure on the voyage to settle a colony at the mouth of the Mississippi in July, 1684.

plorer's own brother—who hoped to convert the Indians to Catholicism. After traveling five hundred leagues to reach the gulf, Thomas had been told, La Salle had gone fifteen leagues out to sea, taking soundings and recording the depth; he had affirmed that big ships could enter. To guard the Mississippi, La Salle had left seventeen men in a stronghouse built upon an island eminence, returning to Canada on the route by which he had come.

La Salle had been told by the Indians that rich mines were to be found near the Mississippi, Thomas related, and that they could be reached only with the expenditure of work and bloodshed. These mines were La Salle's objective; he had brought the infantry soldiers and campaign pieces to help him attain it and to seek other discoveries west of the great river. The land, according to what the natives had told him, was fertile plains, well watered, and with good climate; edible fruits and berries, as well as wild cattle, abounded.

La Salle was prepared to deal with the Indians of the region, by having in his company a native who had been with him on the voyage to France. Thomas many times had seen this Indian, who spoke French fluently. He described him as being light-skinned (by comparison to the natives of Campeche) and obese, having thick black hair. He dressed in red garments as did the French and wore a red hat with points of gold, given him by his master. Although the Indian spoke French, La Salle, his brother (the missionary), and his servant (La Esperanza) were able to converse in the Indian language.[14]

The interrogators pressed young Thomas from every angle: What did he know of the future plans of the corsairs? What part had he taken in the rape of Campeche? Did he not know that it was a crime to rob and kill, as the pirates had done there? The Frenchman knew nothing of Grammont's plans except that he was seeking a place of refuge to careen his ship. The witness claimed that he himself had not participated in the atrocities at Campeche; he had not taken even a sou with which to settle the debts he had contracted at Petit Goâve, and he had found occasion to free two

---

[14] Ibid., pp. 9-10. The identity of La Esperanza can only be guessed at. He may have been Saget, who was slain by La Salle's murderers.

persons whom Grammont had planned to hang. Yes, he recognized the criminality of the assault, but he had embarked solely as a seaman seeking to earn his livelihood.[15]

Others among the captives—including Captain Pedro Bart—corroborated the testimony of Denis Thomas concerning the French settlement on the gulf. Spanish officials reacted instantaneously. It was evident that La Salle, for purposes of conquest and colonization, had landed a force in territory claimed by Spain. The intruders were equipped and provisioned for attacking the settlements of northern Mexico, and they posed a threat to all the shipping in the gulf. Hasty calculations convinced the Spaniards that the "Micipipi" emptied into the gulf through a bay called Espíritu Santo. This natural port, in the hands of the French, they believed, would be "injurious to all America"; Spanish galleons and ships of all kinds—commerce from Florida, Havana, and Campeche, as from all the ports of New Spain—thenceforth would run the risk of falling into the hands of this enemy in control of such a strategic point. No vessel or fleet would be secure. The French, being a populous nation, were certain to form a major settlement. The enemy must be cast out before there was time to strengthen the colony with additional manpower and munitions. Reinforcements were expected the following spring; hence a voyage must begin by February in order to extirpate the colony before that time. The armada must be made ready at once.[16]

The viceregal government of New Spain could ill afford to wait for word from Spain to begin the search for the site of this bold intrusion. Plans were begun immediately. When news of the reported invasion reached the royal court in Madrid the following spring, the War Council of the Indies reviewed the facts with perhaps less surprise but just as much alarm as had colonial officials. "His Majesty's prompt action is necessary," the Council ruled, "to pluck out the thorn which has been thrust into the heart of America."[17]

---

[15] Ibid., p. 12.
[16] Joseph de Murueta Otálora and Francisco García de Arroyo to the Viceroy, October 29, 1685, A.G.I., México, 1678-1686 (61-6-20), pp. 2-3.
[17] Marqués de los Vélez and others, "Junta de Guerra de Yndias," A.G.I., México, 1685-1688 (61-6-20), p. 59.

While concern over La Salle's intrusion upon the coast of Seno Mexicano was uppermost in the minds of colonial officials, there was another matter not to be forgotten: disposition of the 120 pirates captured by Admiral Ochoa. No heed was given to Denis Thomas's plea of innocence. After the Spaniards had obtained from the buccaneers what information they could, a mass execution was held in the port of Veracruz.[18]

[18] Gaspar de Palacios to the Viceroy, September 6, 1686, A.G.I., México, 1685-1688 (61-6-20), p. 110.

2. THE GREAT DESIGN

The principal purpose of Sieur de la Salle in making this discovery was to find a port on the Gulf of Mexico on which could be formed a French settlement to serve as a base for conquests upon the Spaniards at the first outbreak of hostilities . . . the great river he has discovered . . . passes near New Biscay. Sieur de la Salle has found along its borders savages who are at war with the Spaniards of that province . . . and claims he can easily join them together to drive all the Spaniards from New Spain.

–Marquis de Seignelay
Margry, *Découvertes*, III, 56-57

Spain had long lived in dread of a French attempt to plant a colony on the coast of the Gulf of Mexico. Louis XIV espoused an aggressive policy toward Spanish rights in America, according official status to French encroachments on the northern coast of Santo Domingo. The king included in the patent of the French governor of the island of Tortuga full jurisdiction over these settlements. Spain naturally took this action as an indication of French designs upon Santo Domingo, which might well serve as a stepping stone to more formidable aggressions on her mainland colonies; true French intentions, the Spaniards feared, were masqueraded behind the pirate host of the Caribbean.

Still Spain, having found no road to quick and easy wealth in all the early explorations of the region later to comprise the United States, held little interest in it. The geographical knowledge gained through the explorations of Pineda, Narváez, Cabeza de Vaca, De Soto, and Moscoso was all but forgotten. Having lost control of the seas with the defeat of her armada by England in 1588, Spain laid claim to vast regions she was powerless to colonize: specifically, the region north of Mexico, between Florida and New

Mexico. It remained for a threat of conquest by a foreign power to spur her to new efforts of exploration and colonization.

The first awakening from this somnolent stance came as the result of an expatriate, who seemingly had vowed vengeance and ruin to the nation that had humiliated and exiled him: Diego de Peñalosa. Native of Peru, scion of a prominent Spanish family, and knight of the Order of Alcántara, Peñalosa had served as governor of New Mexico from 1661 to 1664. Claiming to have explored in 1662 the regions then known as Quivira and Teguayo, reaching as far east as the Mississippi, he went to Mexico in 1664 hoping to interest the viceroy in the conquest of those provinces. While in the capital he involved himself in a controversy with the Inquisition, which accused him of blasphemous utterances against the church and the holy office. Imprisoned for a time, his property confiscated, he was humiliated—by being forced to march bareheaded through the streets of the capital carrying a green candle[1]—and exiled.

The next year Peñalosa was in England, making proposals to the king for conquest of Santo Domingo or South America, which was most embarrassing to Spain. Unsuccessful with his schemes in England, he took residence in France by 1673 and married a French woman. Not until 1678, however, did his treasonable activities against Spain once again bring him to the attention of Spanish officials. He had made a proposal to Louis XIV for exploration and conquest of Quivira and Teguayo, "assuring that they were very rich in silver and gold, offering to go with the fleet, since he was very well informed concerning the Indies."[2] He was told that the matter could not be considered until the end of the current war.

The full text of his proposal is found neither in French nor in Spanish, but its contents are revealed in the royal decree issued by King Charles II to Viceroy-Archbishop Fray Payo de Rivera. Historians generally have agreed that Peñalosa never had made the expedition into the provinces of Quivira and Teguayo, as he

---

[1] Hubert Howe Bancroft, *History of the North Mexican States and Texas*, I, 389.

[2] Charles II, "Real Cédula," December 10, 1678, A.G.I., México, 1678-1686 (61-6-20), pp. 152-153. This document is translated in part in José Antonio Pichardo, *Pichardo's Treatise on the Limits of Louisiana and Texas*, I, 156. The full text is printed in Spanish in Cesareo Fernández Duro, *Don Diego de Peñalosa y su descubrimiento del reino de Quivira*, pp. 50-53.

claimed. Even at the time, the king's advisers perceived a marked similarity between his description of the region and that contained in the 1630 memorial of Fray Alonso de Benavides, a Franciscan priest.

Benavides, after serving as *custodio* of the new conversions in New Mexico, had issued the memorial on his return to Spain. He cited reports he had heard of great riches of silver and gold to be found in the "Kingdom of Quivira and Aixaos" and urged the settlement of those regions for the enrichment of the crown:

> At all events, it is best that this kingdom of Quivira and that of the Aixaos be settled and that those Indians embrace Christianity so that Your Majesty may enjoy all this. Looking from this site of Quivira toward the point closest to the sea, which is eastward, there is indicated on the sea charts a bay called Espíritu Santo. It is situated at 29°, between the Cape of Apalache and the coast of Tampico, which is the northern coast of New Spain, within the gulf. According to the chart, therefore, from this kingdom of Quivira to this gulf, the distance is not even one hundred leagues, and from there to Havana it is a matter of five or six days along the coast. So that if this port, or bay, of Espíritu Santo were colonized, in that stretch there would be saved more than eight hundred leagues, the distance between New Mexico and Havana by way of Mexico City. It takes more than a year to cover this distance, and four hundred leagues of it is through hostile and very dangerous territory, where Your Majesty expends large sums on escorts of soldiers and on wagons. By way of the bay of Espíritu Santo all this is saved by a journey of only one hundred leagues between the kingdom of Quivira and this bay; and the entire road is peaceful, passing through the country of a friendly and well-known people, who probably are already converted and preparing for Baptism; for it was in that state I left them last year.[3]

Father Benavides's report, designed to win royal approval of his plan to colonize and Christianize the region, can hardly be regarded as objective. He scarcely dreamed that he was providing ammunition to be used by such a schemer as Peñalosa.

Now, nearly half a century later, the Council of the Indies pondered the memorial and weighed it against Peñalosa's perfidious plot. Either the provinces in question were not as rich as the renegade schemer indicated, the Council reasoned, or else their

[3] Alonso de Benavides, *Benavides' Memorial of 1630*, pp. 63-64.

conquest would be an extremely difficult undertaking; otherwise the English from Virginia would have moved in before now. Nevertheless, the Treaty of Nimwegen recently had been made, bringing the peace that Louis XIV had stipulated as a condition for considering Peñalosa's proposal. Precautionary measures should be taken. Accordingly, the king instructed the viceroy to report on the feasibility of occupying Espíritu Santo Bay in order to open a new route to New Mexico and Quivira as suggested by Father Benavides:[4]

> What advantages or disadvantages it would have, and for what reason and what means and effects could be applied in order that the communication with the two said Kingdoms of Quivira and Tagago and the conversion of its natives to our Holy Catholic faith might be attained, and whether in that Kingdom [New Spain] Religious are to be had who may be inspired to undertake these conversions with hopes of fulfilling the purpose, or whether it would be easier from the Provinces of Florida; and whether there are in the vicinity English or Frenchmen who should be distrusted, and any damage which might occur from the proposition which don Diego de Peñalosa has made to the Most Christian King.[5]

This cédula of December 10, 1678, marks the beginning of the reawakening of official Spanish interest in the deserted Mississippi Valley and gulf region of the United States. Vague rumors of foreign encroachment had done more than the repeated petitions of soldiers, settlers, and priests.[6] But still the reawakening was not complete. Responsibility for the matter merely was shifted to the shoulders of the viceroy, and there it rested.

Then, on January 18, 1682, Peñalosa made a second proposal, this time through the French foreign minister, Marquis de Seignelay. It called for establishing a colony at the mouth of the Río Bravo. This colony, he averred, would serve as a base for the conquest of Nueva Vizcaya at the king's will. Capturing the mines

---

[4] William Edward Dunn, *Spanish and French Rivalry in the Gulf Region of the United States, 1678-1702*, pp. 15-16.

[5] Charles II, "Real Cédula," pp. 155-156; see partial translations in Herbert Eugene Bolton (ed.), *Spanish Exploration in the Southwest, 1542-1706*, p. 347, and Herbert Eugene Bolton, *Bolton and the Spanish Borderlands*, p. 114. The "Most Christian King" refers to Louis XIV of France, in recognition of his Catholicism.

[6] Dunn, *Spanish and French Rivalry*, p. 16.

of that province of New Spain would, as Peñalosa told it, be easily accomplished with the help of Indians, mestizos, mulattoes, and Creoles, all oppressed by the yoke of Spain.[7]

On December 23, 1683, La Salle arrived in France, having journeyed down the Mississippi to the gulf the previous year and claimed the immense river valley for Louis XIV. He proposed to the king establishment of a fort at the mouth of the great river, to serve three functions: as a means of extending the Christian religion among the Indians, as a base for subsequent conquest of Nueva Vizcaya, and as a port for the king's vessels and the key to a vast region of natural wealth at the belt of the North American continent.[8]

War again had broken out between France and Spain in October, 1683, over the aggressive policy of Louis XIV in Flanders. La Salle doubtless appealed to the cupidity of the monarch by incorporating into his proposal Peñalosa's designs against Nueva Vizcaya, with its rich silver mines. He proposed a fortification sixty leagues above the mouth of his Río Colbert (the Mississippi), from which he could proceed with two hundred Frenchmen and up to fifteen thousand Indians to attack New Biscay, where he would rally the oppressed classes of Mexico to assist him in an easy victory over the enervated soldiery.

The two plans of Peñalosa bore a marked similarity to La Salle's plan. At about this same time Peñalosa came forward with a third scheme. Geared to the renewal of the state of warfare between France and Spain, it proposed an invasion at the mouth of the Río Pánuco instead of the Río Bravo. After capturing this settlement, Peñalosa proffered, he would proceed with ten or twelve hundred freebooters from Santo Domingo to seize the entire province of Nueva Vizcaya and its mines of Parral, Cuencamé, Sombrerete, San Juan, and Santa Bárbara. As leader of this pirate horde he suggested the notorious rogue, Michel de Grammont, who, Peñalosa assured, was accustomed to the art of war; his buccaneers would gladly follow him for the chance at plunder and pillage,

---

[7] E. T. Miller, "The Connection of Peñalosa with the La Salle Expedition," *Texas State Historical Association, The Quarterly* 5, No. 2 (October, 1901):101. Pierre Margry (ed.), *Découvertes et établissements des Français dans l'Ouest et dans le Sud de l'Amérique septentrionale*, III, 44-48, contains the full text of the proposal, in French.
[8] Miller, "The Connection of Peñalosa with the La Salle Expedition," p. 101.

such as they had committed scarcely more than six months previously on the port city of Veracruz.[9]

Grammont and his pirates were to be denied any official connection with the forthcoming French invasion of the gulf coast. Still the buccaneers—as has been seen and as will be seen further—had a profound influence on the expedition and on Spanish countermeasures, in ways that hardly were anticipated.

While Peñalosa proposed to exploit the sanguinary French pirates in carrying out his plan, he himself was to be the commander in chief. He proudly recited his qualifications, including the fact that he had been governor of the large province of New Mexico. His ruination at the hands of the religious of the Inquisition, who had imprisoned him for thirty-two months and deprived him of his office, had caused him to come to France to offer the Christian king his services in the conquest of that country.

From the easy conquest of Nueva Vizcaya, so defenseless and so remote from outside help, so seething with discontent of the oppressed masses, he expected to bring to France each year 20 to 25 million pounds of silver ingots. It would be a stepping stone eventually to driving all the Spaniards from North America.

For the enterprise he asked two war vessels to transport the silver from Pánuco to Santo Domingo, which would serve as an intermediary port. The vessels should be sent under the pretext of protecting the islands of the Indies, along with an order to the Sieur de Cussy, new governor of the French coastal settlements of Santo Domingo, to gather the buccaneers and provisions for six months. Two commissions should be issued by His Majesty—one to Peñalosa as governor of the region to be conquered, the other to Grammont as the king's lieutenant.[10]

La Salle's plan also was in the hands of the king's minister by this time, and the two proposals were pondered together. The French explorer, too, envisioned an easy conquest that would

---

[9] Robert S. Weddle, *San Juan Bautista: Gateway to Spanish Texas*, p. 10; Juan Domingo Arricivita, *Crónica seráfica y apostólica del Colegio de propaganda fide de la Santa Cruz de Querétaro en la Nueva España, segunda parte*, p. 206; Isidro Félix de Espinosa, *Crónica de los colegios de propaganda fide de la Nueva España*, p. 166. This pirate attack on Veracruz in 1683 occurred just as twenty-four Franciscan priests were arriving from Spain aboard the silver fleet to found the New World's first missionary college, that of Santa Cruz de Querétaro.

[10] Margry, *Découvertes et établissements*, III, 50-55.

result in great riches for the crown. He incorporated certain of Peñalosa's points into his plan, possibly to prevent the renegade Spaniard from outdoing him. But he must have recognized that Louis XIV would be most impressed by a suggestion that included the conquest of new territory and the acquisition of mines, the source of Spanish riches. Some have interpreted these points in his plan as a true indication of his intentions. Thus was born the notion that La Salle, in passing the mouth of the Mississippi, was not the victim of error but of his desire to move closer to the object of his conquest: the northern regions of Mexico itself. In any event, La Salle seems to have assimilated Peñalosa's plan into his own without acknowledgment. Thus he succeeded in eliminating his competition.

Peñalosa, however, was not easily discouraged. He issued a fourth and final proposal in February, 1684. After capturing Pánuco, he would march on Durango, seize Culiacán near the Pacific, capture the mines, and fortify the region. He asked to be allowed to embark at once for Santo Domingo in order to arrive before September, when the freebooters would be returning from their voyages. The following winter would be spent in raising an army among them, and he would launch his expedition in April, 1685. He greatly desired that the king send La Salle with the necessary support to establish himself on his river and assemble the natives. Peñalosa's plan and that of La Salle would support each other. La Salle, with his Indian horde, should spread terror "in that part of New Biscay which is along the river he has discovered" while Peñalosa carried out his plan of conquest to reach the South Sea (Pacific Ocean). Following the king's orders, they would divide their conquests into "two beautiful rich governments, which will bring each year into France considerable riches, and to his majesty a new glory in having extended his victories and conquests into the new world."[11]

Still, in no manner did La Salle ever acknowledge Peñalosa's proposals, or his own debt to them. Undoubtedly the two men became acquainted and quite likely consulted with each other regarding their plans of conquest.[12] But if Peñalosa's scheme was

[11] Miller, "The Connection of Peñalosa with the La Salle Expedition," p. 103; Margry, *Découvertes et établissements*, III, 70.

[12] Bancroft, *History of the North Mexican States and Texas*, I, 396; Miller, "The

approved or acted upon by the French government, documentation is lacking. The naval captain Beaujeu indicated at one point that Peñalosa's forces were expected to follow and cooperate in the establishment of La Salle's colony.[13] Speculation has arisen, therefore, that a double expedition was planned; that La Salle set sail on his ill-fated voyage with the expectation that he would be reinforced the next year by Peñalosa and his freebooters from Santo Domingo; that the second phase of such a conjectural master plan was eliminated by the conclusion of the truce of Tregua at Ratisbon on August 15, 1684—more than three weeks after La Salle had put to sea.

La Salle's landing on the Texas coast instead of at the mouth of the Mississippi, consequently, occasionally has been construed as intentional rather than accidental. His penetration of the country to the west of his colony—even before he had searched out the area that lay to the east—has been taken as an indication that his designs on Nueva Vizcaya were real, and that perhaps he expected to rendezvous with Peñalosa on Mexican soil. But the actions of Grammont's privateer fleet during this period offer contradiction that the pirate chieftain entertained any notion of rallying to La Salle's aid.

New light on the matter comes from the testimony of one of La Salle's survivors, Pierre Meunier, to the effect that a pirate leader approached the great explorer at Petit Goâve with a proposal to accompany him. The buccaneer chieftain, says Meunier, had a large ship and many well-armed men. La Salle, however, declined the offer because he had no authority from the king.[14]

The factor most often overlooked in attempts to evaluate the great explorer's true intentions is the pronounced lack of geographical knowledge of the region in question at the time. La Salle believed, for example, that the Red River, which he called the River Seignelay, ran parallel with and near to the northern border of New Spain. Having crossed it and the intervening margin of forest, he thought, he would be within a short distance of the

Connection of Peñalosa with the La Salle Expedition," p. 104; Margry, *Découvertes et établissements*, II, 428.

[13] Bancroft, *History of the North Mexican States and Texas*, I, 396.

[14] Pierre Meunier, Declaration, August 19, 1690, A.G.I., México, 1688-1690 (61-6-21), p. 193.

coveted mines of Parral and Santa Bárbara. He had little idea of the extent of the vast wilderness between the Mississippi and the Río Grande.[15]

In any event, Louis XIV preferred to have a loyal Frenchman lead his conquests, rather than a dispossessed Spaniard. Instead of the two vessels La Salle had asked for, the king provided four. Including the crews of the ships, almost three hundred persons comprised the expedition. The grant for supplies and munitions was liberal. In view of this munificence and the expense involved, it would be most unusual if the government's plans had included a second expedition, also requiring a large expenditure.

Peñalosa faded from the picture; he died in Paris in 1687. On the horizon of the New World loomed the sails of La Salle's small fleet, bearing a nondescript band of colonists for France's bold venture. Included were one hundred men, "the scum of French towns,"[16] who were recruited as soldiers; thirty volunteers, of noble birth; artisans; laborers, and servants; several families of colonists; a number of young women, whose object was matrimony; three Recollect Franciscans and three priests, one of whom was La Salle's brother, the Abbé Cavelier. In the high spirit of the adventure, they could have had no premonition of the disaster that lurked beyond the seas.

On the hostile gulf shore, La Salle found support neither from the *flibustiers* nor from the natives. Grammont's buccaneers were a thousand miles away, preparing to harass the Spaniards in another area, through a completely unrelated and independent action. From this operation by the pirate fleet, the word of La Salle's abortive conquest reached the Spaniards, to launch them on the three and one-half-year search. The quest was to wax hot and cold. While the Spaniards searched, the French clung to their tenuous colony, battling the Indians, the wilderness, and each other. And over their crude fort on the desolate shore hovered the specter of tragedy.

[15] Bancroft, *History of the North Mexican States and Texas*, I, 397. This source notes that on La Salle's map of this year the region now known as Texas is almost entirely suppressed. Plate 2, reproduced here in the picture section from Christian Le Clercq (*First Establishment of the Faith in New France*, II, 8), obviously was drawn later, but it shows the geographical error responsible for La Salle's miscalculation. Not only is Texas suppressed, but also the coastline turns sharply southward just west of the Mississippi, as it does in actuality west of Matagorda Bay.

[16] Bancroft, *History of the North Mexican States and Texas*, I, 397.

3. BAY OF THE HOLY GHOST

This excessive Toil, the poor Sustenance the labouring Men had, and that often retrench'd as a Penalty for having fail'd in doing their Duty; the Uneasiness Monsieur *de la Sale* was under to see nothing succeed as he had imagin'd, and which often made him insult the Men, when there was little Reason for it; All these things together afflicted very many so sensibly, that they visibly declin'd, and above thirty dy'd.

—Henri Joutel
Journal, pp. 95-96

"Micipipi." That was the name Denis Thomas applied to the river at whose mouth La Salle had gone to plant a colony. It was meaningless to the Spaniards, except possibly for the similarity it bore to the river that Peñalosa claimed to have visited—"Michipi"—and it appears that even this clue was overlooked. To determine the location, colonial officials pored over innumerable maps and came at last to the conclusion that the river called Micipipi emptied into the bay that Fray Alonso de Benavides had designated as Espíritu Santo—the Bay of the Holy Ghost.

Whether holy or not, a ghost it would prove to be. While the name was familiar to Spanish cosmographers, no Spaniard had visited Espíritu Santo Bay in many years.[1] The geographical knowledge gained by the early explorers, such as Pineda in 1519, and De Soto and Moscoso, 1539-1543, was lost to memory. The name had been loosely used, having been applied to several different locations on the gulf coast. Alonso Alvarez de Pineda, while

---

[1] José Antonio Pichardo, *Pichardo's Treatise on the Limits of Louisiana and Texas*, I, 445.

exploring the mainland coast from Florida to Veracruz in 1519, had given it to the mouth of the Mississippi. To the previously unexplored region between Apalache and Tampico—the area that now became the focus of the Spanish search for La Salle—Pineda gave the name Amichel. His map,[2] however, appears to have escaped the notice of those concerned with the quest.

Hernando de Soto had applied the name Espíritu Santo to the Florida bay in which he anchored May 25, 1539, on the feast day of the Holy Ghost. While early maps indicate Charlotte Harbor as the site, the place is generally conceded to have been Tampa Bay.[3] During the search now about to begin, Spanish explorers would come upon Mobile Bay and form the conclusion that this was indeed the Espíritu Santo Bay mentioned in the Benavides memorial. None of these was the actual site of La Salle's colony. Yet all would figure in the quest in one manner or another.

Even Admiral Gaspar de Palacios, the most knowledgeable officer of the gulf region, with fifty-six years in His Majesty's service, had no certain knowledge of the bay's location. From available sources he computed distances and deduced that the site was at approximately 30° north latitude—one degree farther north than Benavides had indicated. His distances, however, serve only to show the great dearth of geographical knowledge of the time. By his calculations the place should be 145 leagues from Tampico, which would have put it near Corpus Christi Bay; from Veracruz, 190 leagues, approximately the distance to the mouth of the Río Grande; from Apalache, 120 leagues, which would approximate the mouth of the Mississippi, where La Salle had intended to land; and from Mexico City, 280 leagues, about the distance to Matagorda Bay, where the French actually had landed.[4]

In 1678 King Charles II had issued instructions to the viceroy, Rivera, to investigate the location of Espíritu Santo Bay mentioned in the Benavides memorial in the light of Peñalosa's original proposal to the French government. In the summer of 1685 it

---

[2] Martín Fernández de Navarrete, *Colección de los viages y descubrimientos que hicieron por mar los Españoles desde fines del siglo XV, con varios documentos inéditos concernientes á la historia de la marina castellana y de los establecimientos españoles en Indias*, III, reproduces this map opposite p. 176.

[3] Garcilaso de la Vega, *The Florida of the Inca*, p. 59 n.

[4] Gaspar de Palacios to the Viceroy, October 27, 1685, A.G.I., México, 1678-1686 (61-6-20), pp. 25-26.

came to the king's attention that these instructions had not been carried out. Rivera had passed from office in 1680 without having acted.

This failure came to the king's attention with the receipt on August 2, 1685, of a proposal from Captain Martín de Echagaray, pilot major of the Presidio de la Florida at St. Augustine (see Plate 4 in the picture section). The plan reached Charles II a month before the capture of the pirate ship *Nuestra Señora de Regla*— which had once been in Spanish service and captained by Echagaray himself—and the startling testimony elicited from her crew. In a most timely gesture, Echagaray asked to be empowered to explore Espíritu Santo Bay to determine whether the region might be occupied by Frenchmen. He, too, undoubtedly acted from the Benavides memorial; the bay he referred to, therefore, was the mouth of the Mississippi. No explanation for his prescience is found. He had left St. Augustine for Spain in July, 1683—a year before La Salle sailed from France—and evidently was in Spain when he wrote the proposal received by the king in August, 1685. It seems inconceivable, therefore, that he could have had prior knowledge of the La Salle expedition, even from the pirate underground.

In any event, Echagaray's timely plan called for immediate exploration of Espíritu Santo Bay, described as being "two hundred twenty leagues from Vera Cruz and one hundred forty from the Port of Apalache." Ascending from the bay, he said, were two copious rivers, one to the extended Province of La Mobila, the other to New Mexico. On all the coastline from Apalache to Espíritu Santo Bay, he noted, not one Spanish settlement was to be found. Whether the French might be settling was not definitely known, because he had been unable to obtain definite news from either Spaniards or Indians who had been there. It was known, however, that the French were to be found in the region bordering the rivers that fed into the bay. Furthermore, the bay, as did the land around it, offered all the conveniences for settlement, including a good, deep port, which could be fortified so that no enemy could enter.

Considering these claims, the king was obliged to order exploration of the coastal region and especially Espíritu Santo Bay. On the same day the proposal was received he instructed the governor of Florida to provide Captain Echagaray with ten soldiers and two Indian guides, provisions, and a vessel for their voyage.[5] It should be done, the monarch informed the Conde de Paredes, viceroy in Mexico City, "in order that from all directions may be had the desired news concerning the points raised, for the greater security and certainty of the attainment which can be had through the discovery of the said Espíritu Santo Bay and the kingdoms of Quivira and Tagago, and their settlement, to insure the provinces of Florida against the menaces posed by the corsairs and pirates who commonly infest that coast."[6]

The king at this point could have had no definite knowledge that French settlers already had landed in Spanish territory. It remained for him to receive the stunning news from Admiral Palacios, by way of the viceroy, the following April. Once again his instructions lagged in the execution. Echagaray never carried out his assignment.

According to computations based on the testimony taken from Denis Thomas before his execution, Admiral Palacios informed the viceroy, the French had now had nine months to establish their settlement; there was not a moment to lose. The appropriate time to act, he asserted, was "today." In his appeal to the official in Mexico City—who would transmit the news to Madrid—he suggested that two fishing barks, each with twelve men, be sent to reconnoiter the long stretch of coastline.

In command of the two vessels should be a leader adept at celestial navigation, who could take depth soundings all along the coast and who would keep a clear and concise diary. In order to take advantage of the favorable wind, the reconnaissance should be launched from Havana, proceeding to Apalache. From that cape on the Florida coast to the French settlement the distance should be no more than 120 leagues. Admiral Palacios closed the letter to His Excellency, Don Tomás Antonio de la Cerda y Aragón, Conde de Paredes and Marqués de la Laguna, on a note of deep feeling: "I ask Your Excellency's forgiveness, but the Lord knows the injury I feel at the misfortunes of the kingdom during the time of your government. If by shedding my blood I could

---

[5] Charles II to the Viceroy, August 2, 1685, ibid., pp. 156-158.
[6] Ibid., pp. 158-159.

remedy it, I would do so. But since this circumstance is unavoidable, we must believe that it is God's will."[7]

To Admiral Palacios's letter was added a summary statement of Admiral Antonio de Astina, who had conducted the examination of the prisoners taken from the pirate vessel captured by Don Andrés de Ochoa. These letters, along with those of officials in the city of Veracruz and a transcript of Denis Thomas's testimony, were forwarded to the viceroy. The high official passed the documents to his *fiscal*, Don Pedro de la Bastida, who promptly summarized the facts and recommended a course of action. The threat posed by the French intruders, Bastida noted, was quite real and dangerous and by no means to be taken lightly. The interlopers must be extirpated before they became entrenched. The plan of Admiral Palacios—a man of great experience and intelligence—should be promptly pursued. Palacios himself should name the officer to carry it out. While the reconnaissance, to be launched from the windward port of Havana, was being conducted, the *armada de barlovento* should be getting ready for action. Once the reconnaissance ship had located the French settlement, the windward fleet should proceed with all its vessels to destroy the colony and seize its people and ships. For the repair of the armada, masts and spars should be gathered from Havana or Campeche by early January. The needs of the fleet should be given top priority, "admitting no excuses."[8]

The following day a general junta met to approve the recommendations of Admiral Palacios and the *fiscal*. The junta decided that Palacios immediately should seek the person of his satisfaction to conduct the voyage and should instruct him as to procedure. The officer chosen must be on the first ship sailing from Veracruz for Havana, where the governor and the royal officers—with special instructions from the viceroy—would make all necessary preparations. Arms, munitions, provisions, and personnel would be provided by the viceroy from the Royal Treasury of Mexico.[9] The viceroy issued his orders the same day, and by November 12 they were in the hands of the royal officers of Vera-

---

[7] Palacios to the Viceroy, October 27, 1685, p. 26.

[8] Pedro de la Bastida, "Repuesta del Señor Fiscal," November 4, 1685, A.G.I., México, 1678-1686 (61-6-20), pp. 20-21.

[9] Fructos Delgado and others, "Resolución de la Junta," November 5, 1685, ibid., p. 23.

cruz. Soon to depart from that port was the frigate, *Nuestra Señora del Carmen*, captained by Gaspar de Acosta. When she sailed, the frigate would carry the two officers chosen by Admiral Palacios to conduct the coastal reconnaissance and the supplies and provisions required for the voyage. The long and diligent search for the ill-starred French colony on the Texas coast was about to begin.

For conducting the voyage to scan the long stretch of coastline from Apalache to Tampico, Admiral Palacios—in conference with Admiral Astina—chose two senior officers of the windward fleet. Juan Enríquez Barroto, chief pilot of *Nuestra Señora de la Soledad*, a ship of the *armada de barlovento*, would be in charge. Noted for his astute mind and navigational ability, Barroto was considered to be the best qualified person for mapping the uncharted coastline and compiling the precise data required for directing the windward fleet to the point of attack. To assist him was Antonio Romero, the admiral's pilot of the windward fleet, who knew much of the coastline to be explored, having sailed "from the Cape of Apalache to the Port of Apalachicole, which is approximately forty leagues from Espíritu Santo Bay."[10]

Impressed with the extreme urgency of their assignment, Barroto and Romero made ready to sail with Acosta for Havana to begin their voyage from that point, which lay to windward of the coast to be explored. To help him arrange his personal affairs for the voyage, each was given an advance in salary of 150 pesos. On the advice of Romero, who had visited among the Indians of the Florida coast, sundry merchandise was obtained and placed on board the *Carmen*: beads, bells, knives, blue serge cloth, and trinkets—items of little value that would appeal to the natives. By means of such gifts, it was hoped, the savages could be induced to tell the location of the French colony. A royal accountant of Veracruz made the purchases, with 125 pesos 6 reales in common gold. Cash was provided for purchasing in Havana salted meat, hardtack, and other items not to be had in Veracruz. Captain

---

[10] Antonio de Astina and others, "Acuerdo," November 13, 1685, ibid., p. 32. This distance reference further bears out the confusion surrounding the location of Espíritu Santo Bay. Neither Apalache (Tallahassee) nor Apalachicola was within 40 leagues (104 miles) of any of the many locations to which this name applies.

Acosta's voyage to Havana was of the gravest importance. His two passengers, in the most urgent service of King Charles II and under orders of the viceroy, must be delivered safely to their destination without fail.[11]

On November 14, 1685, from Veracruz, Admiral Palacios issued his detailed instructions to the two naval officers, Barroto and Romero:

Instruction and course which Juan Enríquez Barroto and Antonio Romero, experienced Pilots, must keep and observe on the voyage and discovery which they are ordered to make to the Bay of Espíritu Santo, to be done on the orders of the Most Excellent Lord, Conde de Paredes, Marqués de la Laguna, Viceroy and Captain General of this Kingdom of New Spain, in the following manner:

With the letters for the Governor and Royal Officers of the Port of San Christóval de la Havana they will embark in the frigate of the Castillian, Gaspar de Acosta, and go on her to Havana. There, by order of the Most Excellent Lord Conde de Paredes, Marqués de la Laguna, Viceroy and Captain General of this Kingdom of New Spain, a frigate is standing by with everything they will need. On her said Juan Enríquez Barroto and Antonio Romero are to embark with the greatest possible haste, to proceed with the reconnaissance of this bay and coast of Espíritu Santo. With all care, zeal and boldness they shall follow from Havana the course to the Cape of Apalache. On arriving there they shall obtain two Indians who are familiar with the coast, who know Spanish, and who should accompany them to serve as translators with the Indians of Apalachicole. And without any delay whatsoever, they shall then proceed on the voyage to the Bay of Espíritu Santo by the Coast, keeping a Diary of daily happenings from the time they leave Havana. They shall proceed in shallow water in order to take soundings, observing and outlining the coast, noting any inlets, the distance from ship to shore, and whether the coast has shoals of sand or stone, noting where these shoals occur, the distance between them and the shore, the depth of the water over them, and the direction they run in relation to the coast. By these instructions they must navigate by day, fixing the location of each river's mouth with the distances between banks, as obtained by the sun; the position and distances from various points, and the various routes of access, with greatest precision.

On arriving at the River and Port of Apalachicole, which is eighty [sic] leagues from the Cape of Apalache, they shall enter it with every caution,

---

[11] Ibid., pp. 33-34.

although the Indians may be friendly, and seek from the Indians knowledge of whether the bay of Micipipi, which is that of Espíritu Santo, is settled by white men, and whether any ships have been passing along the coast and, if so, when. And to induce the Indians to tell these things, they may be regaled with beads and other trinkets of the kind which they [Romero and Barroto] are carrying. They shall take from there, if they can, one or two Indians who are familiar with the coast, to go on the ship to the bay of Micipipi, or Espíritu Santo, telling them that they will be returned to their own ports, giving them the best passage possible and caring for them well. They shall leave the Port of Apalachicole, which is some forty leagues from the bay, with all care and caution, adhering to the shore by day in order to take depth soundings, and to see if along the coast the Indians from Apalachicole can speak with the Indians of the land in order to learn from them whether white people are forming a colony on the bay, and whether there are any ships in it, whether they have built a fortress, on what part of the bay they are settled, and how they might be surrounded. They [Romero and Barroto] shall seek to ascertain from the Indians of the coast any news of its being settled. On arriving at the bay they shall sound it, insofar as possible, by night, to determine whether there are banks or shoals in the mouth and the arms of water which the banks as well as the channel might have. In case the bay is not settled (may God will it), they are to enter it, to reconnoiter the channels and determine the depth of the bay, both at the middle and at the banks; to locate the mouths which the river might have, the depth and point of entrance of said rivers, sketching distinctly the location of all mountain peaks, meanders, and obstructions, and the landmarks of the mouth of the bay, with its latitude, without omitting anything which might facilitate our return to search further.

With an understanding of this Bay and Coast, they shall then come to this port to give account to said Most Excellent Lord Conde de Paredes, Marqués de la Laguna, of what has been done.

In the event that in Apalachicole they are not able to obtain Indians, they shall do everything possible to gain definite knowledge of this Bay and its Colony.

All this will be accomplished by the honest efforts of the said Juan Enríquez Barroto and Antonio Romero, that they shall carry out with the zeal and vigilance to which such conscientious persons are accustomed by being so long in the service of both Majesties. Nueva Vera Cruz, November 13, 1685. Gaspar de Palacios.[12]

[12] Gaspar de Palacios, "Ynstrucción y Derrota," ibid., pp. 40-43; repeated, ibid., pp. 45-48. Veracruz in this period frequently was called Nueva Vera Cruz to distinguish it from the site that appears on present-day maps as Antigua Veracruz. This latter point,

As Admiral Palacios prepared to send a copy of these instructions to the viceroy, however, he suffered misgivings about the effectiveness of the plan. Both he and Don Francisco Osorio de Astorga, governor of Veracruz, expressed their doubts in a letter to the high official. The two officers chosen to conduct the reconnaissance, Palacios wrote, were standing by, ready to sail with Acosta, but the season's first norther was blowing, and they must wait for it to subside before embarking. In trusting the important mission to one expedition only, he pointed out, the Spanish officials were running several risks. In addition to the well-known hazards of the sea, the single vessel might easily fall prey to enemy corsairs, or even be captured by the French colonial forces. Should such a disaster occur, news of it would reach Spanish officials too late for them to dispatch a new expedition to dislodge the intruders before expected reinforcements arrived from France the following spring. It seemed advisable, therefore, to send a land expedition northward from Tampico to seek contact with the Indians. In all probability, it was believed, these natives could give information on the white settlement at Espíritu Santo Bay.[13]

On November 19 the viceroy granted approval for Palacios and the other officers at Veracruz to pursue their plan for a land expedition in addition to the maritime voyage. They should seek the proper person, with knowledge of the region, to lead it. But, since the admiral's first proposal had made no mention of the necessity for the land probe, His Excellency had failed to include it in his plans. He therefore felt it proper that the officials of Veracruz bear the expense of the expedition themselves. Conveniently, Palacios was unable to find anyone familiar enough with the country north of Tampico to be entrusted with the assignment. He learned only that from "the place called Monte Rey del Reyno de León" explorations had been made to the northward, possibly even to the vicinity of Espíritu Santo Bay itself. It was evident, therefore, that the matter should be turned over to the

---

discovered by Juan de Grijalba in 1518, was the landing site on April 21, 1519, of Hernán Cortés, who called it Villa Rica de la Vera Cruz. It was abandoned because it was considered unhealthy (Spain, Consejo Superior de Invistigaciones Científicos, *Colección de diarios y relaciones para la historia de los viajes y descubrimientos,* IV, 114 n.).

[13] Francisco Osorio de Astorga to the Viceroy and Gaspar de Palacios to the Viceroy, November 14, 1685, A.G.I., México, 1678-1686 (61-6-20), pp. 44-45, 48-49.

governor of Nuevo Reino de León. A copy of the instructions to the maritime pilots who would explore the coast from Apalache westward should be sent the governor, so that the two expeditions might be coordinated. These conclusions were borne out by the *alcalde mayor* of the province of Tampico, who had joined in the search for a leader, to no avail.[14]

The investigation by the Veracruz and Tampico officials was not long in producing the name of the military leader who had traversed the region north of Monterrey: the *sargento mayor*, Alonso de León, of the Villa de Cadereyta. Before the month was out, De León's memorial relating his services to the king and his exploits on the northern frontier was in the hands of the viceregal advisers in Mexico City. Thus, before the first maritime expedition in search of La Salle's colony was yet underway, wheels were in motion to choose the leader who would devote a large part of the next four years to probing the wilderness in quest of the French intruders.

Barroto and Romero, meanwhile, had sailed from Veracruz on Captain Acosta's vessel on November 21. Reaching Havana on December 3, they presented their credentials to the acting governor, Andrés de Munibe, and began the month of preparations for their voyage.

[14] Delgado and others, "Resolución de la Junta," November 19, 1686, pp. 58-60; Francisco Osorio de Astorga, "Auto de Acuerdo," December 3, 1685, pp. 61-64.

4. THE BUCCANEERS

If [the French] maintain themselves here, it will become a haven for pirates, which will end the trade of our ports at one stroke; and one may fear they will proceed to waylay our ships, of whose departure from Veracruz they will have news because it is so close, and to windward, and from their port they will come to intercept them in the place of their choosing.

—Admiral Gaspar de Palacios
Report, September 6, 1686, p. 113

From the tenuous colony on the Texas coast, La Salle set out in the autumn of 1685 to seek his "fatal river." By water the band of Frenchmen descended to the mouth of the bay, sank their canoes, and took up the march by land. They traveled west instead of east; the river they found was not the Mississippi but the Río Grande, which La Salle called La Maligne. If later accounts of the Jumano and Cíbolo Indians may be credited—and enough of their testimony coincides with established fact to indicate that they can—the French explorers ascended this river a great distance, reaching a Cíbolo village near present Langtry, Texas. Not until the following March did the tattered remnant of the original band of twenty return to relate their ill fortune to the struggling colony.

During the interim the Spaniards had taken steps to launch their frantic search. Barroto and Romero had reached Havana early in December to begin the month of preparations for their voyage. In Veracruz, Admiral Palacios fretted over lagging efforts to bring the windward fleet to a state of readiness to cope with the French invaders once they were found. And in yet another theater of action, the problems of Spain, so hard pressed by the intrusion of a foreign power, were being compounded by an additional threat.

Pirate vessels plied the gulf and the Caribbean at random, posing a constant menace to the coastal towns. From the governor of Guatemala came word that his province was threatened from "the South Sea" by enemy corsairs. Should those from the north descend upon him, he would be "placed in major conflict."[1] Reliable reports revealed the whereabouts of the pirates of the Caribbean. One band, probably that of "Lorencillo," or De Graff, had gone to the Isla de Roatán, off the Honduras coast. The other, likely Grammont's, had quartered at the Isla Mujeres. Both were poised to strike wherever caprice or fortune should dictate, and rumors often suggested intended targets—usually at such widely divergent points that Spanish forces found it impossible to base their preparations on this idle talk.

A multipronged dilemma confronted the Spaniards. Should the limited forces at their disposal be sent after the pirates, to thwart anticipated attacks on any one of a large number of coastal towns? To follow this course might mean sacrificing the windward fleet's state of readiness; when La Salle's French colony was found, the fleet must proceed immediately and in full force to wipe it out.

Admiral Palacios chafed at the binding problems. His ships of the *armada de barlovento* were far from ready. If the coastal reconnaissance from Havana proceeded on schedule, news of the French settlement should be received in Veracruz in January. Warships must then be dispatched to reach Espíritu Santo Bay by February 20. Delay might mean reinforcement of the French colony: "God forbid that time should be lost. . . . The enemy may come with greater strength than that of our windward fleet."[2]

Time was of the essence, and time was being wasted on cleaning and caulking ships that could hardly be improved by the process; they were scarcely capable of facing the rigors of the sea, not to

[1] Francisco Osorio de Astorga to the Viceroy, Veracruz, November 14, 1685, A.G.I., México, 1678-1686 (61-6-20), p. 45. The enemy corsairs who threatened from "the South Sea"—the Pacific—most probably were the same ones who plied the Caribbean and the Gulf of Mexico. Crossing the Isthmus of Darién with the aid of natives of the region, the freebooters would obtain vessels with which to make forays on Spanish settlements up and down the Pacific coast.

[2] Gaspar de Palacios to the Viceroy, November 26, 1685, ibid., p. 55.

mention those of war. The temporary loss of these vessels to service made it difficult to wage warfare against the pirates and still be assured of having a fleet available to deal with the French colony when it was found. Admiral Palacios devised a plan for doing so, hypothetical though it proved to be.

By Palacios's reckoning, the French force on Espíritu Santo Bay could have no more than 250 men. Five hundred of the windward fleet's best should be able to dislodge them with ease. He proposed sending them, when the time came, aboard four frigates from the armada with an aggregate of sixty-two guns. The larger vessels of the fleet then could be held in reserve to deal with the pirate threat. Should a mishap at sea prevent Barroto and Romero from finding the French settlement, the frigates themselves could take up the search.[3]

The plan quickly won support from the *fiscal*. The admiral's proposal, the viceroy's chief adviser noted, was the only one by which the two important objectives of eliminating the French colony and chastising the pirates could be achieved. The plan should be executed without delay. With the frigates in readiness to strike La Salle's colony, the windward fleet proper, when it was ready for sea, should deal with the larger force, if not the larger problem: it should proceed to Roatán and Isla Mujeres to seize the ships of the pirate chieftains "Lorencillo" and Grammont. The whereabouts of the buccaneers, he noted, had been disclosed to the governor of Campeche by prisoners taken during the recent attack on that province.

But such plans, in reality, were only academic. The pirate fleet was too mobile and too powerful for the windward squadron to be effective against it. The coastal reconnaissance about to be undertaken in search of La Salle would be thwarted first by a lack of geographical knowledge, then by foul weather. A tangled wilderness with savage Indians and impassable streams and marshes would block any attempt to search by land until the intruders were defeated by the wilderness itself.

The buccaneers, meanwhile, would remain a force to be reckoned with, severely afflicting Spanish capabilities. Not only would they continue to harass the settlements and the shipping; they

[3] Ibid., pp. 54-56.

would also create diversions, causing the resources of the Spanish searchers to be dissipated in fruitless efforts.

From the time of conquest Spain had guarded her colonial possessions from foreign encroachment with a zeal that inspired resentment and hatred. This Roman Catholic nation tried to force the trading world, especially the Protestant nations of England and Holland, to honor her claim to the newly discovered continents. The claim was based not only on Columbus's voyage but also on a 1494 decree by Pope Alexander VI. The papal bull accorded Spain all the Americas except Brazil, which was given to Portugal. Spain, while attempting to exclude foreigners, also imposed oppressive restrictions on her own subjects, denying them the right to enjoy the fruits of her discoveries. English and Dutch traders pushed against the restrictions, abetted by Spanish colonists who found it advantageous to evade the fiscal regulations of their own government. As a countermeasure Spain assigned ships called *guarda-costas* to attack strange vessels found in her colonial waters, often with instructions to take no prisoners. Such force was met with similar tactics by the interlopers. Foreign seamen, traders, and colonists drifted into a state of perpetual warfare with the various local governments. Foreign powers licensed "privateers" to prey on Spanish shipping, always claiming when challenged that these corsairs were not subject to their control; Spain was at liberty to proceed against them as she chose. Privateering became a profitable business. The *boucaniers* of the Caribbean isles—originally the wild cattle and swine hunters who cured meat by the *boucan* process—came to indulge in a different occupation. The French word was anglicized as "buccaneer," while the English equivalent, "freebooter," became *flibustier* in French,[4] then was translated back into English as "filibuster." The islands of the Antilles became their bases of operations.

Now from these island bases the buccaneers—corsairs or privateers—moved out into the same area where the Spanish searchers for La Salle operated. And the pirates themselves became a part of the search. When it suited their purposes, the freebooters were effective minions of the government that gave them their letters of

---

[4] Henry Powell, "Introduction to the 1893 Edition" in John Esquemeling, *The Buccaneers of America*, pp. xxiv-xxv; C. H. Haring, *The Buccaneers in the West Indies in the XVII Century*, p. 66.

marque. When their own pernicious goals were not served, their governments found them difficult to control, at times an outright embarrassment.

> The French buccaneers indeed [relates Haring] occupied a curious and anomalous position. They were not ordinary privateers, for they waged war without authority; and they were still less pirates, for they had never been declared outlaws, and they confined their attentions to the Spaniards. They . . . were always ready to turn against the representatives of authority if they believed they had aught of which to complain.
> The buccaneers almost invariably carried commissions from the governors of French Hispaniola, but they did not scruple to alter the wording of their papers, so that a permission to privateer for three months was easily transformed into a license to plunder for three years.[5]

It was with such outdated authority from Governor de Pouançay that Michel de Grammont had perpetrated a bloody attack upon La Guaira (Caracas) in 1680, launching himself upon his sanguinary path of piracy.

Grammont is said to have been a native of Paris who entered the Royal Marine, distinguished himself in several naval engagements, and finally appeared in the West Indies as commander of a frigate armed for privateering. After capturing a Dutch vessel near Martinique, he took the prize to Santo Domingo, "where he lost at the gaming table and consumed in debauchery the whole value of his capture."[6] Not daring to return to France, he joined the buccaneers.

In April, 1683, he was one of eight buccaneer captains—French, Dutch, and English—who gathered for the attack on Veracruz, led by two Dutchmen, Laurens de Graff and one Vanhorn. Though a native of Holland, De Graff had served as a gunner in the Spanish navy and, distinguishing himself for bravery and skill, won the command of a vessel. Later captured by buccaneers in American waters, he, like Grammont, joined their ranks and proceeded to outdo them at their own game. In a quarrel over division of the booty from the rape of Veracruz, Vanhorn and De Graff crossed swords and Vanhorn was slashed on the wrist. He died of gangrene two weeks later.[7]

[5] Haring, *Buccaneers in the West Indies*, p. 240.
[6] Ibid., p. 246 n.
[7] Ibid., pp. 242-243.

In April, 1684, M. de Cussy arrived at Petit Goâve as the new French governor and found the buccaneers at the point of revolt over the efforts of his predecessor, Sieur de Franquesnay, to enforce orders for their suppression. De Cussy restored order, but not without concessions. Grammont and several other captains demanded commissions against the Spaniards, and the governor consented on condition that they persuade all the freebooters driven away by Franquesnay to return to the colony. With peace in Europe so precarious, the safety of French Santo Domingo depended on the presence and good will of the sea rovers. Already De Graff had offered his services to the English of Jamaica, but De Cussy's change in policy induced him to return. He was received "with all the honour due to a military hero."[8]

De Cussy's liberalization, however, lacked official backing. Realizing this, many of the buccaneers transferred their operations over the Isthmus of Darién to the Pacific coast, where they would be safe from interference by French or English governments. For the Spanish colonialists the fight with the pirates became a two-front war.

While the *Señora del Carmen* rode the southeast winds across the gulf from Veracruz toward Havana, bearing the two pilots who would conduct the first official search for La Salle, rumors of pirate activity were rife in the Cuban port. Reports of incursions by the French corsairs came constantly to the ears of Governor Andrés de Munibe. Five days before the ship from Veracruz entered his port a Spanish privateer captained by Mateo Guarín sailed into the harbor bringing exciting news of many kinds. Guarín had discovered the lair of the Dutch pirate captain Laurens de Graff—"Lorencillo"—on the island of Santo Domingo. There the freebooter's mulatto mistress and their bastard child awaited his return. Guarín's vessel, scudding for Baracoa, on Cuba's eastern tip, had overhauled a French ship running between Petit Goâve and Puerto de la Paz (Port de Paix, Haiti). On board was official correspondence that revealed the position of the French government concerning the buccaneers supposedly under its influence. Included was an order from the French minister of marine, the

[8] Ibid., p. 244 and n.

Marquis of Seignelay, to the governor of the Ile de la Tortue (Tortuga) and the coastal settlements of Santo Domingo.

The governor, Monsieur de Cussy, was to dissuade the French privateers from obstructing Spanish shipping, lest they give provocation for war. The energies of the buccaneer fleet were to be diverted from striking the coast of Mexico, as Grammont and De Graff had done recently; the spoils from such raids soon were dissipated in prodigal sprees. This kinetic force should be turned instead to a more sinister enterprise: taking possession of Santo Domingo. Outwardly, at least, the peace attained by the Treaty of Tregua should be kept. De Cussy was to learn whether the Spanish governors of Santo Domingo and Cuba meant to do likewise; it was hoped they would permit freedom of commerce to the French in the ports of their jurisdiction.[9]

If the government of Louis XIV should be successful in using the pirate fleet to such an end, the implications were clear: Spain would be severely impaired in her effort to find and extirpate the colony of La Salle. The explorer then could have all the time he needed for fortifying his colony and obtaining reinforcements. Such a threat, at least in the eyes of Governor Munibe, lent utmost urgency to the matter of locating La Salle and driving him out.

The pirate "Lorencillo," meanwhile, remained unbridled by the new policy of the minister Seignelay. He continued to harass Spanish shipping in exploits that made the Spaniards look with pleasure upon the prospect of setting a trap for him at his lair on Santo Domingo. Early in December his fleet of twenty-two vessels fell upon a Cuban merchant and his four ships, killing eight men and wounding sixteen. At the same time it was rumored that De Graff was mustering his freebooters for an attack on either Cartagena or Havana. Governor Munibe, who could ill afford to take chances as to which, made hasty preparations to withstand such a raid. "I have raised a parapet of buttresses and mud walls [he wrote to the viceroy] for defense of the inner channel of this Port, which is adjacent to the mouth."[10]

The French correspondence captured by the Spaniards perhaps

[9] Marquis de Seignelay, "Letters Translated from the French Language," A.G.I., México, 1678-1686 (61-6-20), pp. 122-127.

[10] Andrés de Munibe to the Viceroy, Havana, December 31, 1685, ibid., p. 148.

explains the actions of De Cussy following the pirate attack on Campeche in the summer of 1685:

> The Spaniards of Hispaniola, who kept up a constant desultory warfare with their French neighbors [writes Haring], were incited by the ravages of the buccaneers in the South Seas, and by the sack of Vera Cruz and Campeache [*sic*], to renewed hostilities; and de Cussy, anxious to attach to himself so enterprising and daring a leader as de Grammont, obtained for him, in September, 1686, the commission of "Lieutenant de Roi" of the coast of San Domingo. Grammont, however, on learning of his new honour, wished to have a last fling at the Spaniards before he settled down to respectability. He armed a ship, sailed away with 180 men, and was never heard of again. At the same time Laurens de Graff was given the title of "Major," and he lived to take an active part in the war against the English between 1689 and 1697.[11]

De Graff evidently became a worthy citizen. In October, 1698, he sailed with Pierre Le Moyne d'Iberville from La Rochelle on the expedition to found the French colony of Louisiana. He died in May, 1704.[12] On the latter voyage he appears once again as a thorn in the Spanish flesh. Grammont also will return to our story before his final disappearance; his influence on the search for La Salle was not yet ended.

An extended norther, meanwhile, delayed the start of the reconnaissance in search of Espíritu Santo Bay. However unfavorable for this sailing, the north wind brought to Havana on January 2 the bark of Francisco Romero from the Presidio de la Florida at St. Augustine. With Romero came three passengers, survivors of a disaster on the Florida coast. The victims of this misfortune were members of what appears to have been the first—unofficial— expedition to go in search of La Salle's colony. Much concerning this voyage is left to conjecture, but one may speculate that word of the La Salle enterprise had spread to the pirate underground from the capture of the *St. François*. The crew of a corsair, with an eye for another such prize, had gone looking for the French colony, but on the wrong Espíritu Santo Bay, when the disaster

[11] Haring, *Buccaneers of the West Indies*, p. 246. After entering the service of the king, says Haring (p. 246 n.), De Graff was styled "Laurens-Cornille Baldran, sieur de Graff, lieutenant du roi en l'isle de Saint Domingue, capitaine de fregate legere, chevalier de Saint Louis."

[12] Ibid., p. 246 n.

overtook it. Thus it seems that Barroto and Romero would not be the first Spaniards to look for La Salle.

The three passengers who now came to Havana with Francisco Romero were members of the crew of the Spanish privateer that had been preying on English shipping in the Caribbean. As they told their story before Governor Munibe's scribe, they had heard the previous spring (1685) that "the enemy" was forming a settlement on Espíritu Santo Bay. They had set out to find it. The story emphasizes again the crucial part that pirates played in the La Salle episode. It also points up the lack of knowledge concerning the location now being so sedulously sought. The Espíritu Santo Bay they went looking for appears to have been the bay so named by Hernando de Soto, that is, Tampa Bay.[13]

All three deponents, though of diverse origins, were residents of Havana. Jorge Nicolás, native of "Venetia," related the activities of the privateer during the three years he had served on her as mate under Captain Juan Corso. He had gone aboard at the Villa de San Francisco de Campeche. From Campeche the freebooters rounded the Yucatán Peninsula and proceeded to the Honduras coast, where they seized three English ships. At the island of Jurabán they captured an English sloop carrying a slave cargo of sixty Negroes, a quantity of cloth, and some gold and silver, the spoils having been divided among the crew after it reached Cuba. Then, after seizing two English ships outward bound from Jamaica, they returned to Cuba to deposit the prisoners.[14]

In April, 1685, the vessel put in at "Tuspa" (Tuxpan) for members of the crew to "fulfill their obligation to the church," and Diego de Castro, native of Maracaibo, joined the crew. The buccaneers sailed on up the coast to Tampico, to take on supplies, according to Nicolás; to look for an Indian pilot who might take them to Espíritu Santo Bay, according to Castro, who claimed news that "the enemy" was settling on that part of the coast; and to make preparations for going to St. George (Carolina), where some English had formed a settlement twenty-five or thirty leagues from Presidio de la Florida, according to Manuel de

[13] Diego de Castro, "Testimonio," A.G.I., México, 1678-1686 (61-6-20), p. 133. Jorge Nicolás ("Testimonio," ibid., p. 137) refers to it as the Bay of Ascensión, which was the name the Spaniards later applied to Atchafalaya Bay on the Louisiana coast (José Antonio Pichardo, *Pichardo's Treatise on the Limits of Louisiana and Texas*, I, 359).

[14] Nicolás, "Testimonio," pp. 137-138.

Munibe, a Cartagena native who was the third deponent. By Castro's account they failed to find the pilot they sought and put to sea again, steering east-northeast for the province of Apalache. Four days later, on May 4, they hit foul weather, and the storm drove them upon the Florida coast "two leagues to windward of Espíritu Santo Bay."[1 5]

While on shore attempting to effect repairs to their storm-ravaged vessel, the Spaniards saw many signs of white habitation. A party of six Indian men and women informed them by sign language that many people with muskets like those of the Spaniards had landed there and gone inland. Captain Pedro de Castro, who evidently shared command of the expedition with Corso, took fifty well-armed men and three Indian guides and went in search of the reported intruders. A day and a half later Castro's men reached the shore of "Espíritu Santo Bay," where they saw barefoot tracks in the sand and many broken casks and bottles. On the other side of the bay they could see half a dozen canoes filled with people, but at such great distance they could not determine whether the people were Indians or Europeans.

About May 19 the galley put to sea again, but mean swells and unfavorable winds cast them ashore in an unknown inlet. The vessel, having lost its anchor, was helpless in the rough water. Twenty-five men were put into the water to try to fashion a mooring. Suddenly the wind shifted, and the galley stood in danger of being hammered to pieces upon the rocks. She quickly rigged sail and turned seaward, leaving the twenty-five men marooned without provisions on the savage coast.

For three days they awaited the ship's return. At last nine of the men went out to look for crayfish to allay their hunger. They returned to find that their companions had been taken aboard the galley, now standing offshore. Not wishing to hazard another landing, Captain Corso signaled to the stranded men his intention to put in at Apalache Bay, which he believed to be only fourteen leagues distant; they should go by land and meet him there. But the distance he gave was in error. Seven starving days later, the marooned men, tramping out the coastline, had not reached the point of rendezvous. Weak from hunger, they surprised a group of

---

[1 5] Probably meaning Tampa Bay (Castro, "Testimonio," p. 133).

Indian boys fishing. They captured one as the others fled, leaving a fish and some pumpkins behind for the hungry Spaniards. The captive told them that a priest lived in his village, promising to return with the cleric if they would free him. Placing a rosary around his neck and a jacket on his shoulders, the Spaniards sent him on his way. All the next day they waited for him to return with the priest, then set out upon his trail. After five days they came upon seven Panzacola (Pensacola) Indians. The natives gave them roasted ground corn to eat, then took them aboard their canoe. Fourteen leagues up the coast they reached the Panzacola village of about 120 men, women, and children.[16]

Three days later twenty Indian warriors from the Río de la Mobila, called Ystamanes (probably Alabamas), came to the village, having followed the Spaniards' trail to the point where they had boarded the canoe. Armed with bows, tomahawks, and lances, they began a scalp dance, thus announcing their plans to kill the white visitors. The Panzacolas intervened, however, pacifying the Ystamanes by inviting the belligerent ones to eat with them. Nevertheless, the hostile savages remained at the village twelve days, regarding the Spaniards threateningly the whole time.[17]

Two or three days after the Ystamanes' departure, the ten white visitors left with an escort of nine armed Panzacolas, traveling along the coast in three canoes. Nine days' travel by sea and five by land, following the sun, brought them to a village of Christian Indians called Chacatos (Choctaws), where they were received by Fray Juan Mercado. The priest gave them directions for reaching Apalache. Taking leave of the friendly Panzacolas, who were resting and trading among the Chacatos, the landlocked sailors proceeded to Apalache. From their account, the lieutenant of Apalache estimated that they had traveled more than two hundred leagues from the point where they had been put ashore. Of Juan Corso the people of Apalache had seen or heard nothing. Perhaps, they speculated, he had gone to the Presidio de la Florida, on the other side of the peninsula. With a harquebus provided them by the lieutenant, the seamen began the eastward trek across Florida. On reaching the presidio at St. Augustine, they again made inquiry

[16] Ibid., pp. 133-135.
[17] Manuel Munibe, "Testimonio," A.G.I., México, 1678-1686 (61-6-20), p. 143; Castro, "Testimonio," p. 136.

of Corso and again received the same answer. After several days, the three men received passage on the Havana-bound bark of Captain Francisco Romero.

During the voyage the three sailors talked with Captain Romero concerning the mystery of Juan Corso and his galley. Romero had recently conversed in sign language with the Indians of "Las Carsos," who told him that six months previously they had seen a long vessel with a deckhouse and a large number of persons on board, off the west coast of the peninsula. Doubtless this was the missing galley. But what had become of her afterward was anybody's guess.

The rescued seamen had a traveling companion, the father guardian of the Convento de la Limpia Concepción at Havana. Fray Martín de Alcano, who had been at the Presidio de la Florida when the nine men arrived, heard their confessions. While Romero's vessel stood outside the Havana harbor the evening of January 2, the padre went ashore in a small boat. He proceeded forthwith to the governor.

The adventures of the nine men from the corsair, he told the official, had been related to him in the confessional: They had been cast ashore by a freak of circumstance after having examined Espíritu Santo Bay. On this "good, large bay with a key adjacent to its mouth" they found no settlements of Europeans—only some Indians who lived there and some remains of vessels that had visited the area in times past. And having traversed, during their eighty days of wandering, many leagues of both coastline and interior, they had found signs of neither English nor French ships and no settlements whatsoever.[18]

It only can be assumed that the buccaneers had learned from the pirate underground of the capture of the *St. François* and her rich cargo, and that they had come, like barracudas at the scent of blood, seeking a similar prize for themselves. The survivors' reports are shot with discrepancies for which there is no explanation. Regardless of stated intentions, they had landed at a bay long known by the name Espíritu Santo. The observations made during their wanderings were considered of importance to the coastal reconnaissance about to begin.

The episode provided Romero and Barroto another task to perform: They should be on the lookout for signs of Juan Corso's galley and the remainder of the crew.

[18] Fray Martín de Alcano, "Certificación," ibid., pp. 151-152.

5. MUD CAPE

They were in a bad Condition, their Cloaths ragged, Monsieur *Cavelier's* short Cassock hung in Tatters; most of them had not Hats, and their Linen was no better; however, the Sight of Monsieur *de la Sale* rejoyc'd us all. The Account he gave us of his Journey reviv'd our Hopes, tho' he had not found the fatal River, and we thought only of making ourselves as merry as we could.

–Henri Joutel
Journal, p. 107

A brisk westerly wind carried *Nuestra Señora del Carmen* into the port of Havana on December 3, 1686. She brought not only the two officers who were to conduct the coastal reconnaissance but also the spate of orders that would spur the port town to action. Don Andrés de Munibe, the governor of Cuba, went immediately into conference with Captains Barroto and Romero concerning the selection of a vessel to make the voyage. From the few available craft, they chose a frigate, *Nuestra Señora de la Concepción y San Joseph*, captained by Juan Rodríguez Manzano, in port for overhaul. Rodríguez was ordered to hasten the repairs and make ready to put to sea as quickly as possible.

With munitions and supplies for ninety days, the vessel was to return to Veracruz at the end of the voyage. She was manned by forty-two seamen, all able to bear arms, and carried a small boat for negotiating bars and shoals where the larger vessel could not go.[1]

[1] Andrés de Munibe to the Viceroy, January 3, 1686, A.G.I., México, 1678-1686 (61-6-20), p. 121.

Before the end of the year the *Concepción* was rigged and ready to sail, but the norther that brought the bark from St. Augustine with the survivors of Juan Corso's galley kept her in port. Change of wind and fortune came the morning of January 3. Barroto and Romero, after hearing Father Alcano's report of the lost galley, set sail without waiting to hear firsthand testimony of the survivors.

Two days later the voyagers sighted the Marquesas Keys and logged the position of 24° 30′ north latitude. "From there they began to run the coast from the Ensenada de Carlos, making observations of the sun, sounding river mouths and coves, to the port of Apalache, where they took refreshment and began their new discovery."[2]

The Florida mainland was sighted on the seventh, at 25° 50′. The ninth brought the frigate within view of the point at Tampa Bay, 27° 40′, according to the diary of Juan Jordán de Reina, a pilot from Havana who had come along "without salary or subsistence, to perform this service for His Majesty."[3] At five o'clock on the afternoon of the eleventh the Spanish mariners passed the mouth of the Suwannee River, which they called San Martín, and logged the latitude of 29° 30′. On January 17 they dropped anchor in the port of Apalache, at 30°.[4]

Here the searchers were partially fogbound for several days but continued to explore the various offshoots of the bay. Almost a week later, on the twenty-third, Manual Gómez, "the Lieutenant of the Province of Antimuqua, who temporarily was in charge of the Province of Apalache,"[5] came on board the reconnaissance vessel. The pilots quizzed him for any clue he could offer as to the whereabouts of La Salle. On the Apalachicola River, Gómez informed them, some Englishmen were engaged in trading among the Indians. The lieutenant of Apalache, Antonio Mateos, at the head of thirty infantrymen and eight hundred Indians, had gone out with orders to seize the invaders, ascertain their designs, and punish the Indians who were dealing with them. Three days later word came from Mateos that he had captured three native

[2] Gaspar de Palacios, Report, September 6, 1686, A.G.I., México, 1685-1688 (61-6-20), p. 110.
[3] Ibid.
[4] Juan Jordán de Reina, "Diario y derrotero del viaxe," March 16, 1686, A.G.I., México, 1685-1688 (61-6-20), p. 26.
[5] Ibid., pp. 26-27.

pueblos, but the inhabitants had fled. On the bank of the Apalachicola River he had found a storehouse of English trading goods, containing peltry, worsted stockings, and glass beads. The lieutenant and his company pressed on, hoping to capture the English and their native allies.

But Romero and Barroto could scarcely afford to concern themselves with these intruders. Their quarry was the French colony on Espíritu Santo Bay. Obtaining two Indian guides, they set sail at sunset on the thirtieth to begin the important part of the voyage. The following day the *Concepción* scudded along the coast to the west-southwest on a favorable wind, passing the mouths of three rivers. Thirty-three leagues from Apalache she changed course to conform with the coast, at Cape St. George (Punta de Abiñes), and sailed northwest two leagues. Then, becalmed, she dropped anchor.

The wind came back with the dawn, and no effort was made to enter the mouth of the Apalachicola River. By first light the frigate's crew weighed anchor and sailed northwestward. At nine o'clock a point covered with pine trees was sighted by the prow, with breakers rolling over the shoals extending a league and a half into the sea. The frigate took a southward tack to escape the shallow water. Even so, her bottom gouged the sand but cleared safely to anchor in six fathoms beyond the point.

> The Indian pilot told us that a very large ship had been lost on this point [Jordán recorded], where were seen a liquor case, a musket barrel, a pile of deer and bird bones, many deck timbers, and the tracks of a large number of people. It is believed that the galley of Captain Pedro de Castro [and Juan Corso] was lost here, and that the deck timbers were from his having made a small ship or boat in which to escape. But to this day nothing is known of [these men], except for the ten [actually nine] whom the Panzacola Indians found.[6]

"Punta Brava," as Jordán called it, evidently was Cape San Blas. It was seven leagues from the anchorage of the day before and three leagues from the mouth of the Apalachicola River, "which we could not reach because of the high wind that blew upon us from the southeast."[7] It was with considerable risk that the vessel

[6] Ibid., p. 28.
[7] Ibid.

had made the turn of the shore from the southwest with reduced sail, to travel northward.

On February 6 the *Concepción* reached "the bay the Indians call Panzacola"—in Jordán's words, "the best bay I had ever seen in my life."[8] Traveling "almost north," the vessel made the entrance with almost ten fathoms under her keel, then sailed northeastward the distance of a cannon shot to anchor in seven fathoms. Climbing to the maintop, Jordán could not see land to the north or northeast. Putting the launch over the side, some of the officers went with the Indian guide the following day to the village of the Panzacola Indians. With demonstrations of "love and good will" the natives conducted the Spaniards to the house of their cacique, "where they took out a cross for us to kiss, which we did with great devotion, kneeling down."[9] Seated with tribal council, the Spanish leaders asked if the Indians had knowledge of any white people in the region. The natives told of the marooned sailors from Juan Corso's galley, almost dead from hunger, who had been found by some fishermen of their tribe. After bringing the unfortunate ones to their pueblo, the Panzacolas had shared with them their meager provisions before taking them to the Apalachicola River, whence they proceeded to Presidio de la Florida.

Asked if they had seen any ships on the coast, the Panzacolas replied that many moons ago—April of the preceding year, as the Spaniards understood them—a ship had sailed into the bay, then departed to the westward one day later, leaving no one behind. Again, they must have referred to Juan Corso's galley.

Sorely afflicted by their wars with the Indians of "La Gran Mobila," the Panzacolas had lost many of their tribesmen and had seen their crops burned by their relentless enemy. Nevertheless, they shared what they had with the Spaniards—mainly corn torti-

---

[8] Ibid., p. 29.

[9] Ibid. The portion of the diary dealing with the rediscovery of Pensacola is translated in the Introduction to Irving A. Leonard (trans.), *Spanish Approach to Pensacola, 1689-1693*, pp. 13-14. This source (pp. 1-19) gives a concise summary of the La Salle expedition with emphasis on events relating to Pensacola Bay. The Jordán diary is translated in its entirety in Irving A. Leonard, "The Spanish Re-exploration of the Gulf Coast in 1686," *Mississippi Valley Historical Review* 22, No. 4 (March, 1936):547-557. Leonard errs, however, in attempting to identify landmarks mentioned by Jordán with present-day names.

llas. The Spaniards in turn regaled the natives with beads, and the
Panzacolas were happy with the exchange. "They advised us to
proceed with caution along the large bay and river of La Gran
Mobila, because those fierce and warlike Indians have three mighty
villages there."[10]

Back on board their vessel on the eighth of February, the Spaniards took sun shots and determined their latitude to be 30° 30'.
Their longitude they considered to be the same as that of the Bay
of Sisal, on the Campeche coast (Yucatán)—a calculation that
modern maps show to be somewhat in error. The distance from
Punta de Abiñes was estimated at sixty leagues (about 158 miles).
At three in the afternoon the frigate got underway and moved
near to the mouth of the bay, where it anchored in seven fathoms
"near the leeward shore, which extends three leagues, northeast to
southwest."[11] Entering the bay nearby was a waterfilled creek
adjacent to a high bank of red clay, "an easily recognizable land-
mark."

A northeasterly wind on the ninth carried the frigate southwestward a short distance. Then she sailed west-southwest, skirting the
coast and its beach of clean white sand. Anchorage was made in
ten fathoms, eight to ten leagues from that of the previous day.
Mindful of the Panzacolas' warning of hostile Mobilas, the Spaniards took care to arm themselves with cutlasses and firearms on
setting out the following day, again sailing west-southwest until
sunset.

On the eleventh the explorers felt their way slowly along an
island, finally putting the launch over the side to go ashore. To the
north of the island—distinguished by its growth of chinaberry
trees—the mariners saw a large body of water—Mobile Bay—which
they entered by an opening between the island and the mainland
to anchor in three fathoms. As darkness fell they could see many
Indian fires spaced at intervals along the shore. Latitude was computed at 30° 10', the distance from Pensacola Bay at sixteen to
eighteen leagues.

The reconnaissance vessel remained in Mobile Bay until Febru-

[10] Jordán, "Diario," p. 30.
[11] Ibid.

ary 25, but a hiatus in the diary's narration obscures the mariners' activities during that two-week period. The first day after resuming the voyage the frigate made good only five or six leagues on a slight wind. The following day the *Concepción* felt her way among the islands and shoals of the Mississippi Sound, not daring to attempt to get inside them, making good ten leagues to the southwest. That she missed grounding on the shoals was considered a miracle.

The vessel continued on the same course proceeding cautiously among the Chandeleur Islands and playing tag with the shallow mud bottom, until Monday, March 4, when she came to land's end. At eleven o'clock that day she stood off the shoals of mud at the end of the Mississippi Delta. The pilots, observing the mighty river as it emptied into the sea, failed to recognize it as the "Micipipi" mentioned by the frightened young Frenchman Denis Thomas, or as the Espíritu Santo Bay described by Pineda, Benavides, Peñalosa, and Echagaray. Instead they saw a river's mouth choked with logs to such an extent that they believed no mariner in his right mind would attempt to enter it. And from the logs, they gave the river a name: El Río de la Palizada. They computed the latitude at 29° 03', indicating a location in Garden Island Bay, near Port Eads. The distance from Apalache was given as one hundred leagues.

But no sign was there to indicate that such a disgusting place—their feeling expressed in the name of Cabo de Lodo, or Mud Cape, which they gave it—was the intended site of La Salle's colony. The pilots concluded, therefore, "that the Bay of Espíritu Santo for which we came to search is not in the latitude at which it is placed on the charts, but somewhat farther west."[12]

While the pilots were pondering the advisability of attempting to enter the river's mouth, a storm arose and drove them southward across the gulf to Cayo Arenas, less than a degree of latitude from the Yucatán Peninsula. With less than ten days' provisions

[12] Ibid., p. 33. Luis Gómez Raposo ("Diario del descubrimiento que hizo el Capitán Don Andrés del Pez," in Spain, Consejo Superior de Investigaciones Científicas, *Colección de diarios y relaciones para la historia de los viajes y descubrimientos*, IV, 132) says the Barroto-Romero expedition sighted the river mouth at North Pass, latitude 29° 20'. See Chapter 11 of this study.

left, they considered it unwise to return to the mouth of the Río de la Palizada to resume the reconnaissance. Instead they set sail for Veracruz, where they arrived March 13 at eight o'clock in the evening.[13]

The following day Barroto and Romero met with Admiral Palacios and the provincial officers to give them an oral report of the voyage. The local officers then reported by letter to the viceroy, sending a copy of the diary of Juan Jordán de Reina.

Two important results of the voyage stand out, one positive, the other negative. First, Pensacola Bay was rediscovered, and glowing reports of the site eventually led others to urge its settlement. The second, negative, result was the failure of the expedition's leaders to recognize the importance of the mouth of the Mississippi. Their cursory report influenced observations of later explorers, clearing the way for the French ultimately to gain a foothold there in effective challenge of Spanish claims to the coastal region and its hinterlands.[14]

Palacios and the other writers acknowledged that the first official expedition in search of La Salle had fallen short of its principal objective: the reconnaissance of Espíritu Santo Bay. Yet the admiral was firm in the conviction that the navigators had done the best they could under the circumstances, which included the shortness of provisions and the storm that had driven them almost all the way across the Gulf of Mexico.[15]

All were in agreement, however, that a new voyage should be undertaken immediately. Barroto and Romero were willing to try again, but it was agreed that this time they should go in two long barks, to be specially made in the port of Veracruz. The vessels would be equipped with both sail and oars, and each would be manned by twenty men and supplied for four months. These specially designed craft could maneuver the shallow water along the coast without running the hazard experienced by the frigate *Concepción* in the shallows off Cape St. George and among the Chandeleur Islands.[16] The new expedition should get underway

---

[13] Palacios, Report, p. 111. The storm is not mentioned in the diary.

[14] Leonard, "The Spanish Re-exploration of the Gulf Coast in 1686," p. 550.

[15] Joseph de Murueta Otálora and Francisco García de Arroyo to the Viceroy, March 15, 1686, A.G.I., México, 1678-1686 (61-6-20), pp. 159-161; Gaspar de Palacios to the Viceroy, March 15, 1686, ibid., pp. 161-162; Palacios, Report, pp. 110-113.

[16] Otálora and García to the Viceroy, pp. 160-161.

by the end of April, to seek anew the Bay of Espíritu Santo, which Admiral Palacios believed would be found twenty to twenty-five leagues west of the Río de la Palizada.

The viceroy's advisers, the *factor* and the *fiscal*, agreed generally with Admiral Palacios's recommendations. The former official suggested that the viceroy reopen the question of having the coastline explored by land. The province of Nuevo Reino de León, he noted, was believed to extend within one hundred leagues of the elusive Espíritu Santo Bay; the governor of Nuevo León, the Marqués de San Miguel de Aguayo, should be charged with making an entrada, aided by the friendly Indians who were obedient to the Spaniards. "By this means it is possible to thwart the evil intention of these pirates, by which they would settle as far as New Mexico and make themselves Lords of many Kingdoms and Provinces."[17]

The *fiscal* noted that steps already had been taken in that direction. The previous December he had searched the files for a record of explorations made from Nuevo León, and the governor had been instructed to make inquiry of the distances involved and to seek a suitable leader for conducting the land reconnaissance.[18]

On March 18 a general junta met to consider the various reports and proposals. It noted that the king, the previous August 2, had issued approval for Martín de Echagaray to undertake the search for Espíritu Santo Bay, with assistance provided by the governor of Florida, Don Juan Márquez Cabrera. Since it was not known in Mexico whether Echagaray had begun the exploration, the junta ruled, plans for further maritime expeditions should be held in abeyance.[19] Meanwhile, the search was to be taken up by land on the northern frontier, under the leadership of a tough frontiersman whose name would thenceforth be remembered in connection with that of La Salle—Alonso de León.

[17] Sebastián de Guzmán y Córdoba, "Ynforme," A.G.I., México, 1678-1686 (61-6-20), p. 164.

[18] Pedro de la Bastida, "Repuesta," ibid., pp. 166-167.

[19] Antonio de Morales, "Junta General," ibid., pp. 168-174. Although the junta met on March 18, the report is dated April 3.

6. TO THE RÍO BRAVO

Today all the coast of the Gulf of Mexico has been discovered and explored except for that section between the mouth of the Río de la Empalizada [sic], at 29 degrees latitude, and the River of Tampico, which is at twenty-one and one-third. This is a distance of a hundred leagues, more or less, in which lies Espíritu Santo Bay and, farther west, the Río Bravo. . . . That the French dwell in this place is quite apparent, since it is contiguous with Nueva Vizcaya, where so many mines, the object of their settlement, have been discovered.

—Admiral Gaspar de Palacios
Report, September, 1686, p. 113

In their search for a military leader familiar with the region to the north, the officials of Veracruz and Tampico were unsuccessful. Vague rumors came to them of a frontiersman from the Nuevo León town of Cadereyta who had led explorations as far as the unknown Río de las Palmas[1] and who had discovered some salines in the vicinity of the Río de San Juan. It was held likely that both these rivers flowed into Espíritu Santo Bay, no more than six or seven days' journey from Monterrey. Perhaps, suggested the officials, the archives of the viceroy would yield information on these expeditions; if so the documents should be forwarded to the governor of Nuevo Reino de León, that he might seek out this adelantado, who unquestionably could be of help in conducting the proposed search by land.[2]

[1] The Mexican river presently known as Soto la Marina. The Río Grande is frequently said to be the stream called Río de las Palmas by Pineda (see Walter Prescott Webb [ed.], *The Handbook of Texas*, II, 474). Documents of the period of our narrative, however, identify the Soto la Marina as the Río de las Palmas (see Chapter 14, n. 7).
[2] Pedro de la Bastida, "Repuesta del Señor Fiscal," December 20, 1685, A.G.I., México, 1678-1686 (61-6-20), pp. 75-76.

The archival search soon turned up the documents in question. Included was the report of the *sergento mayor* Alonso de León on his discovery of four abundant salines on the San Juan, and his petition to the viceroy for a franchise to work the salt mines for his own profit. De León represented himself as the son of the noted captain by the same name, one of the first settlers of Cadereyta, and claimed twenty-eight years in the service of the king, as a soldier in the Royal Armada and in pacification of the Indians of Nuevo León. His most recent exploit—as related in his petition of 1682—had consisted of exploring the seacoast for a distance of fifty leagues, discovering two promising ports. One of these was at the River of Palms where, he estimated, no less than 200,000 Indians lived. In addition he had discovered the salines of San Lorenzo and the Río de San Juan, for which he now sought the franchise. He had been informed by natives of precious metals to be found in the coastal region, and he claimed actually to have seen specimens. It would be to the advantage of the crown, he suggested, to have the salt deposits worked, since it would stimulate settlement and result in the opening of ports and roads. Discovery of gold and silver mines also might result, as well as settlement of the natives, who would be brought from a place called Las Ciénagas de los Apóstoles to work the mines.[3]

On recommendation of the *fiscal*, the viceroy granted De León a fifteen-year franchise (he had asked for twenty), on termination of which all rights should revert to the crown. In return the grantee should settle the Indians by the most suitable nonviolent means. De León also was conceded the right to discover the mines of which the Indians had informed him.[4]

To what extent he took advantage of the official grant, once he had received it, is not definitely known. Any failure to fulfill terms of the franchise might have been caused by the departure of the governor of Nuevo Reino de León, Juan de Echeverría, his health broken, on his terminal journey to Mexico City. He died the following December. At the end of February, 1683, Alonso de León took the office of governor on an interim basis "to the great

---

[3] Alonso de León, Petition, ibid., pp. 64-67.
[4] Bastida, "Repuesta del Señor Fiscal," December 13, 1682, pp. 67-70, and the viceroy's decree of January 26, 1683, ibid., pp. 71-74.

pleasure and satisfaction of everyone." During the relatively short time he served, it is said, "he looked after the affairs of state and the citizens like a true native son."[5]

Arriving from Spain at the port of Veracruz, meanwhile, was the new governor-appointee, Agustín Echeverz y Subiza, Marqués de San Miguel de Aguayo. He reached the province to take office February 4, 1684. It was he, the *junta general* decided on December 20, 1685, who should be asked to initiate the land search for Espíritu Santo Bay and its reported French colony. The papers relating De León's explorations, together with instructions for beginning the quest, should be dispatched to the new governor without delay, the junta ruled.[6]

By the time the papers relating to De León's exploits had been found and examined and the viceroy's orders prepared, it was May 1.[7] Not until June 8 did the documents reach the governor of Nuevo León. The Marqués de Aguayo hastily dispatched riders to the outlying ranches and settlements of his province to bring in those persons most knowledgeable of the region. On June 11 twenty-six military officers "and other citizens, encomenderos, and officers who have served in the militia of this Kingdom" responded to the governor's call. All frontier veterans, these men had traveled over the province in pursuit of hostile Indians and on reconnaissance, and, by the governor's statement, some of them had crossed the Río Grande at the ford that lay beyond Cerralvo, penetrating as far as five or six leagues into present-day Texas.

Among the officers were the *sergento mayor* Alonso de León, the former interim governor who presently was serving as lieutenant governor; Captain Juan Bautista Ruiz of the presidio of Cerralvo; Captain Antonio Leal of the presidio of Cadereyta; and Captain Diego de Villareal, *justicia mayor* and captain of the jurisdiction of the salines—presumably those for which De León had

---

[5] Alonso de León, and others, *Historia de Nuevo León*, pp. 192-193.

[6] Fructos Delgado and others, "Junta General," December 20, 1685, A.G.I., México, 1678-1686 (61-6-20), p. 77 (erroneously cited by William Edward Dunn, *Spanish and French Rivalry in the Gulf Region of the United States, 1678-1702*, p. 66, as January 20, 1686).

[7] Marqués de San Miguel de Aguayo to the Viceroy, June 15, 1686, A.G.I., México, 1685-1688 (61-6-20), p. 79. Aguayo ("Testimonio," ibid., p. 83) refers to a letter from the viceroy dated January 20, 1686, in which instructions were given for ascertaining the truth behind reports that the French had settled on Espíritu Santo Bay. None of the documents, in any event, reached Monterrey before June 8.

been granted the franchise.[8] But none of the group had traveled as far as Espíritu Santo Bay, where the French were said to have settled.

Missing from the documents sent by the viceroy was the itinerary from Admiral Gaspar de Palacios; the junta was forced to consider the matter without complete information. Missing also were documents cited by the *fiscal* as saying that Espíritu Santo Bay was only six or seven days' journey from Monterrey. "In this Kingdom," Aguayo reported, "there is no information of the direction to be taken to reach said bay, because the land has not been traversed that far." It was claimed that in ancient times, the junta noted, expeditions had been made to the Villa de Tampico and the province of Huasteca, and that communication and trade had been opened between Nuevo León and those places. Actually, Aguayo pointed out, such results had not been attained, because of the distance and the many nations of hostile Indians who blocked the Spaniards' travel.[9]

It was recalled that Don Juan de Echeverría, as governor of the province in 1682, had sent Alonso de León with a company of soldiers to Huasteca and the Villa de los Valles (west of Tampico). On the return portion of this journey, De León had discovered the salines for which he was given the franchise, but, unfortunately, these journeys had not provided information on the route to Espíritu Santo Bay.

Members of the junta, however, agreed that the bay in question must lie to the northeast. The "big river"—*río grande*—which some of them had crossed on previous expeditions, was taken by Aguayo to be that which appeared on navigational charts as the Río Bravo.

Since the region was infested by "many barbarous Chichimeco Indians" and no person was available who was familiar with the route and its landmarks, the governor decided to raise a force of fifty men from the military garrisons and the citizenry. The expedition was to assemble at Cadereyta on June 25 to proceed to the Río Grande and follow its course to the sea.

Shortly after the junta adjourned, Aguayo received the first

[8] Aguayo, "Testimonio," pp. 85-86.
[9] Ibid., p. 84.

direct news of La Salle's settlement to reach officials of New Spain. The bearer was a Pelón Indian who had visited among the Blanco and Pajarito nations. His hosts had told him that white people who resembled the Spaniards had been seen on the banks of the Río Grande.[10] These people were said to have come from a larger settlement somewhere north of the river, where they planted corn and tobacco by hand, since they had no oxen and few horses.

Along with the white people who had come to the Río Grande was an Indian who wore trousers, a cassock, and a large hat, and carried a "knife"–probably meaning a saber. This Indian had come with a companion to call on a native *ranchería,* but the two visitors were not kindly received. Inhabitants of the village killed the companion, and the Indian, though wounded, managed to escape. Befriended by the Blanco Indians, he dwelt among them until he recovered from his wounds, then returned to his masters.

In the opinion of the Pelón Indian, the distance to the white settlement itself could be covered in ten days. He offered to guide the Spaniards as far as the land of the Pajaritos and Blancos; the road beyond, he believed, was easy and not inhabited by hostile Indians.[11]

The account of this Indian sheds new light on the movements of La Salle as he explored southern Texas, supposedly in search of the Mississippi River. Having set out to the west from Matagorda (Espíritu Santo) Bay in the fall of 1685, he evidently had reached the lower Río Grande valley in the area soon to be explored. The Indian who had gone as emissary of the French to the native *ranchería,* where he was wounded and his companion was killed, almost certainly was La Salle's personal servant and interpreter, Nika. Further information on this expedition of the French explorer would be carried later to the Spanish mission settlement at La Junta de los Ríos by Indians of the Cíbolo and Jumano nations.

With the news that the native informant had brought from the wilds to the north, the coming expedition gained added significance: "It was determined [in the junta] that no one would be

---

[10] Aguayo to the Viceroy, pp. 79-80. Although "Río Grande" as it is used here might mean any big river, De León (*Historia*, p. 202) establishes that the Pajaritos, at least, lived on the river presently known by that name.

[11] Aguayo to the Viceroy, pp. 79-80.

able to carry out a project of such importance better than General Alonso de León . . . no one was found who was better qualified by experience."[1][2]

On receipt of the letter from the Marqués de San Miguel de Aguayo, the *junta general* in Mexico City ratified, ex post facto on July 6, the decision of the junta held in Monterrey almost a month earlier. The expedition had been underway more than a week.

In preparation for the reconnaissance one company of thirty soldiers, led by Captain Nicolás de Ochoa, marched from Monterrey for Cadereyta on June 26. Accompanying the Monterrey company was the governor himself. At Cadereyta, meanwhile, another company of twenty, with Captain Antonio Leal at its head, was gathered. Joined near the village on the twenty-seventh, the entire troop passed in review before the governor, who replaced the temporary leaders with Captains Carlos Cantú and Nicolás de Medina. In overall command he placed Alonso de León, who noted that he received the commission from the governor "more by his generosity than by my own merit." In the Cadereyta company marched two of the commandant's kinsmen, Sergeant Miguel de León and Captain Alonso de León III. In addition to the fifty soldiers were nineteen "muleteers, servant boys, and pages," an Indian guide who was chief of the Zacatil *ranchería*, and two other natives; forty muleloads of provisions—flour, biscuit, meat, and chocolate—and 468 horses. Fray Diego de Orozco, father-president of the Villa de Cadereyta, went as chaplain. As special aides to De León, the governor assigned his brother, Don Pedro Fermín de Echeverz, the sublieutenant Francisco de Benavides, and Juan Bautista Chapa.[1][3]

The review over, De León took up the march immediately, traveling eastward along the upper portion of the Río de San Juan. Turning toward the northeast on the third day, to conform with the river's course, the troop traveled through dense woods to reach a ford, sixteen leagues from Cadereyta. After crossing the river, the expedition was forced to detour around a large wood the following day. Bearing northeastward along the river, it stopped

[1][2] De León, *Historia*, pp. 193-194. De León was not at this time a general, though he later attained that rank,

[1][3] Ibid., pp. 194-196. The last named, it will be noted, was one of the co-authors of De León, *Historia*. This source names all those who accompanied the expedition.

near the present village of General Bravo, where it was noted that "the river straightens toward the north at this point."[14] The *ranchería* of De León's Indian guides, the Zacatiles, was nearby.

On Monday, July 1, the troop bore eastward, inclining slightly to the north. During the day forty-four Indians of the Cuarame nation joined the Spaniards. Camp was made that night on smooth ground, near some pools of rainwater, and De León's scouts came in to report that a *ranchería* of Indians who were enemies of the Cuarames had been sighted. The following day the leader took twenty men and went to seek the Indians, hoping to obtain two of their number as guides. But the chary savages, evidently fore-warned of the Spaniards' approach, had abandoned their camp. Pressing on northeastward, the Spanish troop encountered after eight leagues a wood too dense to penetrate with horses and pack mules and made camp at a small marsh. The Indian guide Alonso brought news that the Río Grande was near, and De León, by means of a path into the forest, succeeded in reaching the river, two leagues distant. He noted that "at this point it runs wide, the water very muddy. It appears to be navigable by small ships. I had no means of sounding it. It was the width of a harquebus shot, and this part runs toward the north."[15]

Wednesday, July 3. Not finding passage through the dense wood, I was forced (though with great labor) to take the troop around it. We traveled no more than two leagues today, because I was obliged to reconnoiter the route which we would follow the next day. To that purpose I went downriver with twelve companions. Unexpectedly, we came upon a *ranchería*, whose people, having observed us, had abandoned it and all their belongings. I ordered that nothing should be taken. Returning to the river, we followed it downstream, where we saw some Indian men and women swimming across. Although we called to them in peace, I could get no one to come. One did come to the narrowest part to shoot arrows at us, at less distance than a harquebus shot, from which we surmised that they had never seen Spaniards before, for he did not fear the harquebus shot. The course [today] was to the east.[16]

Finding dense woods along the Río Grande, De León traveled

[14] Ibid., p. 196.

[15] Ibid., p. 197. He apparently reached the stream opposite the present Texas village of La Joya, Hidalgo County.

[16] Ibid.

downstream four leagues the following day, staying outside the timber, and stopped at a gulch a league from the river bank. From the camp he and the twelve companions went to examine the river. Because of the dense growth it was necessary to travel three leagues to reach it. The river still ran wide and appeared to be navigable, but its steep banks afforded no place for the horses to go down to drink. On July 5 the expedition followed a narrow path, dangerously exposed to ambush by lurking Indians, and came to a watering place on the river, near some large hills. The stream still appeared to be navigable by small ship. De León went out with ten companions to explore the area, but the detail became entangled in "a wood so dense we could not penetrate it."[17]

During the days that followed, the expedition wormed its way downstream, four, then six leagues. Keeping close to the river, it frequently had to detour around dense woods, filled with briars and wild roses. Toward the end of the day on Sunday, July 7, De León and his scouting party of seven climbed the highest of a group of large hills to get a view of the countryside. They saw an expansive plain stretching out toward the river two leagues distant. Making preparations to spend the night on the eminence, they were startled by the sudden appearance just before sunset of some forty Indians. As the Spaniards mounted their horses, however, the Indians took flight. De León left a white cloth, biscuit, tobacco, and other tokens of friendship and returned to the main camp.

Passing by the hill the next day, he found the items where he had left them. The leader went forward with twenty men, still hoping to obtain an Indian guide. At last twenty of the natives came out of a wood, but, despite friendly gestures by the Spaniards, none would approach the visitors. Again De León left friendship tokens—a cloth and a knife—and withdrew. This time the Indians came to claim the gifts. They placed in their stead a banner made of feathers and another feather ornament (*plumero*), making signs that the Spaniards should come and take them, which they did.

As the explorers continued on their way, the Indians followed, always at a safe distance, in the shelter of the wood. After trav-

[17] Ibid.

eling eight leagues the Spaniards had to backtrack three to find water for the horses. The river afforded a good watering place, but the stream now appeared less favorable for navigation than it had farther upstream.

While De León led a scouting party over eight leagues in search of the next watering place, the main force remained an extra day at this place, then took up the march over the charted route. As the mules were being harnessed, thirty Indians sprang with a yell from the brush on the opposite bank of the river, making signs that the Spaniards took to mean the natives had united and come to put them to death. Two of the number danced about playing flutes. The savages then disappeared, only to return a short time later with doubled strength. As the Spaniards marched eastward along the river, they were conscious of the Indians lurking in the brush, following on the opposite bank. That night camp was made on a plain, away from the timber that afforded shelter for the menacing savages. Even the open place contained a reminder that the natives were close at hand, for the ground was trampled, indicating that as many as three hundred had taken part in a dance on the spot.

On the twelfth the expedition made camp at an estuary. The scouts found two lakes, one of them a league and a half long and half a league wide, the water much too salty for drinking. These salt lakes, just below present Matamoros, Tamaulipas, indicated that the coast was near. A meandering course the following day brought the Spaniards to an Indian village, which De León adjudged had been abandoned fifteen days previously. A barrel stave found in the village indicated that Europeans once had been in the area. De León, with his smaller force, traveled six leagues farther, keeping the river in view. At six in the evening they came unexpectedly upon a native village in the act of taking flight. The soldiers managed to capture three of the natives, who "were treated in a friendly manner and questioned by signs as to where there might be Spaniards and people who wore clothing." Pointing northward, the Indians indicated that two settlements of white people were to be found in that direction, and De León "inferred that they were not to be found at the mouth of the river that we had been following."[18]

[18] Ibid., pp. 199-200.

The nearest of the two settlements, by De León's understanding, lay to the northwest and was called Taguila; the other, more to the north, Zaguili. The savages could give no indication of the distance: "By no stretch of the imagination did they understand us or we them." Found in the village were a piece of the bottom of a wine cask, a broken bolt from a ship, a link of chain, and a small piece of glass. There the leader and the scouting detail made camp, and in the stillness of night was heard the roar of the sea.[19]

On Sunday, July 14, feast day of St. Buenaventura, De León sent four men to guide the main force forward to a point of rendezvous and proceeded with the rest of his scouts to find the coast. "Conquering marshes, cane brakes, willow thickets and the dense woods along the river, bearing northeast, we reached it, two leagues distant. No sign was found of either Spaniards or foreigners ever having come to the mouth of this river." The soldiers marched one league up the coast to the mouth of the Río Grande, which was the distance of a musket shot wide, muddy, and vermilion colored. From a crude raft built by the soldiers, soundings were taken in five or six places. The mouth was found to be eight fathoms at the deepest place—"sufficient for a seagoing vessel to enter some two leagues within."[20]

Exploring the coast four leagues in the direction of "the Río de Palmas,"[21] De León found fresh Indian trails and some staked enclosures where huts had stood long ago. Though the gulf breeze was gentle, a heavy sea rolled upon the smooth beach, which was littered by not a single pebble, though many logs and timbers lay along the shoreline where they had been left by the tide. With an astrolabe—"badly aimed and somewhat out of order"—a sun shot was taken at noon on July 15, and latitude was computed as 25° 45' north (actually about 25° 57').

With little pasture available along the smooth beach, De León ordered the main force to begin the homeward trek, while he took twenty-five soldiers to reconnoiter the coast once more. Covering eight leagues of shoreline, again in the direction of the Río de las Palmas, they found ship's planking, a bowsprit, masts, pieces of

---

[19] Ibid., p. 200.
[20] Ibid.
[21] Obviously meaning Soto la Marina, not the Río Grande, which the expedition had been following since July 2.

keel and rudder, bottoms of casks, staves, buoys, four wheels from artillery pieces, a cask with willow hoops, three broken canoes, and a small round glass flask sealed with a cork and containing a little stale wine. De León, noting the shape of the flask, believed it not to have been made in Spain. From the wide variety of ships' ruins, some old, some more recent, he surmised that many vessels had been wrecked upon the shore over a long period of time. "What surprised me the most was seeing some stalks of corn carried in by the surf. It appeared to have been grown this year, since it had begun to tassel, and the stalk had roots on it. From this evidence I surmised that a settlment was near, and that a flood had carried it from some field."[2] [2]

Still there was no solid evidence that the Frenchman La Salle had come to this river. De León must retire without being able to afix meaning to the evidence he had found.

Not until Wednesday, July 17, and only after punishing their horses, did the smaller band of soldiers overtake the main force at the rendezvous on the estuary where camp had been made five days previously. Traveling homeward, the force moved much faster than it had in coming. By Sunday, July 20, it had advanced up the Río Grande thirty-three leagues from the estuary and came to a halt near the native village where the savages had shot arrows at the Spaniards. Then they spied more than fifty Indians and moved to attack. Major Lucas Caballero, hoping to capture one of the natives, advanced into a thicket and was struck in the breast by an arrow. In return the Spaniards fired a volley, killing two of the savages; two Indian boys were captured.

On the twenty-third the troop departed from the course by which it had come in order to reach the village of the Pajaritos and stopped for the night at a place called Pool of the Skulls. Passing by the *ranchería* of the Cuarames the following day, the explorers came to the ford on the Río de San Juan, which they had passed on the third day out. On July 26, with jaded horses and tired men, the company reached Cadereyta, and De León made his report to the governor.

Despite the contents of the diary that De León filed with the Marqués de San Miguel de Aguayo the following day, the governor

----

[2] [2] De León, *Historia*, p. 201.

remained firm in the belief that the French settlement was to be found on the gulf, perhaps farther up the coast than the mouth of the Río Grande. Seven months after the return of the first expedition, a second was preparing to march. Three companies—led by Martín de Mendiondo, Pedro Fermín de Echeverz, and Nicolás de Medina, with De León in overall charge—set out at the end of February, 1687. Their orders called for proceeding to Cerralvo to cross the Río Grande twenty leagues distant (either near the latter-day towns of Zapata-Guerrero or Rio Grande City-Camargo), where a good ford was known to exist.

Proceeding past many nations of Indians "who gave ample sign of their hostility," the soldiers meandered across the tip of Texas to reach the coast on March 20. Tramping out the shoreline, they at last found their way blocked by a "big salty river"—probably Baffin Bay, southeast of present-day Kingsville. The one meager account of the expedition suggests that, had the force gone farther north, it might have found the crossing that would have taken it on to the discovery of the French colony it sought. As it was, however, the force turned back, having found neither a settlement of Frenchmen nor natives who could give a report of it. Much to the regret of everyone, the purpose remained frustrated. Especially disappointed was the governor, who was coming to the end of his term without having realized his greatest aspiration.[23]

---

[23] Ibid., pp. 202-203.

7. AWAKENING IN FLORIDA

All these Designs being disappointed, he resolv'd to set out a second Time, and travel by Land, to find out his River. He staid to rest him a while, and to provide for his Departure, but having neither Linen nor Cloaths, I supply'd him with some I had. . . . All Things being thus provided, Monsieur *de la Sale* took twenty Men along with him. . . . Each of the Travellers made up his Pack, and they set out towards the latter End of *April* 1686.

—Henri Joutel
Journal, pp. 108-109

While the Spaniards looked for the French colony, the Frenchmen continued their search for the Mississippi. Misfortune still stalked the colonists. The loss of the *Belle*, at about the time of La Salle's return from his voyage to the westward, dashed all hopes of going by sea to find "the fatal river." Also nullified was a plan taking shape in La Salle's mind to use the vessel to go "up one of the Rivers he had discover'd, to advance towards those Nations with whom he had contracted some Friendship," as well as an alternate scheme to send back to the Caribbean islands for assistance.[1] No course remained open but to continue the quest by land.

On April 22, after mass and prayers in the chapel, La Salle and his band of twenty issued from the gate of Fort St. Louis to undertake the trek across the silent prairies to the east. Anxious eyes of men, women, and children followed them until they became specks upon the farthest hill, those within the palisade

---

[1] Henri Joutel, *Joutel's Journal of La Salle's Last Voyage, 1684-7*, p. 108.

doubtless wondering which of the twenty they would ever see again. And whether, before their return, the Spaniards would find Fort St. Louis.

Slow and tedious as the hunt for La Salle's colony was, the Spanish searchers had in two expeditions considerably narrowed the area of the search. The Barroto-Romero voyage had examined the coast from the tip of Florida to the mouth of the Mississippi; Alonso de León and his troop from Monterrey and Cadereyta had tramped out the lower Río Grande and the coastal region adjacent to that river's mouth. By such an eliminative process, the Spaniards could infer that the French settlement lay somewhere between the estuaries of the Mississippi and the Río Grande. In all that mass of tangled wilderness between the two, there hardly seemed to be a hospitable site for civilized human habitation. In short, it appeared likely that the French, in their attempt at intrusion, already had met failure, either at the hands of sanguinary natives or from the wilderness itself. In certain quarters a feeling of complacence settled over Spanish officials. Why should they concern themselves, when the vast, unexplored, unsettled country offered so adequately its own defense?

Still the rumors wafted, and smugness could not endure. The continuing war with the French pirates alone was enough to keep the Spaniards on edge. As one band of captured corsairs had served to alert them to the intrusion, another bade fair to keep their fear alive. The French buccaneers, following the rape of Campeche, had split up and gone seeking new conquests. While plans were being made in Mexico for launching the search for La Salle's colony from New Spain's northern frontier, the pirate chieftain Michel de Grammont aimed a blow at the Florida coastal settlements.

The Florida governor, Don Juan Márquez Cabrera, at St. Augustine, was well aware of the threat that hovered over Spain's colonial possessions as a result of the rumored French colony. It was his subordinate at the port of Apalache who had provided Indian guides for Captains Romero and Barroto to take them westward on their costal reconnaissance the previous January. From the viceroy he had received word of that expedition's failure. The news distressed him, for during the previous three years French and English pirates had made repeated thrusts at his coastline, bent on finding the Achilles' heel of his presidio's defenses.

During the six years of Cabrera's tenure as governor, the English traders from St. George (Carolina) had steadily pushed against his coastal outposts from the north, gradually driving back the Spanish line until, in this year 1686, it had been withdrawn to the St. Marys River.[2]

The Carolina traders, led by "Captain Juan Enríquez"–Dr. Henry Woodward–spread their operations among the various tribes of the Apalachicola confederacy, steadily marching westward. By early 1686 they had penetrated the wilderness more than one hundred leagues, "disturbing the provinces of Caveta, Casista, and Apalachicola." From the direction they took, it appeared to Cabrera that they were themselves seeking Espíritu Santo Bay, perhaps to form a liaison with the French for driving out the Spaniards. To thwart the English intruders he sent Lieutenant Antonio Mateos of the Presidio of Apalache with six Spanish soldiers and five hundred armed Indians. But the poachers already had won friends among the natives, who concealed them from the searchers. No sooner had the Spaniards withdrawn than the English again emerged and renewed their activities. Again Mateos went out, this time with twenty soldiers and six hundred Indians. Again the native caciques sheltered the intruders.

Refusing to be frustrated a second time, Mateos ordered the burning of four principal native villages. "It was because of these *entradas*," Cabrera reported, "that the Indians of the Province of Chicasa [Chickasaw] who live in the vicinity of Espíritu Santo Bay, rendered obedience [to the Spanish crown]."[3] The repentance of the natives, however, was short-lived. As early as May 20

---

[2] See Herbert Eugene Bolton, "Spanish Resistance to the Carolina Traders in Western Georgia, 1680-1704," in *Bolton and the Spanish Borderlands*, pp. 133-139, for a discussion of the Anglo-Spanish conflict during this period. Much background information also is found in Mark F. Boyd, "Introduction," in Boyd, Hale G. Smith, and John W. Griffin, *Here They Once Stood: The Tragic End of the Apalachee Missions*, pp. 1-19.

[3] Juan Márquez Cabrera to the Viceroy, July 22, 1686, A.G.I. México, 1671-1685 (61-6-20), p. 320. According to Bolton ("Spanish Resistance," p. 140 n.), Mateos ascended the Chattahoochee River in September, 1685, and again in December. He evidently was on the latter expedition when Romero and Barroto stopped at Apalache in January, 1686, and were informed of his efforts by Lieutenant Manuel Gómez (see Chapter 5 of this study).

Cabrera reported that the English were continuing their intercourse with the natives in Spanish-held territory.[4]

Against this backdrop of troubles with the English, the French corsairs moved in to galvanize Cabrera to action. On April 30 a galley manned by a crew of forty and flying the Spanish flag approached the Florida coast at Matanzas Bar,[5] five leagues south of the Presidio de la Florida at St. Augustine. Four soldiers in a launch came out to hail the vessel and were invited in Spanish to come on board. Accepting the invitation, they soon found themselves prisoners of the French pirates. The corsair then put several men ashore to seek provisions and an Indian interpreter. While the landing party was away, the buccaneers on board tortured two of the Spanish soldiers to extract information concerning the nearby presidio.

As those on shore returned with another Spanish prisoner, several Indian captives, and some provisions, the pirates espied a band of soldiers approaching from the presidio. The Spanish flag already lowered, they made ready for battle.

Sentinels posted by the governor in the Matanzas area had carried the alarm to St. Augustine. Cabrera, receiving the news at ten o'clock at night, acted within the hour to send four men to Matanzas, dispatching another four as scouts. At two in the morning one of the scouts returned to apprise Cabrera of the situation. Within two hours the governor had roused twenty-five musketeers from their beds and sent them marching for Matanzas. At six o'clock sixteen more men marched. The two details arrived

[4] Pedro de la Bastida, "Repuesta del Fiscal," July 19, 1686, A.G.I. México, 1671-1685 (61-6-20), p. 255; Viceroy Conde de Paredes to the King, same date, ibid., pp. 137-138.

[5] According to Herbert Eugene Bolton (*Spanish Borderlands*, pp. 146-147) the place still called Las Matanzas (The Massacres) was so named for a massacre perpetrated by the Spaniards upon bound French captives in September, 1565. General Pedro Menéndez de Avilés, having just founded St. Augustine, had marched on the French stronghold at Fort Caroline, where his men slaughtered 132 Frenchmen. Then he learned that 140 Frenchmen who had sailed from Fort Caroline to attack St. Augustine had been shipwrecked near the Spanish settlement. After inducing the castaways to surrender, he marched them, with hands bound behind their backs, toward St. Augustine. At Matanzas the Spanish soldiers, on Menéndez's orders, fell upon the Frenchmen and slew 130 Protestants. Ten Catholics who had been set apart were spared. The foul deed was repeated on a grander scale a short time later when the French captain Jean Ribaut was marooned on the bar with 200 men. Following their surrender to Menéndez, with their hands bound for the march to St. Augustine, they were massacred on the same spot. Only 17 who professed to be Catholics were spared (ibid., p. 148).

at the bar within an hour of each other—sometime after ten o'clock in the morning. As they approached the anchorage, the pirates came to meet them in two launches. A four-hour battle followed. The soldiers, getting the worst of the battle, withdrew with one dead and four wounded.

The Spaniards bivouacked on the shore till dawn, then attacked. The pirate galley, driven by heavy groundswells during the night, now was aground on the bar. The buccaneers, carrying their arms in their mouths, waded ashore and dug holes in the beach from which they poured a heavy fire into the Spanish troops. At last reinforcements arrived, first nine soldiers with Captain Antonio Arguelles, then forty with Major Pedro de Aranda y Avellaneda. Again the Spaniards were held off. Captain Arguelles took a musket ball in the breast, and his nephew, Diego Arguelles, was killed. A Spanish prisoner, Antonio Rutinel, attempted to escape from the pirates and was mortally wounded. Two other soldiers were killed, another six wounded, before the Spaniards again withdrew.[6]

The Spaniards attempted to keep watch until dawn, but the night was cloudy and dark, punctuated by frequent showers. The pirate captain, Nicolás Brigaut, first sent out a launch with five men to carry a message to Grammont, whose forty-eight-gun vessel and a sloop lay offshore farther to the south. Grammont was informed that the crew would forsake the grounded galley and go by land to the Bar of Mosquitos, thirteen leagues down the coast. Brigaut asked the buccaneer chief to send the sloop to pick up his men there. Then, with the sound and sight of their movements obscured from the Spaniards by rain and darkness, the beleaguered pirates stole ashore and marched down the coast undetected. Clothing and provisions from the galley were carried on the backs of the prisoners as the pirates began the five-day trek. The rain obliterated their tracks.

The same night Grammont's ship approached Matanzas Bar near the grounded galley and dropped anchor. The Spaniards naturally assumed that Brigaut's crew had escaped in their boats and boarded the other vessel. On receipt of such a report the governor ordered part of his force withdrawn, leaving twenty-five men to guard the galley until it could be salvaged.[7]

[6] Juan de Ayala, Report, Havana, June 23, 1686, A.G.I., México, 1685-1688 (61-6-20), pp. 105-107.
[7] Ibid., p. 107.

When Brigaut's men were five leagues from the Bar of Mosquitos, having made a noon stop, they were approached by fifty or sixty Indians, who offered signs of friendship. The natives proposed to take the Frenchmen to their canoes to eat with them, but Brigaut, suspecting trickery, warned his men to put no trust in the warriors. Without warning the Indians began shooting arrows at the buccaneers, six of whom fell wounded. The attack, Brigaut perceived, was designed to free the prisoners. As he ordered his men to open fire upon the Indians, the natives fled.[8]

With a canoe that had been washed up on the beach, the thirty-five pirates and five captives crossed to the bar to await arrival of Grammont's sloop.

Among the prisoners held by the buccaneers was an Apalachino Indian, Juan López, from the Pueblo of San Luis (Tallahassee). When the pirates talked among themselves, López listened carefully. The grounded galley, he learned, was but one of a fleet of French privateers in Florida waters, bent on putting men ashore on the coastal islands or bars in order to surprise and capture the presidio of St. Augustine.

After four days López found opportunity to escape. Plunging into the water, he swam for shore amid a hail of musket fire and three days later reached St. Augustine to inform Governor Cabrera. Thus the official learned the whereabouts of the galley's crewmen who had slipped from the Spaniards' grasp. Most interesting of all was López's statement, though erroneous, that the captain of the pirate galley was the well-known Spanish renegade Alonso de Avesilla. Such a possibility served as a spur to the sanguine officers of St. Augustine.

Cabrera, with news that two enemy vessels lay off the island of Santa María, twelve leagues north of St. Augustine, already had dispatched eighteen men to that sector to forestall a landing. From friendly native chieftains to the south word had come of seven vessels' having approached the shore near the Bar of Ais, some days previously. The ships had withdrawn, but now forty men were said to be running up the coast in launches. Cabrera hastily called a council of his officers to determine his course of action.[9]

---

[8] Nicolás Brigaut, "Confesión del Capitán de la galeota de nación francés Corsario pirata," May 30, 1686, A.G.I., México, 1671-1685 (61-6-20), pp. 152-154.
[9] Juan Márquez Cabrera, "Autos," May 26, 1686, ibid., pp. 139-141.

The seriousness with which he viewed the situation is reflected by the fact that, in the face of numerous enemy threats on his province during his six years in office, the governor had never previously called his captains to such a *junta de guerra*. They gave him full support. Notwithstanding the cost, and the shortage of personnel as a result of Cabrera's having deployed his troops in appropriate places to prevent the pirates from landing on the mainland, they advised dispatching up to forty men in two piraguas to pursue the enemy as far as the Bar of Ais. "The principal goal to which the pursuit of said enemy should be directed," the officers declared, "is that of taking Alonso de Avesilla prisoner, as the prime mover and principal leader of the invasions which for three consecutive years the said enemies have attempted against this presidio."[10]

Cabrera acted immediately to send Captain Francisco de Fuentes with fifty men to seek the French corsairs from whom Juan López had escaped at the Bar of Mosquitos. Marching to the bar, the Spanish force caught the pirates ill prepared. Nineteen of the Frenchmen under Brigaut's leadership had left the bar to swim ashore, carrying their muskets and powder in waterproof bags. The presidial soldiers evidently made short work of the nineteen corsairs, then proceeded to the bar to deal with the rest. Motivated by a desire for vengeance on the hated renegade Avesilla, the Spaniards massacred them to a man, apparently killing even the five— three Spaniards, a mulatto, and a Negro—whom the buccaneers held prisoner. Of the forty-five men, including the five innocent, only Brigaut, a Negro pirate named Diego, and a nine-year-old boy were left alive. Brigaut and the Negro were taken to Presidio de la Florida and given an opportunity to confess before being put to death on the gallows. Ironically, Alonso de Avesilla, the principal target of the Spaniards' wrath and vengeance, was not to be found among the dead.[11]

[10] Francisco de la Rocha and Francisco de Ligaroa (or La Garroa), "Repuesta de oficiales reales," San Agustín, May 26, 1686, ibid., pp. 144-145.

[11] The five men sent by Brigaut with a message for Grammont evidently had rejoined the crew to make the total number of forty-five. William Edward Dunn (*Spanish and French Rivalry in the Gulf Region of the United States, 1678-1702*, p. 70) says that forty-five of the buccaneers were "summarily executed," indicating that they were captured, then shot or hanged. Rather, the documents, though hazy, imply that forty-three were slain in the battle in which they were shown no quarter, with the two hanged later.

On May 30 Nicolás Brigaut was brought before the governor and the public notary of St. Augustine to confess his crimes against the Spanish crown. It was this confession which aroused in the breast of Governor Cabrera a deadly fear of the consequences of the rumored French settlement on Espíritu Santo Bay, and convinced him that such a settlement in fact existed.

Brigaut declared himself to be thirty-three years old, a native of the Ile de Ré on the coast of France (three leagues from La Rochelle), of Protestant persuasion, and a mariner by trade. Seven years previously he had sailed from France for Martinique to obtain a cargo of sugar, but his ship was lost at sea, fifty leagues from Puerto Rico. Rescued by another vessel, he was taken to Santo Domingo, where he signed on with a fleet bound from Petit Goâve for Maracaibo. Later he left the ship in New England, where he purchased a forty-tun sloop.[12] Sailing to Isla de la Tortilla, off Caracas, he joined the fleet of French privateers headed by Grammont and Laurens de Graff, which boasted seven hundred men and was preparing for the assault on Campeche. Following the rape of the Mexican port, in which six hundred men from ten ships went ashore,[13] he took command, on commission from Grammont, of a captured forty-man galley at Campeche. This was the same galley that now lay on the Bar of Matanzas, five leagues from St. Augustine, and whose crew had been massacred by the vengeful Spaniards.

After Campeche, Grammont and De Graff had a falling-out. While the latter put to sea intent on sailing down the South American coast, Grammont put in at the Isla de Roatán, off Honduras, to careen his vessels. Then the chief's forty-eight-gun vessel, a sloop, and Brigaut's galley set sail for Carolina—St. George—to raise a force of six hundred men for capturing St. Augustine. The plan was communicated to Brigaut by Grammont himself. The

See Brigaut, "Confesión," p. 155; Juan Márquez Cabrera, "Ynforme," July 22, 1686, A.G.I., México, 1671-1685 (61-6-20), p. 319.

[12] "Tunnage in England and France at this period meant a ship's capacity in *tuns*, double hogsheads in which they shipped wine. From this developed the modern standard for a maritime ton as 40 cubic feet" (Samuel Eliot Morison, *The European Discovery of America: The Northern Voyages, A.D. 500-1600*, p. 124).

[13] Denis Thomas ("Declaración," A.G.I., México, 1678-1686, p. 11) says that seven-hundred men went ashore at Campeche, with the entire expedition comprising eleven or twelve ships with up to twelve hundred men.

scheme had gone awry when Brigaut attempted to land on the Florida shore to pick up provisions and interpreters, encountered Spanish soldiers, and had his galley washed up on the bar.

The pirate captain, asked if he knew of any new settlements being formed along the North Sea (Atlantic) or the South (Pacific), repeated the story told many months earlier in Mexico by another ill-fated participant in the rape of Campeche, Denis Thomas:

Two years previously "Monsieur Acale" (La Salle), who had discovered for the king of France a river called "Misipipi," had come with a ship of fifty-four guns and three hundred men captained by a French naval officer; the king had given ten thousand pesos to defray the cost of the expedition, a *pingue* laden with provisions and artillery, and another smaller ship; with the two smaller ships the noted explorer had planned to cruise up the river from the bay as far as possible, and thence by land to a suitable place for building a fort; at Petit Goâve three months previously the larger vessel had passed on its way to France, leaving the two smaller ships and the settlers behind to build the fort; from having talked and dined with the French governor at Petit Goâve he knew that this official had planned to take some settlers from Petit Goâve and others coming from France to the new French settlement, though the governor's advanced age and illness caused Brigaut to doubt that such plans had been carried out.[14]

Quizzed further the following day, the Protestant Brigaut—whose confession, it was noted, was not taken legally, because he was not a "Christian"—testified that the pirate chieftains Grammont and "Lorenzo" operated under orders from the king of France. One part of those orders, he attested, spelled out French plans to capture the Spanish-held portion of Santo Domingo.

His answer to the next question made mockery of the Spaniards. Was he acquainted with one Alonso de Avesilla, native of this city of St. Augustine, who it was said had been captain of the captured pirate galley? Brigaut replied that he had known him well, before his death two and a half years ago in Petit Goâve. The galley mentioned had never had any captain save Brigaut himself, to whom it had been delivered by Monsieur de Grammont.[15]

[14] Brigaut, "Confesión," pp. 150-157.
[15] Nicolás Brigaut, "Otra ratificación," May 31, 1686, A.G.I., México, 1671-1685 (61-6-20), pp. 158-160.

The "confessions" of Brigaut and Diego were read to them, and they affirmed the facts set forth therein. Thus their death warrants were signed and sealed.

If Cabrera previously had regarded the search launched from Mexico with detachment, his complacency now was shattered. Hearing the report of La Salle's settlement from a Frenchman captured in the act of assaulting his own presidio was not the same as receiving word in a dispatch from Mexico City. The governor began immediately to formulate his plan of action, and on June 28 he wrote to the viceroy of the course he had decided upon: he would send Marcos Delgado,[16] a Florida native with expert knowledge of the territory and the languages of its inhabitants, with a force from Apalache to seek the French settlement in the unexplored wilderness between Florida and New Spain.

[16] Delgado is described as a soldier of the presidio at St. Augustine, but no military rank is ascribed to him (Mark F. Boyd, "The Expedition of Marcos Delgado from Apalachee to the Upper Creek Country in 1686," *Florida Historical Quarterly* 16, no. 1 [July, 1937]:29 n.).

8. LAND OF TIQUI PACHE

Whilst we thus pass'd away the Time the best we could, Monsieur *de la Sale* had penetrated very far up the country. . . . He had travell'd through several Nations, the Inhabitants whereof were, for the most Part, sociable, and had concluded a Sort of Alliance with them, and particularly with the *Cenis* and others. . . . We were extraordinary glad to see our Commander in Chief return safe, tho' his Journey had not advanc'd his Design. Monsieur *de la Sale* had not found out his River, nor been towards the *Islinois* as we had hoped. Only eight Men return'd with him of twenty he carry'd out, and all the visible advantage of that Journey consisted in five Horses, laden with Indian Wheat, Beans and some other Grain, which was put into the Store.

—Henri Joutel
Journal, pp. 113-114

As La Salle returned to Fort St. Louis in August, 1686, from his first journey to the Cenis, or Tejas, the Florida expedition was about to begin its westward thrust in search of the French colony. Governor Cabrera, on the same day he wrote to the viceroy informing him of his plans, issued instructions to Marcos Delgado.

From St. Augustine, Delgado was to proceed to Apalache, where he would be joined by twelve soldiers armed with muskets or carbines and by forty Indians, half with firearms, half with bows and arrows. Then he was to proceed, if possible, to the viceroy's presence in Mexico City, crossing on the way the land supposedly occupied by the French. Under no circumstances were his men to harm the person or property of any Indians of the provinces they would traverse; they were cautioned to make due payment to the natives for supplies and services. Delgado carried gifts to be presented in the name of the king to the chiefs who were friendly and helpful.

And thus it is ordered that he shall go with great attention and care, reconnoitering the provinces and territories, the rivers, lakes, and streams, approaches to the sea . . . to make soundings insofar as possible, at high and low tide; as also the plants and animals . . . the width and depth of the fords and passages of the rivers he will cross; the kind of people, their manners and customs, and origin; whether there are any veins of metals; the shape of their pueblos and houses, and the personal disposition of the Indians; their ceremonies and manner of government; the kind of goods and merchandise they use.[1]

Should Delgado find himself in danger of being captured by the French, he was to make every effort to burn his orders; the only paper to be shown was the letter addressed to the viceroy. And should he himself decide to turn back, he was authorized to surrender the letter to any of his men who might wish to take it on to its destination for appropriate reward.[2]

On July 22 Cabrera received an order from the viceroy to report on whether Captain Martín Echagaray had come to Florida to carry out the plan he had proposed to the king for exploring and settling Espíritu Santo Bay. The governor replied immediately that he knew no more of Echagaray than what His Excellency the Viceroy had told him. Echagaray, he opined, could know nothing of the country beyond the port of Apalache. Furthermore, the captain's grandiose plans always were found lacking in the execution. Further delays, in the opinion of the governor, might prove costly indeed.[3]

For the viceroy, Cabrera summarized the circumstances that had forced his decision to send Delgado. Figuring prominently were the repeated intrusions of the English traders of St. George, pointing themselves always toward Espíritu Santo Bay. When the chiefs of Casista, Caveta, and Panzacola had come to pledge their obedience to Spanish rule, they had brought signs that they were deal-

[1] Juan Márquez Cabrera, "Derrotero y Orden que ha de guardar Marcos Delgado que va al descubrimiento de la Bahía del Espíritu Santo," A.G.I., México, 1671-1685 (61-6-20), pp. 296-297.
[2] Ibid., pp. 296-298.
[3] Juan Márquez Cabrera, "Ynforme," ibid., pp. 318, 321.

ing with the French colonists: bottles of wine and salt, rosary beads, and some bells. These items, they said, had been given them by "some men like the Spaniards" who were not of that nationality. Also influencing the governor's decision was the testimony of the pirate Brigaut concerning the La Salle colony. All doubt of the settlement's existence now seemed to have been removed.

To backstop the Delgado expedition, Cabrera continued, he was sending a frigate to sea; the captured French galley was being manned with Spaniards and Indian oarsmen; a bark equipped with oars had been built at St. Augustine. Expecting that Delgado would send back news of the discovery of the French settlement, he hoped that his vessels, aided by two ships of the windward fleet, could take a force by river and dislodge the French poachers.[4] Although the idea would rise again, Cabrera's plan for a maritime operation of his own was not to be carried out.

On August 28, 1686–"day of the glorious St. Augustine"– Delgado and his twelve soldiers, accompanied by the forty armed Apalachino Indians, marched from the Presidio of San Luis de Apalache. They set their course west-northwest, toward the Río de Palos (Little River), to reach the village of the Sabacolas. This way point was adjacent to the Mission Santa Cruz de Sabacola, at the juncture of the Apalachicola and Pedernales (Flint) rivers.[5]

At the Sabacola village Delgado inquired concerning the availability of canoes from the Panzacola Indians farther on. He apparently intended to travel by water, making portage from one stream to another. The Sabacolas advised against such a plan, however, and he decided to proceed by land, notwithstanding Cabrera's orders to examine the "approaches to the sea" and take soundings.

Cabrera received news of Delgado's change of plans in a letter

---

[4] Ibid., pp. 318-324.

[5] Near the present town of Chattahooche. The Sabacola Indians of the Apalachicola, or Creek, Confederacy were settled in the Mission Santa Cruz in 1681, according to Herbert Eugene Bolton ("Spanish Resistance to the Carolina Traders in Western Georgia, 1680-1704," in *Bolton and the Spanish Borderlands*, p. 138), "near the recently formed mission of Chatots." The Chatots proper, says Mark F. Boyd ("The Expedition of Marcos Delgado from Apalachee to the Upper Creek Country in 1686," *Florida Historical Quarterly* 16, no. 1 [July, 1937]:29 n.), should not be confused with the Choctaw, to which the Panzacolas probably were ethnically related.

from Lieutenant Antonio Mateos of the Presidio of Apalache: "The road he took is better and does not go by Panzacola, since from Savacola [*sic*] to Tavasa is no more than five days' travel. From there to La Chata would be only six days, and he wishes to go by the Province of La Chicasa, hardly more than forty leagues from Tavasa, according to what the Indians from Tabasa [*sic*] say." There he should be able to obtain guides to take him to the French settlement on Espíritu Santo Bay.[6]

Despite a raging fever, Delgado departed from the Sabacola village about the first of September. Crossing the Apalachicola, he noted the width and depth as per orders and emerged on the opposite bank at a village of Christian Chacatos (Choctaws), evidently the Pueblo of San Carlos. On September 2 he left San Carlos, plunging into the trackless and tangled wilderness on the northwesterly course that would take him to the province of Tavasa.

As the Spaniards slashed their way through nearly impenetrable forests and cane brakes, fording treacherous streams and bogs, Delgado kept careful record of each league traveled and the direction, of the terrain, and of the vegetation. His observations should prove invaluable today to the ecologist seeking knowledge of western Florida and southern Alabama in their primeval state. Unfortunately, dates are not given to coincide with distances, and it is difficult or impossible to fix precisely the location of certain events chronicled in the letters. These reports and the diary together, however, give eloquent testimony of the catalytic effect La Salle's attempt to settle at the mouth of the Mississippi had on Spanish exploration of the southern United States.[7] This expedition constituted the first extensive Spanish reconnaissance in west-

---

[6] Antonio Mateos to Cabrera, September 29, 1686, A.G.I., México, 1671-1685 (61-6-20), p. 300. Tabasa, or Tavasa, says Boyd ("Expedition of Marcos Delgado," pp. 6, 29), was a village belonging to the Alabama group of the Muskohegan stock, near present-day Montgomery, Alabama.

[7] Marcos Delgado, "Derrotero," A.G.I., México, 1671-1685 (61-6-20), pp. 258-265; Delgado to Juan Márquez Cabrera, September 19 and October 15, 1686, ibid., pp. 302-304, 314-317. See Boyd ("Expedition of Marcos Delgado," p. 6) for an appraisal of the Delgado diary, which parallels the one given here. Prior to reading the Boyd article, I translated the documents pertaining to the expedition and plotted my interpretation of Delgado's route on a map, bringing him to approximately the same destination as did Boyd. The Boyd article (pp. 9-28) includes translations of several of the documents, including Delgado's "Derrotero" (pp. 21-28).

ern Florida and Alabama during the seventeenth century and
marked a revival of Spanish activity among the Indian tribes of
that region. "For these reasons Delgado well merits a place among
the early explorers of the southern portion of the United States."[8]

As he proceeded on his northwesterly course, Delgado observed
these features: five leagues from San Carlos on the Apalachicola a
copious spring flowing into a deep river,[9] which watered a dense
cane brake with stalks of cane as thick as a man's body; six leagues
beyond, a wood so dense that it was necessary to cut a road
through it, then in the next four leagues a plain on which grew a
thin stand of pine, with a slough so boggy that horses would be
unable to cross it in the wet season (seen here, near Dothan,
Alabama, for the first time were buffalo,[10] which Delgado felt
called upon to describe: "a kind of animal like cows"); five leagues
of walnut forest with three springs close together and, nearby, a
moribund Chacata village called San Antonio; a nine-league stretch
punctuated by cane brakes and running creeks, then hills fringed
by a dense wood of chestnuts and laurel, sheltering bison and bear,
with a small river running through; high wooded hills, with a creek
flowing over bedrock to join a wide river, then a dense chestnut
grove, more hills, and a wood so dense that the soldiers had to use
axes to cut a road (evidently near Spring Hill, Alabama); fourteen
leagues beyond, a grove of chestnut trees so big it took two men
to reach around one.

As the expedition proceeded, the hardwoods of the lower
country gave way to sassafras and pine, the terrain became more
rugged, and water was scarce. It was evident that the land was in
the clutches of severe drouth. Nine leagues beyond the giant
chestnut trees, the explorers began a three-day trek of seven
leagues over steep hills, during which they found not one drop of

---

[8] William Edward Dunn, *Spanish and French Rivalry in the Gulf Region of the United
States, 1678-1702*, p. 74. The expedition did not, as Dunn states, approach "within a
short distance of Mobile Bay." Boyd ("Expedition of Marcos Delgado," p. 4) calls it
"perhaps the first penetration into Central Alabama by white men since the time of De
Soto and De Luna." Although no Spaniards are known to have penetrated this area
during this interim, it seems likely that English traders had.

[9] Blue Spring and the Chopola River, according to Boyd ("Expedition of Marcos Delgado, p. 7).

[10] Boyd (ibid.) says that this is the only record of buffalo "ever having been observed
within the limits of the present state of Florida." It is problematical as to which side of
the Alabama-Florida state line Delgado was on at this point in his narration.

water. "The people half drowned themselves when we arrived at a spring." So steep were the banks that the men had to draw water in their hats for the horses.[11] Encountering smooth ground again, they at last reached a river where they found the first village of "the Province of Tiqui Pache." Four leagues beyond was a Chocata village called Aqchay. Three leagues farther west, on the banks of "the River which goes to La Mobila" (probably the Alabama, near Selma) was a place called Quita.[12]

On September 15, almost two weeks after departing from San Carlos on the Apalachicola, Delgado's force had reached the first village of "the Province of Tavasa," having traveled two days without water. The time required to reach this point was almost three times the five days estimated by Mateos. Well received by the chief, Delgado presented the cacique with gifts in the name of the governor of Florida and told him of "the affection, fondness, and love with which Your Lordship regards them."[13] Next day six chiefs of different bands came to the village, received like gifts, and at Delgado's bidding seated themselves on the ground while the Spanish leader addressed them in the name of the governor. Assuring the caciques that he came in friendship, Delgado informed them of his need for provisions in order to continue. But the natives had none to offer; it had not rained all year long and the corn crops had withered in the drouth.

With this disheartening news, the Spaniards took up the march for the village of Culasa, six leagues distant, where they again were well received. Four chiefs from neighboring villages told them of an attack by the Mobila Indians upon a neighboring tribe and asked their help in avenging the deaths of their native kinsmen. Delgado, wary of commitment, responded that he had come for many purposes that were vital to the service of the king. He expressed his desire to talk with the chiefs of La Mobila, "without

[11] Delgado, "Derrotero," pp. 261-262. This is the only definite indication that at least part of the troop went mounted. Later on Delgado refers to the footsore infantrymen and Indians.

[12] Ibid., p. 262, The Province of Tiqui Pache, as that of Tavasa, refers to the upper Creek country. Boyd ("Expedition of Marcos Delgado," p. 30) says that the former name has come down to modern times as Tuckabahchee and refers to Indians of one of the Muskogee groups, perhaps of Shawnee origin. The Mobilas, according to Boyd (p. 29 n.) are identified as "a tribe of Choctaw living adjacent to Mobile Bay."

[13] Delgado, "Derrotero," p. 263.

getting them aroused." The chiefs, warning that the Mobilas were bellicose by nature, advised him to send a messenger telling them of his wish. Delgado, on September 19, dispatched his emissary, then penned a letter to Governor Cabrera.

As a result of his visits with the natives in this sector, the leader wrote, four villages had pledged obedience to the king: Miculasa, Yaimamu, Pagna, and Cusachat, all of whom were agreeable and friendly. Although he continued to suffer from his recurring fever, and his infantry soldiers and the Apalachino Indians were footsore from their difficult journey, he would press on to the fulfillment of his task—or at least until forced to turn back for want of provisions. The large axes he had brought had been worn out in cutting a road through the wilderness. While Delgado awaited a reply from the Mobila chiefs, he would march on to the province of Tiqui Pache, still hoping to find provisions.[14]

At Tiqui Pache the Spaniards obtained "thirty measures" of corn. "With this provisionment," wrote Delgado, "I marched for the lands and villages which in all their life had neither given obedience to nor even seen Spaniards or Christians."[15] Farther up the "Río de la Mobila," he came first to a place called Qusate, whose people were not known in the region, because they had come recently from the north, fleeing from "the English of Chichumeco." One league to the northeast, still traveling up river, the explorers found a village called Pagna, populated by a people who had fled the interior to escape the wars made on them by the savage tribe of La Chata (Choctaw).

On up the river Delgado marched, visiting among the various Indian villages whose inhabitants had fled from the English, the Chichumecos (Yuchi), the Chatas, or the Chalaques (Cherokee). Meandering with the course of the river, his general direction now was northeast, no longer pointed toward the Mississippi. Successively, he came to the pueblos of Culasa and Aymamu, whose inhabitants were in the act of fleeing from the Chatas, and Tubani.

[14] Marcos Delgado to Juan Márquez Cabrera, Miculasa, September 19, 1686, A.G.I., México, 1671-1685 (61-6-20), pp. 302-304. Miculasa is identified by Boyd ("Expedition of Marcos Delgado," p. 30 n.) as a Creek town on the Tallapoosa River, Pagna as a village on the Coosa River. Yaimamu and Cusachat he was unable to identify.
[15] Delgado to Cabrera, Río de la Concepción (probably the Alabama River), October 15, 1686, A.G.I., México, 1671-1685 (61-6-20), p. 314.

The Tubani pueblo, of the Qusate nation (Alabama), had been sorely pressed by the English, the Chichumecos, and the Chalaques.

From the Qusates, Delgado was grieved to learn that the English had discouraged their friendship with the Catholic Spaniards. He made good the opportunity to counteract this influence, telling the natives on behalf of the governor of "the love, affection, and good will with which Your Lordship regards them." While the English had provided the natives with guns and ammunition with which to kill each other, Delgado urged them to peace with other nations and friendship with the Spaniards. He told them he had opened the road for them to come to Apalache.[16]

As Delgado prepared to leave the Tiqui Pache region to begin the return journey, an answer came to the message he had sent to the Mobila chiefs. The caciques of La Mobila, Tome, Ysache, Canuca, and Gaussa arrived after dark, taking necessary precaution in the land of their enemies, who in Delgado's words were in the habit of "killing like Arabs." The Spanish leader played the role of peacemaker, however, and no effort was made to work treachery on the visitors. As for himself, Delgado assured them, he would lay down his life rather than offend them. Impressed by such rhetoric, the chiefs viewed the Spaniards' coming as an act of divine providence. They assured the white visitor of their desire to be at peace with the tribes in whose province they were visiting, and their wish to make war on no one.

"I gathered the chiefs from one province and the other," Delgado related to the governor, "and gave them to understand the evil they were doing by being at war and killing each other daily."[17] He passed out gifts and assured them of the governor's good will and His Lordship's wish to treat them as Christians rather than as infidels.

At Delgado's invitation the chiefs of the once-warring factions rose, embraced each other, and gave the sign of friendship, made by linking the hands together by the little fingers, "our having drawn them from the darkness of night and shown them with our coming the brightness of day."[18]

[16] Delgado, "Derrotero," pp. 261-264.
[17] Delgado to Cabrera, October 15, 1686, p. 315.
[18] Delgado, "Derrotero," p. 264.

Though the wording is not clear, it seems that Delgado obtained the agreement of the chiefs to send to the missions near Apalache forty-six apostate Christians, including some who were married to heathen women. Although these Indians were at war with those of La Chata—"which borders the inlet of Espíritu Santo Bay"—they would pass to them the word of the governor's redemption, in compliance with Delgado's request.[19]

Delgado then consulted the Mobila chiefs concerning the possibility of continuing his journey. "They told me that it was impossible. In La Mobila they had no provisions whatsoever with which to aid us because the drouth had been so great.[20] The Indians' crops had dried up, forcing them to sustain themselves with shellfish. The Spaniards themselves had managed to survive thus far only because they had guns with which to kill deer. Half the men were ill with the fever, and virtually all had suffered cuts and bruises on the legs from trekking through the dense woods. It did indeed seem impossible to continue. Furthermore, Delgado felt that he already had achieved a worthy result. He therefore gave the letter he carried for the viceroy to a Mobila chief, who agreed to send ten of his braves to take it around the province of La Chata, whose people were said to eat each other, to the territory ruled by a friendly chief. Thence it would be passed on toward its intended destination.

In response to the visitors' inquiry, the chief could offer no news of a settlement of English, Spaniards, or any other nation on the great river to the west. Once a long time ago, he related, a large ship had come down the river to Espíritu Santo Bay, taking soundings; the Chata Indians had fallen upon the sailors, killing more than half of them. The survivors had withdrawn to an island at the mouth of the river, where they had remained until a ship appeared from the sea discharging cannon. The marooned men had answered with a smoke signal, and the ship took them away. This incident had occurred many years ago, and as far as the Indians knew, no white men had been on the river since.[21]

As for the fruits of his journey, Delgado assured the governor that eleven chiefs—including six of La Mobila and five who had

[19] Ibid., pp. 264-265. This document is dated October 30, 1686, "in the Pueblo de Trave, Provincia de Cosate."

[20] Delgado to Cabrera, October 15, 1686, p. 315.

[21] Ibid., p. 316. This incident evidently had not occurred during the chief's lifetime.

fled the English to the north—had pledged obedience to the king of Spain, choosing friendship with "the Spaniards and all Christians." There now remained for him no wise course but to return; all that was possible had been achieved. "God only knows when we will arrive among Christians."[22]

Cabrera, on receipt of the first letter from Delgado, was filled with enthusiasm. In reports to the viceroy and the king he cited Delgado's successes in treating with the natives. The door had been opened, the governor declared; to follow up these achievements the six missionary priests whom the king had previously ordered to Florida to work among the natives should be hastened on their way, along with settlers from Spain's island possessions. With such help, he believed, great benefit would come from Delgado's discovery, and the French settlement at Espíritu Santo Bay could be extirpated; communication could be effected between the newly settled provinces of Florida and those of New Spain, and it certainly would be proved that the distance between the two was not as great as imagined. Should Delgado be forced to turn back because of illness or lack of provisions, Cabrera proposed to send him on a new expedition. But his real expectation was that Delgado soon would send him "very good news."[23]

Even with Delgado's return—reported to the viceroy by a letter of January 4, 1687—Cabrera's optimism hardly diminished. The worth of the land his representative had discovered was evident from its fruits, he declared, sending His Excellency as evidence a box of chestnuts "like those of Spain."

With better preparations, Cabrera arranged to launch another effort, "carrying provisions in piraguas as far as the province of La Mobila" and thence by land a shorter distance than Delgado's men had traveled. Having discarded his plan to send Delgado again, he now intended sending thirty men and one hundred Apalachino Indians with the lieutenant of Apalache, Antonio Mateos. He already had equipped the French pirate galley captained of late by the ill-fated Nicolás Brigaut, and had built two piraguas of war. He awaited only the return of another seven vessels from the north,

---

[22] Ibid., pp. 315-317.
[23] Juan Márquez Cabrera to the King, October 6, 1686, A.G.I., México, 1671-1685 (61-6-20), pp. 306-307.

where he had sent them to dislodge an island settlement of Englishmen formed three years previously.[24]

As if the designing English and French were not detriment enough, however, Cabrera was to see his plans thwarted by opposition from another quarter: his own officers. The government officials of Florida opposed Cabrera on the grounds that he was squandering royal funds needlessly. After all, had not Captain Echagaray agreed to explore the gulf coast without expense to the royal treasury? With his territory threatened by civil war, the governor abdicated, to have his office arrogated by one of his own trusted lieutenants, Pedro de Aranda y Avellaneda. When Cabrera returned to reclaim his post, Aranda threw him into jail. Eventually Cabrera was exonerated and Aranda banished from Florida.[25] But during the early stages of this tragic interlude the search for La Salle had shifted to another theater.

[24] Dunn, *Spanish and French Rivalry*, pp. 74-75; Cabrera to the Viceroy, January 4, 1687, p. 267.
[25] Dunn, *Spanish and French Rivalry*, p. 75.

9. NO STONE UNTURNED

... and after some Time of Rest, [La Salle] propos'd to undertake a Journey towards the Islinois, and to make it the main Business, by the Way, to find the *Missisipi*; but it was thought proper to let the great Heats pass, before that Enterprize was taken in Hand.

—Henri Joutel
Journal, p.114

While Marcos Delgado was hacking his way through the Alabama wilderness and La Salle was planning an attempt to reach the Illinois, the Conde de la Monclova sailed into Veracruz. He was armed with the king's royal orders to succeed the Marqués de la Laguna, Conde de Paredes, as viceroy of New Spain. He came with strong escort and firm resolve to take whatever action necessary for finding and rooting out the French colony said to have been formed in Spanish territory.

The distressing news had reached Spain the middle of March (1686), when a special dispatch vessel sent by the general of galleons at Havana arrived in Cádiz. The ship brought letters from Admiral Antonio de Astina, new commander of the windward fleet; Manuel de Murguía, acting governor of Cuba; and Admiral Gaspar de Palacios, the pilot major of the Indies.[1]

Accompanying Astina's report were the declarations taken from the six deserters from La Salle's expedition who were captured with the French privateer *Regla*—notably that of Denis Thomas,

[1] Marqués de los Vélez and others, "Junta de Guerra de las Yndias," April 8, 1686, A.G.I., México, 1685-1688 (61-6-20), p. 53; Gaspar de Palacios to Pedro de Oreytia, November 17, 1685, ibid., pp. 6-13; Antonio de Astina to the King, November 18, 1685, ibid., pp. 1-3.

who had been the Spaniards' star witness concerning the motives behind La Salle's mysterious movements, before he and the other pirates were executed. Palacios's report to the president of the Casa de la Contratación (House of Trade), Pedro de Oreytia y Vergara, told of plans for the voyage then about to be undertaken by Captains Barroto and Romero to seek the La Salle settlement.

Reaching the War Council of the Indies at about the same time as the letters from Havana was a report from "a trustworthy person who lives in Cádiz and has connections in Paris." The statement of this informant corroborated the news from Veracruz and Havana. The unidentified source refuted the popular rumor that it was the pirate Grammont who had made a landing in Spanish territory; it also gave the number of ships as five instead of four, and that of the settlers as more than one thousand families.[2]

Understandably, the Council was alarmed at the reported magnitude of the enterprise. It believed that the viceroy had taken the proper course in ordering Palacios to send out the first maritime expedition; but if La Salle's strength was as reported, all the resources at his command, including the *armada de barlovento*, would in insufficient to cope with the situation. If the French colony should be given reinforcements, as expected, Spanish dalliance could well mean the loss of the Indies. The Council, therefore, believed "that in order to remedy such grave damage, the greatest force and effort possible should be applied."[3] Steps should be taken immediately to reinforce the windward fleet; there must be no premature confrontation with the intruders, terminating in a Spanish disaster.

Plans were changed hastily to cancel an expedition to the Isthmus of Darién to subdue the Indians and the pirates who were finding refuge among them. As important as this mission was, the Council readily saw that extirpation of the French colony on Espíritu Santo Bay was more vital to the interests of the crown. The buccaneers who were crossing the isthmus to prey on the coastal settlements on "the South Sea" were an irritation, but their depredations were of slight importance when weighed against the threat posed by the French. A base on

---

[2] Text of this report is appended to Junta of April 2, 1686, to the King, ibid., pp. 43-44.
[3] Vélez, "Junta de Guerra," p. 57.

Espíritu Santo Bay would enable Spain's foremost enemy to control the shipping of the entire gulf region. From such a position the French also could march by land upon Nuevo Reino de León, a scant thirty leagues distant (according to the Council's meager knowledge of the region's geography). Since not one fortification was to be found among all the Spanish settlements in northern Mexico, France could, by sending a force of four to six thousand men, confuse and conquer the whole of New Spain. Therefore, the Council ruled, the reported French intrusion must be considered the more critical matter: "Upon it depends the preservation of the Indies and of all the Monarchy of Your Majesty. Prompt action is necessary . . . to remove this thorn which has been thrust into the heart of America. The greater the delay the greater the difficulty of attainment."[4]

The expedition intended for Darién was not yet ready to sail. The Council therefore recommended that two of the best ships of the ocean armada be assigned to escort the fleet that would sail for New Spain with the viceroy-elect, the Count of Monclova. The largest number of infantrymen possible, equipped with the best of arms, should be transported on the two vessels sailing under the guise of escorts. On arriving at Veracruz, the new viceroy should order the ships to join the *armada de barlovento*, which at the proper time should be dispatched to the task at hand. It was expected that the fleet would arrive at Veracruz late in August. A new reconnaissance mission then should be sent out to find the French settlement. After it had pinpointed the quarry, the major Spanish naval force would be able to launch a fullscale expedition to dislodge the French by early May, 1687, when the season of unfavorable winds would end and the *armada de barlovento* would be free from its commitments elsewhere.

The sloop carrying the new viceroy and the two large warships, according to plan, were to accompany the fleet bound for San Juan, Puerto Rico. France, however, still maintained a threatening posture as the outgrowth of an unsatisfactory settlement following the war of 1683-1684. In June it was determined that, as a precaution against a recrudescence of hostilities, the fleet should not sail that year. Only the two ships required for transporting the

[4] Ibid., p. 59.

quicksilver needed for the operation of the mines of New Spain and a third to carry the new viceroy could be spared for the Atlantic crossing.[5]

It was just as well, the junta rationalized; the fleet still could sail from Spain the following February, complete its circuit of the Indies, and arrive at Veracruz the first of May, the time for beginning the maneuver against the French on Espíritu Santo Bay. With the information gathered by the new reconnaissance expedition, the united fleets should be able to proceed quickly to the French settlement and make short work of destroying its vessels, dismantling the fortifications, and putting the French intruders to rout. Blockade tactics should not be relied upon; the settlement should be taken by storm, with superior naval forces and an aggressive landing party.

If everything went according to plan, the ships from Spain should be able to return to Veracruz in time to sail with the merchant fleet before the advent of the storm season. Thus they could augment the convoy, "this increased protection for the return of the treasure being of great importance in such uncertain times."[6] This plan failing, the viceroy should gather what ships he could to escort the merchantmen bearing precious metals to the homeland, for the treasure ships must sail ahead of the storm season at all costs.

While the viceroy-elect, Conde de la Monclova, awaited the sailing, the king's messenger reached him in the port of Cádiz. In a dispatch dated June 25, His Majesty spelled out Monclova's orders. They closely followed the recommendations of the junta but allowed him room to exercise his own judgment after gaining first-hand information.

Taking on their load of quicksilver in the harbor were the two cargo ships, their hulls recently lined with lead for the purpose. Monclova himself boarded the escort vessel, and the three ships, commanded by Admiral Francisco de Navarro, put to sea on the summer breeze.

On reaching Veracruz, the new viceroy was to inform himself on the condition of that settlement. Then he should seek out the

---

[5] Junta de Guerra de Indias to the King, June 18, 1686, A.G.I. México, 1685-1688 (61-6-20), p. 35.
[6] Ibid., p. 37.

officers Barroto and Romero, who had made the initial coastal reconnaissance in search of La Salle's colony. In launching a new maritime expedition to find the French, he was to use even the three vessels with which he had come from Spain, if necessary, as well as those of the *armada de barlovento* and any others that might be available. The colony destroyed and the French driven out, a fort should be established on Espíritu Santo Bay to keep them out.[7]

On September 13 the two quicksilver ships and the escort sailed into the port of Veracruz. The Count of Monclova disembarked and went to Veracruz Castle, where he soon was called upon by Admiral Antonio de Astina, commander of the *armada de barlovento*. In response to the viceroy's rapid questions, Astina briefed him on conditions in New Spain, particularly the coastal region bordering the Seno Mexicano, where La Salle's settlement was believed to be. Astina also summarized the statements he had taken from the French pirates who had given the Spaniards their first news of the French intrusion.

When the admiral departed, Monclova turned his attention to the dispatches that awaited him. Among them was a copy of the report of the Marqués de San Miguel de Aguayo. The governor of Nuevo León adumbrated the land expedition that Alonso de León had made three months previously from Cadereyta in quest of Espíritu Santo Bay. As much as the *marqués* had desired otherwise, it was evident to the viceroy that no solid accomplishment had been made. Monclova then sought out the pilots of the first maritime expedition, Barroto and Romero, who were in port with the *armada de barlovento*. They gave him oral verification of the reports that had been carried to Spain by the ship *Santa Teresa*, arriving after Monclova's departure.

The incisive intellect of the king's representative cut through the excess verbage of both reports, oral and written, and reached a summary conclusion: Nothing had been accomplished toward finding La Salle's colony. With a sense of urgency, he called a meeting with Admiral Navarro and other officers of the quicksilver

[7] Actual orders received by the Conde de Monclova are summed up in Monclova to the King, December 30, 1686, A.G.I., México, 1685-1688 (61-6-20), pp. 126-127. Second part of the letter (pp. 127-131) relates steps the new viceroy had taken to carry out his instructions.

ships, the two pilots and Admiral Astina from the windward fleet, and others "experienced in matters of the sea." Without mincing words he laid before them the task that confronted them: in order to take advantage of the maritime forces that would be in Veracruz the following spring, the location of the French colony must be determined. These forces would be available for a limited time only, for they must return to Spain with the annual shipment of gold and silver in advance of the coming year's storm season. It would be unthinkable to await the return of the fleet in 1688, the viceory proclaimed, "for each day that dislodging this enemy is delayed, the more difficult it will be."[8]

Under Monclova's forceful leadership the council reached agreement on two vital points: first, that until the French colony was found and its proportions known, nothing could be done toward attacking it; and, second, that once the discovery was made, hopefully by the first of May, 1687, the ships already at hand (the three vessels under Admiral Navarro that had just come from Spain and those of the windward fleet) should be ready in all respects for sea.

A map of the coastline, from Tampico to Cabo de Lodo, was laid out in front of the group, its character studied assiduously. While Barroto and Romero had failed—so it was thought—to reach "Espíritu Santo Bay, otherwise known as the Misipipi," they were able to make invaluable recommendations for the second attempt. Their fellow officers all agreed to the wisdom of their plan. For the success of the enterprise it would be necessary to construct two piraguas[9] —"as they are called in this country"—each to carry sixty men. Each vessel, in addition to carrying sail, should be equipped with twenty oars per side. Should these shallow-draft ships encounter storms, they would be able to seek shelter in the nearest cove instead of scudding homeward ahead of the gale, as Barroto and Romero had done. They could even land on the coast, if necessary. Convinced of this reasoning, Monclova promptly ordered the vessels built and manned by the best officers, soldiers, and sailors the *armada de barlovento* had to offer.

[8] Ibid., p. 128.
[9] The piragua was a craft most often used by the pirates of the Indies. It carried only one large sail, says John Esquemeling (*The Buccaneers of America*, p. 89), and was highly maneuverable, often capable of gaining the advantage over the large and cumbersome ships of the Spanish fleet by coming in so close that the guns of the larger vessel could not be lowered sufficiently to fire directly upon it.

To head the expedition the viceroy chose two "captains of sea and war" whom he considered outstanding "because of their youthful spirit." But the high official was frustrated in his choice, first by the death of Juan Duo, then by the severe illness of Andrés de Arriola, who was destined to be the unwilling founder of Pensacola. Faced with the necessity of going on to Mexico City to deal with other problems of his charge, Monclova left the building and manning of the vessels to Admiral Navarro.

Axemen were sent immediately into the woods to begin felling the timber required for the construction. Under the viceroy's orders a *pingue* that had come from Spain with a cargo of much-needed masts proceeded from Havana to Veracruz.[10] With great bustle the shipbuilders laid out the twin keels on the ways at Veracruz. Watching the daily progress as timbers went into place to give shape to the hulls were the two officers chosen to command them: Captain Martín de Rivas, a seasoned veteran of the sea and the most senior captain of the windward fleet, and Captain Pedro de Iriarte, who was much younger. Rivas was to command the ship called *Nuestra Señora del Rosario*, Iriarte *Nuestra Señora de la Esperanza*. The two officers, who between them possessed the attributes of both experience and youthful vigor, were the most highly rated of the *armada de barlovento*. Each vessel was to carry, in addition to the crew, two natives who were expert in their knowledge of the sea coast as far north as the "salines of Tampico," two surgeons, and two carpenters.[11]

By early December the small ships were completed; their crews of sixty-five men each gathered to begin the task of procuring and placing on board the supplies and provisions for a three-month voyage. Admiral Navarro proudly sent to the viceroy sketches of the piraguas, each of which was equipped with six bronze swivel guns, appropriate arms for each man, and powder of the best quality. Also added to the equipment were launches to be used in exploring the shallower coves and river mouths.

The munitions of each vessel included fourteen incendiary grenades, twenty-four hand grenades, one hundred cutlasses, a number of pikes, and six pairs of fetters on loan from the Veracruz

[10] Monclova to the King, pp. 129-130.
[11] Francisco de Navarro, "Relación de las dos piraguas," December 30, 1686, A.G.I., México, 1685-1688 (61-6-20), pp. 114-115.

prison. There also were spare sails and cord; pitch for caulking; grease for protecting masts, hull, and rigging; two cases of pharmaceuticals; a piece of linen for bandages; carpenter's hatchets, nails, tacks, and spikes; and tallow for candles.[12]

In addition to the *bizcocho* (biscuit, or hardtack) and other provisions sufficient for more than three months, each carried a cask of wine, and twenty earthen jars of *aguardiente* (brandy) between them—probably as much for an antidote to scurvy as for the pleasure of the crew.

As the time of sailing neared, Navarro relayed to his captains the orders he had received from the viceroy. They would proceed to Tampico, pick up their native guides, and gather all the information they could of the region beyond. From that point on, until they reached Espíritu Santo Bay at latitude 30°, they would sail only by day. The vessels would keep within sight of land in order to observe all inlets and coves, taking soundings, making sketches, and fixing the position of each. Natives enountered should be questioned carefully concerning their knowledge of a French settlement on the coast, and those with whom they dealt should be treated well and regaled with food and trinkets.

Should any other ship be met on the voyage, the officers of the piraguas should assess its capabilities, then capture it if possible, to learn its purpose. They should exercise extreme caution at all times, carefully scanning the horizon at each daybreak before unfurling sail and keeping a lookout aloft, at the block of the mainmast, during the day.

In the event of definite news that the French had settled at Espíritu Santo Bay or anywhere else along the route, the Spanish mariners should endeavor to enter the bay by day in order to sketch it, take soundings, observe the latitude, note signs along the shore and the character of the coast—whether the beaches were of sand or of stone. But if a French lookout were posted near the entrance of the bay, the explorers should not attempt to enter but merely should observe the latitude.

Care should be taken to make the rations last out the voyage. Beyond Tampico there was no source of provisions, and every-

---

[12] Navarro, "Razón de lo que llevan las dos piraguas," December 24, 1686, ibid., pp. 123-124.

thing needed should be obtained in that port. Whatever the duration of the voyage, Navarro noted, the viceroy would be upset if it were necessary to end the reconnaissance for lack of provisions. But if the voyage were carried out according to the instructions, he had the viceroy's word that each would be rewarded according to his services, and all would be commended to the king.[13]

An air of excitement prevailed in Veracruz as the time for sailing approached. In mid-December a brisk north wind swept down on the little coastal city and continued to blow for six days. The norther was viewed as a good sign. Navarro wrote of it as a blessing with which the endeavor had been favored by the Virgin of the Rosary. When the winds should cease, it was almost certain that a period of fair weather would follow, and the voyage would be off to an auspicious beginning. While he waited, Navarro recruited the two Indian guides who were familiar with the coast to the north and with the native languages. They boarded the piraguas at Veracruz.

At last the north wind subsided. With the supplies already loaded, the crews came on board and the two small ships sailed out of the harbor on Christmas Day, 1686. It was a public occasion, and the townspeople responded accordingly. Navarro personally arranged with all the churches for rogation to be said for the success of the voyage. In the chapel of Our Lady of the Rosary a *novenario*, or nine days of public worship, was observed, with rogation and unveiling of the Divine Image of the Virgin.[14]

Hardly had the piraguas disappeared on the northern horizon when a new task was begun by workmen in the Veracruz shipyard; preparations had to be made for their return, in anticipation of the news they might bring. The three ships that had arrived from Spain the previous September were careened, and the chore of cleaning and caulking was begun. The same was to be done with the ships of the *armada de barlovento*, some of which had to be fitted with new masts. Once the location of La Salle's colony was known, there must be no delay waiting for the Spanish maritime forces to get ready to sail. They should be prepared to get underway at a moment's notice and proceed to Espíritu Santo Bay—

---

[13] Navarro, Instructions, December 12, 1686, ibid., pp. 116-119.
[14] Navarro to the Viceroy, December 25, 1686, ibid., p. 120.

wherever that will-o'-the-wisp might prove to be—to extirpate the thorny intrusion upon Spanish lands.

When Viceroy Monclova received news five days later that the piraguas had sailed, he communicated his satisfaction to the king. Admiral Navarro had carried out his urgent assignment of building and manning the vessels with total dedication, and he had performed the feat in record time. The viceroy was convinced that the ships were manned with the best crews possible, and that they were adequately provisioned. "No stone will be left unturned," he wrote, "in making the discovery which seems so vital to the security of this kingdom and the reputation of Your Majesty's arms."[15]

[15] Monclova to the King, p. 131.

10. DERELICT AT SAN BERNARDO

Monsieur *de la Sale* being recover'd of his Indisposition, Preparations were again made for his Journey; but we first kept the *Christmas* Holy Days. The Midnight Mass was solemnly sung, and on
Twelve-Day, we cry'd, *The King drinks* (*according to the Custom* of
France), tho' we had only Water: When that was over we began to
think of setting out. Monsieur *de la Sale* gave the Command of the
Settlement to the Sieur *Barbier*, directing him what he was to do in
his Absence.

–Henri Joutel
Journal, p. 116

Despite the prayers that went with them, the Spanish piraguas
proceeded ponderously. Although the coast between Veracruz and
Tampico was well known, Rivas and Iriarte explored it as carefully
as they planned to survey the unknown region beyond. The passage consumed more than a month. Because of the deliberate pace
they encountered foul weather. On January 28 they reached
Tampico, the small vessels already mauled by the heavy seas and
groundswells that made coastal navigation especially hazardous.
Many of their provisions were soaked with seawater and had to be
replaced.

Because of this misfortune, and the advice of mariners with
whom they conversed at Tampico, they decided to wait out the
month of February before proceeding. In the meantime they
wrote to the viceroy requesting fifty *quintales* (5,000 pounds) of
bizcocho to replace that which already was consumed or spoiled.
The Count of Monclova responded by ordering that twice the
amount requested be delivered from La Puebla de los Angeles to

the vessels. The viceroy's munificence was to save the day for the officers and crews of the piraguas, who acknowledged later that "if they had carried only the biscuit they had asked for, they would have met with grave misfortune, or else they would not have finished the reconnaissance. On such little things," the count moralized, "the large ones may depend."[1]

While the reconnaissance vessels lay in Tampico, La Salle's small band pushed deep into the wilds of East Texas, each day bringing closer the bloody tragedy that had stalked from the outset. And in the settlement the group had left behind, the grim contest of survival went on, the wilderness and its savage inhabitants biding their time to inflict the stroke of death.

Not until March 7 did the piraguas sail from Tampico. Progress was better from that point, the weather somewhat improved. As the two small vessels cruised northward, they made the most thorough examination of the coast that had been made up to that time, and probably the first complete reconnaissance since the conquest. A detailed diary, complete with maps, was kept, but great caution was considered necessary to keep it from falling into enemy hands. It has not come to light to this day.[2]

By March 30 the expedition was well up the Texas coast. It came that day to a river or bay that the Spaniards called Las Flores, evidently San Antonio Bay or the break between St. Joseph and Matagorda islands. Here they made their first significant find. Seizing two Indian canoes, which apparently had been left behind by natives fleeing as the Spaniards approached, the explorers found them laden with ship irons, hinges, and other items of European origin. The relics obviously had come from a large ship, and the officers were able to tell from the marks on some of the iron that it was from France. They concluded that this was from the 250-tun vessel of the La Salle expedition, probably lost in a severe storm, a likely circumstance, since the French

---

[1] Viceroy Monclova to the King, July 25, 1687, A.G.I., México, 1685-1688 (61-6-20), p. 176.

[2] See ibid., p. 178, concerning the diary. The viceroy states that he was keeping a copy of the diary for himself, while sending the original to the king, adding, "I have ordered Juan Enríquez Barroto not to make any other copy of the diary." Details of the voyage are gleaned from this report and other correspondence cited herein.

colonists had left Petit Goâve at the approach of winter.[3] But the Indians evidently had transported the ship's hardware for some distance in their canoes. The Spaniards now sought the scene of the disaster in which the French Captain Aigron had lost the *Aimable* through suspected disobedience of La Salle's orders.

Eight or nine leagues up the coast, to the northeast, they came on April 2 to a bay to which they gave the name San Bernardo— that presently known as Matagorda Bay—and deduced that the large ship had been lost at the bay's entrance. As the explorers proceeded in their light craft to enter the bay, they were convinced that no ship of 250 tuns could possibly enter it.[4]

They set about taking soundings in the mouth and inside the bay itself, a task that consumed four days. On April 4 they made the most significant find of their entire voyage. Inside the bay, four leagues (10.4 miles) from its mouth, they came upon a fully rigged vessel of fifty or sixty tuns, aground a musket shot's distance off the coast. Emblazoned on the stern of the ship was the fleur de lis—incontrovertible proof that she was French. From the condition of her rigging, it appeared the vessel had been lost more than a year before. "Because she had the number of artillery pieces and swivel guns which the declarations attribute to the *patache* of Monsieur de Salas, we judge her so to be, and that her people have perished at the hands of the Indians and from hunger.[5]

As near as this surmise was to the truth, it was not yet completely so. Even at this moment, a few miles inland, the remnants of the miserable little French colony huddled in their rude fort. Hopefully they awaited news of their leader—not knowing that he already had met his cruel fate—their own lives secure only as long as the savage coastal Indians willed it. Yet the judgment of Rivas and Iriarte and of their pilots, Romero and Barroto, was sound in

[3] Martín de Rivas and Pedro de Iriarte to the Viceroy, Apalache, May 27, 1687, A.G.I., México, 1685-1688 (61-6-20), pp. 168-169.

[4] Andrés de Pez and Juan Enríquez Barroto, "Paracer de Pez y Barroto," June 12, 1689, ibid., pp. 311-312.

[5] Rivas and Iriarte to the Viceroy, p. 168. Herbert Eugene Bolton ("The Location of La Salle's Colony on the Gulf of Mexico," *Southwestern Historical Quarterly* 27, no. 3 [January, 1924] :175) says, "In 1687 the wrecks of the Aimable and the Belle were seen by members of two . . . expeditions, who took from them four pieces of artillery "and three painted fleurs de lis." Only one expedition saw the wrecks, as will be seen.

one respect: Any Frenchmen who might have gone ashore here a year or two before no longer could possess capabilities for doing harm to the interests of Spain.

The Spaniards spent one more day in taking soundings of the bay, whose mouth they fixed at 28° 23′, and which they believed extended as far north as 29°. Inside the bay the deepest part measured two fathoms. But most of the bay was so shallow that it could be navigated only by small boats.

Their efforts to learn more about the wrecked French vessels from Indians in the vicinity were fruitless; the natives could tell them neither when nor how the ships were lost.

Navarro's instructions called for exploring the coast as far as Espíritu Santo Bay, and Rivas and Iriarte could not be certain that the bay they had reached was the one they sought. Perhaps there was another bay, they reasoned, where other French ships had landed more successfully; with such a thought in mind they sailed on eastward. On May 20 they reached Cabo de Lodo, where the reconnaissance of Romero and Barroto had terminated more than a year earlier. They spent little time there, failing to discern that the "Mud Cape" was formed by sediment deposited by a great river.

Passing the Mississippi by, they arrived two days later at Mobile Bay. Two days were spent examining this place without entering; the reconnaissance of the year before should have been adequate. Since the Indians who lived on the shore had such close communication with the soldiers of the Presidio of Apalache, it appeared unlikely that an enemy could settle here without attracting notice.

Two days later, May 26, the piraguas reached San Marcos (St. Mark's), where the lookouts from Apalache (Tallahassee) were posted. The mariners thus made their first contact with other white men since sailing from Tampico on March 8. The Apalache soldiers "gave them a badly needed refreshment."[6]

Sometime before reaching Apalache the Rivas-Iriarte expedition picked up two survivors of Juan Corso's galley, wrecked on the Florida shore more than two years previously. Living among the *indios alarbes* on an unidentified river, the mariners found a Mexican boy and an Apalachian Indian, who told them of the fate

---

[6] Monclova to King, p. 177.

of the rest of the crew of the Spanish privateer: all had perished at the hands of the Indians or from starvation. The two were taken on board one of the piraguas to be returned to civilization.[7]

From Apalache, Rivas and Iriarte reported to the viceroy, emphasizing their belief that the French settlers' ships had been lost in the severe storms for which the gulf was noted. Citing the hazards of the coast during the winter, they observed that "if God had not worked a miracle at every turn, no doubt we also would have perished upon it."[8] Short of provisions, the two captains planned to exchange the remaining goods they had brought as gifts to the Indians for corn and beans to sustain them on the return voyage.

"Your Excellency surely awaits us with great concern, and the Royal Admiral Don Francisco Navarro, chief of the quicksilver ships, together with our armada, will be awaiting us, ready to dislodge the enemy. For this reason we cannot await your Lordship's reply."[9] On May 27 they sailed from St. Mark's, proceeding by way of Cayo de Huesos to Havana, where they arrived June 17. At Havana they took on the needed provisions while some ailing crew members convalesced; they got underway again June 22, to return to Veracruz by way of Campeche.

With great concern indeed did the viceroy await news of the Rivas-Iriarte expedition. Two days before the two small vessels sailed from Havana, he wrote to Navarro: "It having been more than three months since the two piraguas left Tampico, their delay causes me grave concern. The time that has elapsed is out of all proportion to what was planned. Since the circumstances of their reconnaissance cannot be known here, it would be well to consider a new one, as this matter is of such vital concern to His Majesty."[10]

Of all the ships then at Veracruz, Monclova ordered, Navarro should choose the two best suited for the mission and send them over the same route that Rivas and Iriarte had embarked upon.

---

[7] Rivas and Iriarte to the Viceroy, p. 168.
[8] Ibid., p. 169.
[9] Ibid.
[10] Monclova to Francisco Navarro, June 20, 1787, A.G.I., México, 1685-1688 (61-6-20), p. 170.

Not an hour should be lost, for the season of favorable winds would soon pass; delay would mean that the new voyage could not be completed before autumn northers set in.

Navarro reported four days later on the action he was about to take. The frigate (*patache*) that had come with the quicksilver ships and one from the windward fleet, *Santo Cristo de San Román*, already had provisions on board and would be ready to sail within five days. Each of the two vessels, commanded by Captains Francisco Gamarra and Andrés de Pez, was manned with forty seamen and thirty infantrymen. Since many of the men were practically naked, Navarro wrote, it would be necessary to give them an advance in wages to buy clothing.[11] The *pataches* set sail from Veracruz on June 30 and proceeded to Tampico to take on board two large launches, each capable of carrying twelve men, for use in exploring the shallow coves and inlets. But they might well have spared themselves the trouble.

On the night of July 3 one of the overdue piraguas reached Veracruz from Campeche. The other arrived the following morning. A fishing bark was dispatched promptly to overtake the vessels of Gamarra and Pez. But the two *pataches* had reached Tampico the afternoon of July 3 to hear disturbing rumors emanating from neighboring Indian tribes to the effect that the Rivas-Iriarte expedition had met disaster. Although the captains did not give full credence to the report, it nevertheless caused them to hasten on their way; they had sailed from Tampico at five o'clock the afternoon of July 5. The entire voyage of Rivas and Iriarte was to be duplicated.

On the return of Rivas and Iriarte, Viceroy Monclova called the pilots and the captains to the capital to report. Iriarte, Romero, and Barroto reached Mexico City on July 14, bringing the two members of Juan Corso's crew recently rescued from the Florida wilds. Rivas was ill and unable to heed the viceroy's summons.

Monclova went over the voyage with the three officers step by step. His reaction was one of unbridled optimism. The whole of Seno Mexicano, he observed, had been surveyed without finding on its coast a port, river, or bay inhabited by Frenchmen or other Europeans, or even signs to indicate that any part of it ever had

[11] Navarro to the Viceroy, June 24, 1687, ibid., p. 172.

been fortified or settled by a foreign power. The exploration should lay at rest the circumstantial accounts emanating from persons in both Spain and Mexico that "told as fact what they had not seen."[1][2] One question, however, remained unanswered: Where was the elusive bay or river's mouth that the French were supposed to have settled? He pressed the three officers for an opinion, and they agreed unanimously.

> All of them find that Mobile Bay is similar to that which it is said the French call Espíritu Santo or Missipipi [*sic*], because of its suitable anchorage and the island in its mouth that forms two entrances, one with a shallow channel, the other with six fathoms. But the large river which is said to flow into this bay, extending from New France with a large lagoon between, has not been found. From the middle of Mobile Bay it is clearly seen that no single large River empties into it, but six rivers or creeks, which have so little water that even the fishing piraguas could not enter them; in some even the canoes ran aground.[1][3]

On the same day that the officers arrived to give their report, another interesting document reached the viceroy from the Spanish ambassador in England. Don Pedro de Ronquillo, who had made fast friendship with the English king, the Catholic James II, sent an account of La Salle's voyage, which he had gleaned from pirated French documents, and which he described as "a compendium of the report Beaujeu has made to Monsieur de Seignelay of his voyage and the condition in which he left La Salle."[1][4] Monclova had the account read to Iriarte, Barroto, and Romero, who commented on various points. Their observations were entered in the margin of the report.

The noted French explorer La Salle, Ronquillo inferred, had falsified his report of the discovery of the mouth of the river called Mississippi: " . . . those who accompanied him assure that he did not find salt water, and what he took for the sea was only lakes, or a large body of water separated from the sea by a sandbar.[1][5]

[1][2] Monclova to King, p. 176.
[1][3] Ibid., p. 177.
[1][4] Ibid.
[1][5] Pedro de Ronquillo, "Copía de la Ralación hecha al Rey Xpmo tocante a la Bahía del Espíritu Santo," A.G.I., México, 1685-1688 (61-6-20), p. 139.

On returning to France, the ambassador set forth, La Salle was welcomed by the minister Seignelay, "to whom he presented a map showing latitude and longitude conveniently arranged to make his propositions plausible."[16] Thus he had won approval for his enterprise, promising to build two forts at the mouth of the river to intercept the passing shipments of Spanish treasure.

Iriarte, Barroto, and Romero carefully studied that portion of the report which listed the vessels of the La Salle expedition, attempting to reconcile them with the wreckage they had seen on the Texas coast. The thirty-six-gun vessel mentioned, as the report itself stated, was the one in which Captain Beaujeu had returned to France; the smaller frigate of 50 to 60 tuns, which the report said had been lost, was the very one they themselves had seen, aground in the bay they had named San Bernardo. The "ship of 250 tuns, chartered in La Rochelle for carrying the equipage,"[17] was the one whose remnants they had found in the captured Indian canoes on the bay they had named Las Flores (see Plates 3 and 6 in the picture section).

The fourth vessel of the La Salle expedition provoked interesting comment, for it was the ketch of forty tuns, which the report noted "was captured by the Spaniards on its arrival on the coast of Santo Domingo."[18] Although the capture of the ketch was attributed to Spaniards, it was not from this capture that news of the expedition had reached Spanish ears. Had it been so, La Salle's remaining three ships might have been intercepted by the Spanish fleet before they ever reached the gulf shore.

"As for the ketch [the captain and pilots noted on the margin of the report], Spaniards might confess that they had captured it on the coast of Santo Domingo, and these pilots and captains present [i.e., Iriarte, Barroto, and Romero] say that they have sailed with some of those who seized it, and report of said prize has gone to Spain."[19]

The report referred to must have been a letter from the president of Panama, Don Pedro de Ponte, a copy of which Ronquillo

---

[16] Ibid., p. 140. Ronquillo referred to a map similar to that reproduced in this volume as Plate 3.

[17] Ibid., pp. 140-141.

[18] Ronquillo, "Copía de la Relación," p. 141.

[19] Ibid.

had enclosed. Ponte said that a Spanish corsair from Portobelo reported having seized one of La Salle's ships, bringing the news that up to five hundred Frenchmen had gone on to the place called Espíritu Santo Bay. There it was to join a force marching by land from New France at the mouth of a lagoon through which a large river emptied into the sea.[20]

Ponte's letter was written February 12, 1687—two years after La Salle's landing on the Texas coast. There is no evidence to indicate where the Spanish corsair had been since it had captured the *St. François* off Santo Domingo in October, 1684, or why a report of the incident had not been made sooner.

The news transmitted by Ronquillo also verified for those most directly concerned with the search for La Salle their conclusions as to his fate. For one thing, they were convinced that the French themselves had no idea where they really were; the location given for the settlement (27°30′ north latitude, 292° longitude) was impossible. According to the Ronquillo report, Beaujeu had remained two months at the place of debarkation, which was described as a kind of sandbar "that prevails the entire length of Florida, and from there to Carolina."[21] When he left them, the distance from the bank to the mainland had not been determined; he had sailed fifteen leagues to the north without finding anything but small islands inside the bay, in which soundings revealed depth of from five to nine feet. This narrow sandbar, fifteen to twenty leagues from the point where the rivers entered the bay, afforded only brackish water, which made almost everyone in the colony ill. Dysentery was so rampant that hardly 10 healthy persons were to be found among the 150 who remained behind, and 5 or 6 colonists were dying each day.

"On their arrival at that place [Beaujeu had related] they encountered an Indian nation of four hundred to five hundred members, dressed in skins of a kind of wild ox which the Spaniards call *Sybolas* [*cíbolas*]. They had never seen Europeans, nor were they familiar with tobacco. The French met them amicably until there was a falling-out over some trivial thing, which cost the lives of

<hr/>

[20] Francisco de Amolar to Antonio Ortiz de Otálora, July 14, 1687, A.G.I., México, 1685-1688 (61-6-20), p. 173.
[21] Ronquillo, "Copía de la Ralación," p. 142.

three Frenchmen, whom [the Indians] killed with arrows, and they wounded two others."[22]

At last Beaujeu had left La Salle "in very bad condition" upon the sandbar without fresh water. The large supply ship already had been lost because of the master's insubordination, the Indians pilfering its cargo before the Frenchmen could effect salvage. Those on the departing ship hardly dared let themselves consider the probable fate of the ones who remained behind. As the gulf breeze filled Beaujeu's sails the colonists were laboring to repair the launches from the wrecked vessels, which they hoped to use, along with some Indian canoes, to look for the Mississippi.

Since Beaujeu's return to France, the report continued, Seignelay had sent a large ship of seven hundred tuns to Santo Domingo, carrying 130 women to marry the buccaneers, with whom the French maintained close ties. Beaujeu had proposed sending aid to La Salle on that ship, but, because of a financial pinch, French officials had not chosen to heed the suggestion. "A reliable source," said Ronquillo, "assures me that this enterprise already has cost the king [of France] more than the discovery of America cost Ferdinand and Isabella."[23] Indications were that no thought of sending aid for the suffering colonists remained unless La Salle should offer positive evidence that the settlement could be redeemed.

Understandably, the viceroy and his maritime officers were heartened by the report. No doubt remained among the captain and the pilots that the wrecked vessels they had seen were La Salle's. Just as certainly, Monclova asserted in his report to the king, the attempt at settlement was a complete failure, posing no threat whatsoever to Spanish territorial claims. The people may have sailed away in the small boats and perished at sea. Otherwise, they must have died of starvation or been killed by Indians. "The entire monarchy of Your Majesty is to be congratulated, since never [again] will this kingdom be endangered by an enemy settlement along its coast."[24]

[22] Ibid., p. 144.
[23] Ibid., p. 145.
[24] Monclova to King, p. 175.

But the matter was not to rest there. Almost by the time the viceroy's optimistic news reached the royal court in Madrid, new reports of the French intrusion sent the Spaniards scurrying once more in search of the enemy settlement and the elusive Espíritu Santo Bay.

11. RÍO DE LA PORCIÚNCULA

[La Salle] went downstream with 18 or 20 men, as many French-men as savages, in three or four canoes as far as the pretended mouth of this river, although those who accompanied him assure that he did not find salt water, and what he took for the sea was only lakes, or a large body of water separated from the sea by a sandbar. . . . Upon this pretended discovery of the discharge of the Missisipis into the sea . . . he presented a map showing latitude and longitude conveniently arranged to make his propositions plausible."

—Pedro de Ronquillo
"Copía de la Relación," pp. 139-140

While the evidence from previous expeditions was being pondered in Mexico City, the two vessels commanded by Captains Andrés de Pez and Francisco de Gamarra hastened northward along the gulf shore, unaware that Rivas's and Irarte's vessels were safe in port. Having sailed from the port of Presidio de San Juan de Ulúa at Veracruz on June 30, they anchored off Tampico at four o'clock the afternoon of July 3. Luis Gómez Raposo, pilot of Pez's frigate, *Santo Cristo de San Román*, kept a diary, carefully noting the prominent landmarks, the terrain, and the depth of each anchorage, as well as frequent positions. But he failed to make mention of having heard rumors in Tampico that disaster had befallen the previous expedition. Pez and Gamarra, anchored at the mouth of the Río Pánuco, remained at Tampico until July 5. They set sail at noon.[1]

[1] Luis Gómez Raposo, "Diario del descubrimiento que hizo el Capitán Don Andrés del Pez," in Spain, Consejo Superior de Investigaciones Científicos, *Colección de diarios y relaciones para la historia de los viajes y descubrimientos*, IV, 115, with a foldout map showing the route of the expedition following the text.

On the morning of July 8, with the two frigates anchored at the Tropic of Cancer, the launches of both vessels went ashore to converse with some friendly Indians. While the natives said they had seen no other ships pass, they had heard rumors of a settlement of white people farther north. These people were said to wear jackets and trousers like the Spaniards. When the Indians asked in sign language to board the vessels and pay their respects to the captains, they were obliged. They then departed with great show of friendship. The Spaniards weighed anchor and continued along the smooth coast of white sand.

From an anchorage at 23° 36', near the Río Miopate (Maupate), or Río de las Palmas,[2] they descried a hundred Indians on the beach, waving a flag and making gestures. Taking the precaution to load the launches with armed men, the Spaniards went ashore to find the friendly natives led by a chief called Pedro. This leader, who spoke fluent Spanish, said he lived with his family at Tampico.

Having come from Tampico seeking news of "the galleys"— presumably those of Rivas and Iriarte—the chief said his band had penetrated nine leagues to the north, where a warlike tribe had blocked the way. The chief had found friends among these savages, however, and asked them to go to the Río Bravo (Río Grande), find the white settlement said to exist there, and seek news of the galleys. Most of the natives of his own following, Pedro related, were inhabitants of the Tampico area who had fled to this region because they had been harassed by the men of Juan Corso's piragua. Under Pedro's persuasion they now were returning to their homes. The rumored settlement on the Río Bravo, these Indians reported, had horses, cattle, and sheep. Chief Pedro's followers were convinced that the settlers were not Spanish but French or English.[3]

Taking leave of the natives, the mariners sailed on northward the next day, reaching the southern Laguna Madre. As the white

---

[2] The position given here identifies the Río de las Palmas as that presently known as Soto la Marina. Carlos Eduardo Castañeda (*Our Catholic Heritage in Texas*, I, 13-14) offers what he calls "incontrovertible evidence" that the Río de las Palmas, on which Alonso Alvarez de Pineda and his men spent forty days in 1519, was the Río Grande. Documentary sources, however, agree with Gómez ("Diario," p. 118) that Río de Maupate (or Miopate), Río de las Palmas, and Río Soto la Marina were all the same stream.

[3] Gómez, "Diario," pp. 117-118.

sand beaches gave way to flooded marshland and mangrove swamps, the frigates anchored on July 11 near the mouth of the Río Grande. Despite the tales the Spaniards had heard from the Indians, no effort was made to reconnoiter the mouth of this river. On the twelfth, favorable wind and current carried the ships northeastward along the Texas coast.

Two days later the frigates stood off Mustang Island. With a contrary sea and a southeast wind threatening to carry them aground, they were unable to explore for a break in the bar. From the topmast they could see a large bay, set in the midst of marshland. This was Corpus Christi Bay, observed between latitudes 27° 34′ and 27° 46′.

The following day, reaching 28°, the mariners dropped anchor and sent the launches to explore what appeared to be interruptions in the long, sandy island. They hoped to find access to another sizable bay, but in every case the water over the bar was too shallow for passage. Aransas Bay, which lay within, could not be reached. On the sixteenth the launches explored along St. Joseph Island, sounding outside the bar, but the slight channel did not afford the ships entry. On the bar they found many signs of human activity, including footprints, remains of a cooking fire, some smoked fish, a piece of net, and fragments of earthen pottery. A rawhide shield was found, with short hair indicating that it was made from buffalo skin.

After advancing up the coast to a point near the channel between St. Joseph and Matagorda islands, the captains again sent the launches out, but the passage was narrow and the sea heavy. The boats succeeded in entering this "river mouth" next day. Finding the water salty inside the bay, the mariners concluded that it joined the lagoon they had observed the previous day, five leagues back. They called the "river" Carimbas.[4] Doubtless the same feature that Rivas and Iriarte had called Río de las Flores, it probably was nothing more than the stretch of water between the island bars and the mainland, somewhere near the mouth of San Antonio Bay, at 28° 08′. On the beach the Spaniards found some holes dug by the natives to bring up drinking water, many barefoot tracks, and a freshly notched shaft.

[4] Ibid., pp. 121-122.

On the evening of July 17 the frigates must have anchored very near the mouth of Matagorda Bay, where the French ship *Aimable* had been lost during La Salle's landing. Gómez's diary, however, makes no direct mention of the huge body of water through which the ships would have had to pass to approach the French settlement. Neither the derelict *Belle* nor the scattered remnants of *l'Aimable* was observed.[5]

Although a brisk headwind caused the mariners to tack southeastward the following day, they were never far from land. Forward progress was slight. That night they anchored a league and a half from land, waiting out the stormy weather. On the twenty-first they got underway again, advancing up Matagorda Peninsula to shelter in the cove of a small island surrounded by shoals, half a league from the mainland—or from the peninsula—in excess of 28° 30′ latitude. Considerable time was spent taking soundings around the island, during which operation "20 palmos of water and three river mouths were found between the island and *tierra firme*.[6]

Continuing on toward the northeast, Pez and Gamarra, at latitude 29° 15′, observed three pine-covered mesas and what they took to be another river mouth—probably West Bay, the southwestern offshoot of Galveston Bay, for the latitude reading places them near the present city of Galveston. They called it Río del Pinar. Strangely, it is recorded that the "boca de río" was the first fresh-water inlet they had tested since passing Tampico. The following day, July 24, the mouth of Galveston Bay itself opened up at 29° 20′.[7] They named it La Bahía de Barra Seca. Although the mouth was sounded, no attempt was made to enter the bay with the frigates, as the water was no deeper than 12 palmos, too shallow for the deep-draft vessels. Anchorage for the night was at the upper end of East Bay, on a cape they named Cabo de Santi-

[5] Ibid., pp. 122-123. William Edward Dunn, who did not have access to the Gómez diary, says (*Spanish and French Rivalry in the Gulf Region of the United States, 1678-1702*, p. 80) that Gamarra and Pez found the same wreckage at San Bernardo Bay as the previous expedition and brought "corroborative evidence to prove that the French colony had met with disaster." The diary clearly shows that this was not the case.

[6] Gómez, "Diario," pp. 123-124. Assuming that "*tres bocas de río*," as it is written in the diary, refers to three mouths of the same river, and that "28° *y* 1/2 *largos*" could have been as much as 28° 35′, this must have been the mouth of the Colorado River.

[7] Ibid., pp. 124-125. It is by such unmistakable landmarks as this that the general accuracy of the sun observations for latitude taken on this expedition is affirmed.

ago. Because of the marshy shoreline they named the place, near present Gilchrist, Ensenada de la Ciénaga. Looking west-northwest (across Galveston Bay) from this point, they were unable to see land.

As the sandy beaches gave way to pine-covered knolls, then to dense forests, the shoreline curved eastward. Gómez continued to note landmarks in detail, recording data that might be useful, he says, should some ship be cast upon these shores by a hurricane, as once had happened to him. Passing the mouth of Sabine Lake on July 25, the name Los Morros de Santiago was given some nearby knolls that formed a triangle. The course became east, then southeast, to conform with the Louisiana coastline. Passing well out of sight of land to avoid the shallows on July 29, the *Santo Cristo de San Román* was forced to turn about to allow the other vessel to catch up. Twenty leagues of coastline went unexplored because the mariners dared not hazard the shoals that lay to the east of a point called El Pinar de San Cristóbal, at latitude 29° 30'. The course dipped southward as far as 28° 50'.

Regaining sight of the marshy coast on July 31, the Spaniards found themselves the following day at the mouth of a river that gushed muddy water from two channels, discoloring the sea two leagues from shore. The frigates now stood off the Mississippi Delta, at West Pass, which was marked by numerous shoals, the sea crashing wildly upon them. Feeling their way cautiously, they proceeded two leagues to the north-northeast and dropped anchor. Fierce winds and rain lashed the ships in their anchorage. When the storm subsided at three o'clock in the afternoon, they got underway again and sailed northeast until sunset. To the tablelands of the delta they gave the name Las Mesas de la Porciúncula, because it was the eve of the Franciscan festival.[8]

On August 2, the day of the festival, the second stream with two mouths was found and named Río de la Porciúncula. This was the arm of the Mississippi River that empties into the gulf at Port Eads (South Pass). Navigation was complicated by the absence of the sun, which did not become visible again until the fifth, and by high wind and poor visibility. That day the navigators sailed up the east side of the delta, steering northeastward to come back in

[8] Ibid., pp. 129-130.

sight of the coast. From a distance they sighted a large cove, at latitude 29° 10′, with swift current issuing from it. Having gone beyond Southeast Pass, they had reached a third major arm of the Mississippi, at Northeast Pass. The launch was lowered to take soundings and the water was found to be fresh. The cape was named Cabo de las Nieves, since the day before the crews had celebrated the feast day of Our Lady of the Snows.

On August 7 the frigates steered southeastward to clear the cape, then sailed up the coast until signs were seen of another copious stream discharging a great quantity of fresh water and logs into the sound. The Spaniards gave the name San Luis to the cape and cove (La Salle himself could scarcely have done better). They dropped anchor one league from land, sounded the depth of twenty-two fathoms and took a sunshot to compute a latitude of **29° 20′**, at North Pass.

This cape [writes Gómez Raposo] is that to which Julio Enríquez Varroto [*sic*] gave the name Cabo de Lodo, and the river the Río de la Palizada. From here he withdrew and went no farther. He says only that from the topmast of his ship he managed to see land to the southwest. That of certainty was the Cabo de las Nieves, where the other river disembogues, and it also carries much timber. On all the coast, from Vera Cruz to these capes, there are no other rivers which empty out so much fresh water or carry so many logs. Also, this coast is well known as a good anchorage. Three leagues from land there are 40 fathoms and in places 22. Such depths are found from the bar of the Porciúncula to this Cabo de San Luis.[9]

At last the mouth of the Mississippi had been examined thoroughly from the sea. Barroto and Romero had found but one of its mouths on the first maritime expedition; Rivas and Iriarte had passed the delta without realizing its great significance. But Pez and Gamarra, though hampered by four days without a sun from which to obtain a fix, by raging winds and pouring rain, had ferreted out, one by one, the four main channels emptying into

---

[9] Ibid., p. 132. Gómez evidently refers to the diary kept by Barroto himself, which has not come to light, rather than that of Juan Jordán de Reina ("Diario y derrotero del viaxe," A.G.I., México, 1685-1688 [61-6-20], pp. 26-33), which is cited in Chapter 5 of this study. Jordán ("Diario," p. 32) places his Río de la Palizada at 29° 03′, which approximates the latitude of South Pass and the mouth of Gómez's Río de la Porciúncula.

the gulf. They may not have realized that all these streams were fed by one great river, but they at last had ascertained the true magnitude of the Mississippi Delta.

This work done, they turned northeastward across Breton Sound. On the ninth they stood near the Chandeleur Islands, on the tenth at the mouth of Mobile Bay. Captain Pedro de Quintanilla, a pilot of the *Santo Cristo de San Román*, went with the launch to sound around the islands at the entrance and to mark the channel with buoys. Barroto had reconnoitered this bay in February, 1686, reporting a channel six fathoms deep. Quintanilla, however, spent the entire afternoon taking soundings without finding such a passage, a fact that stirred confusion among the navigators.

Gómez himself went next day to look for the channel, following closely the bearings given in the diary of the Barroto-Romero expedition. But all his soundings revealed less than four fathoms. Where Barroto had reported fresh water inside the bay, he found it to be salty. He concluded that the difference in seasons accounted for the variance in depth, the lack of spring rains for the difference in water quality. The prevailing southeast winds had altered the character of the shoals near the entrance.[10]

Eighteen leagues to the east—as opposed to the thirty generally ascribed to it—Pez and Gamarra came to Pensacola Bay, which Pez particularly wanted to enter. But the wind was too slight to give steerage against a contrary current. While Gómez recorded detailed descriptions of the coastline adjacent to the bay, Pez would have reason later to regret that he had not examined the bay thoroughly.

The following day, August 16, they cruised along Santa Rosa Island, looking for an entrance to the body of water that lay beyond. Finding the opening at one o'clock, they anchored half a league off the point and lowered a launch to sound and reconnoiter what is known today as Choctawhatchee Bay. They called it San Roque, because it was this saint's feast day. The found the channel narrow, with only two fathoms of water and shoals on either hand. Inside lay an open body of water extending to the west and northeast. Though there were four fathoms immediately beyond the entrance, the rest of the bay appeared uniformly

[10] Gómez, "Diario," pp. 135-136. See Jordán, "Diario," p. 31.

shallow. On its shores the mariners found some Indian huts, amid plantings of squash and other green crops and wild grapevines in fruit, which they gathered and took back to the ships. The inhabitants of the place had fled.

The vessels then sailed southeast to conform to the coast. On the eighteenth the navigators reached Cape San Blas, which carries the same name today. It was the one that Juan Jordán de Reina, diarist of the Barroto-Romero voyage the year before, had called Punta Brava.[11] Gómez, however, suffered confusion as to names and error in his navigation, referring to this point as

Apalache Cape, which Julio [*sic*] Enríquez Barroto named Cape San Blas, referred to in the *cartas sevillanas*, the reef of which runs from east to west two leagues on the outside of the cape, a league out to sea. The southernmost part is at latitude 29° 30′ [actually 29° 40′] and the *cartas sevillanas* place the longitude at 301° 31′. Concerning the longitude, I have used the Port of San Juan de Ulúa as an anchor point to compute the difference [from there] to Cabo de San Blas or Apalache as 10° 11′ [actually about 10° 50′ by present-day charts, corrected by Gómez on the return voyage to 10° 57′], and by this means I place this cape at 302° 31′. . . . This place is known, and it is not necessary to proceed farther, but to return and report to the Most Excellent Lord Count of Monclova on the course of the voyage. We have run the entire coast, leaving nothing not seen and explored, and have found neither cargo ships nor a port where such vessels could enter, but only [bays] capable of accommodating barks or sloops drawing as little as one and a half or two fathoms of water. All the bays are marshes and subject to flooding. On these matters the Captains and Pilots of these frigates conferred today upon the cape and unanimously agreed that the obligation to His Excellency has been fulfilled.[12]

From Cape San Blas, Pez and Gamarra headed their vessels southward on the home voyage, driven by a tempestuous northwest wind that kept the decks awash. The hard blow gave way to

[11] Jordán, "Diario," p. 28.

[12] Gómez, "Diario," pp. 138-139. Longitudes in this period, which were estimated, were computed from Tenerife, rather than Greenwich, with measurements from 1° to 360°. To this portion of the diary Barroto affixes a "correction" (p. 139), stating that Cape San Blas and Apalache Cape are not the same, which is true, since Cabo de Apalache lay somewhat farther east, around the bend in the coastline. Barroto identifies Cabo de Apalache as being the Punta de Abiñes, mentioned in Jordán, ("Diario," p. 27), and gives the latitude as 29° 40′, the same as the correct latitude of Cabo de San Blas. Barroto notes a 35-minute difference in the longitudes of the two capes.

calm, then to smooth sailing. On the twenty-first, at about latitude 26°, the frigates changed course to the southwest, and at three o'clock the morning of August 30 the lookouts of the *Santo Cristo* espied a sandbank dead ahead. As the ship steered to larboard to miss it, a musket was fired to warn the other vessel, whose lantern was clearly visible astern. The other frigate answered, and the *Santo Cristo* crowded on sail to carry her away from the danger of grounding. With daybreak she returned to the island to reconnoiter it, but still failed to find the other vessel. The island was determined to be Isla de la Bermeja, known today as Arrecife de Alacrán, seventy miles off Yucatán.

On Tuesday, September 3, the Sierras de San Martín rose out of the sea ahead, and the crew of the *Santo Cristo* knew they were drawing near the end of the voyage. Becalmed off the Sierras de Villa Rica during the night, they steered into the port of San Juan de Ulúa at four o'clock the following afternoon. Gómez, recording his computation of a difference of 10° 57′ longitude from Cape San Blas, wrote finis to his diary, thus ending a voyage of sixty-seven days.

The diary then was submitted to a reading by Captains Iriarte, Barroto, and Romero, who commented:

... we find that from Tampico to the Río Bajo [Bravo], because of the condition of the coast and shallowness of the bars, there is little difference [between their observations and ours]; and because their ships draw much water, they examined no more than the mouths of the rivers. As a result they encountered neither Indians nor the wreckage of the two French ships that we discovered, for good reason; and the coast being shallow from Río Bajo to the Cabo de Lodo, they did not see the Río Dulce, Río del Mexicano, Río de Tocaic, Río de la Ascensión, and Río de San Bernardino, nor even the land from the topmast in most places. Also, we have noted that they arrived at Mobile Bay and that they found outside, between the two bars they crossed, a sandbank with three and two and a half fathoms of water, which surprises us, since, to the contrary, we sounded five and six fathoms well beyond the channel; and also that it is said the water of the bay is salty, because between the island and the mainland we drank the water, although it was not exceptionally good. This being the case, the reason doubtless is that mentioned on the 11th: since it was the rainy season when we saw it, we found the channel clean and deep, with the water from the bay fresh in the course of the river, the opposite from August (the dry season); without the hindrance of the swift current outside, the sea from the southeast could form the bank. This cannot be denied, although we are certain that it was Mobile Bay which they saw and describe.[13]

Although Pez and Gamarra had contributed little toward finding La Salle's colony, they did much to advance geographical knowledge of the gulf coast. Not only had they established the true nature of the Mississippi Delta, of which their examination probably was the most thorough that had been made up to that time, but they also had made observations against which to check those of other expeditions.

Despite the optimism of the viceroy, the precise fate of the French intruders remained undetermined. Until Monclova's assumptions were proven fact, the search must go on. Before many months had passed, the two officers who during previous searches had become most knowledgeable of the gulf coast must sail again aboard the *Santo Cristo de San Román*. Captains Pez and Barroto were chosen to follow the directions of a fraudulent Englishman who claimed he could lead them to the elusive French colony.[14]

---

[13] Gómez, "Diario," p. 149.

[14] The part of Captain Andrés de Pez y Malzarraga in the maritime search, beginning with this expedition, may be compared to that of Alonso de León in the overland quest. Of Basque descent, Pez was born in 1657 in Cádiz, where his father was an officer in the royal navy. He served eight years as a common sailor, distinguishing himself in the battle of Palermo, in which his father and his brother died heroically. Transferred about 1681 to the windward squadron in the Indies, he took part in three voyages in search of La Salle, as will be seen. The prime advocate of settling Pensacola Bay, he was prevented from actual participation in the project by a charge of cowardice in a battle with corsairs off Cuba in 1697, of which accusation he was cleared in 1701. Winning the confidence of Philip V, he became a member of the Supreme War Council in 1715, was appointed president of the Council of the Indies in 1717, and was named secretary of state and of the Despacho Central de Marina in 1721. He died in 1723 or 1724, and a street in Madrid was named for him (Irving A. Leonard [ed. and trans.], *Spanish Approach to Pensacola, 1689-1693*, pp. 20-22).

12. THE GRAND HOAX

[L'Archevêque] rejoined with increased insolence, drawing back as he spoke, toward the ambuscade while the incensed commander advanced to chastise him. At that moment a shot was fired from the grass, instantly followed by another; and, pierced through the brain, La Salle dropped dead.

—Francis Parkman
La Salle, p. 308

During the months consumed by the second and third maritime expeditions, events surrounding La Salle's small band marching for the Illinois ascended rapidly to a climax. Near the border of the land of the Indians called Cenis the bloodletting began with the murder of the great explorer's nephew, Moranget. Before it ended, five others lay dead, including La Salle himself. The survivors, innocent and guilty, divided. Seven proceeded onward for Fort St. Louis of the Illinois, six of these eventually to return to France. Another six remained among the natives, their fate to be determined by circumstances that none could foretell. No word of the multiple tragedy was carried back to the struggling colony on the gulf shore, whose inhabitants unknowingly awaited their own cruel fate.

Self-defeating as the French intrusion was, the Spaniards possessed no definite knowledge on which to base their complacency. Even before the two piraguas of Rivas and Iriarte had landed in Veracruz, events were transpiring in another part of the hemisphere that would shatter their new-found confidence. A month before Viceroy Monclova had penned his exuberant message to the king, two English vessels about to enter the Bahama Channel on their homeward voyage were set upon by a Spanish privateer from Havana and taken captive. The whole episode, Spanish officials were later to realize, was born of an ill wind. Among the captives was an English carpenter and sometime buccaneer who called himself Ralph Wilkinson. Wilkinson's wild tales once again filled Spanish hearts with fear of French intrusion and again sent the viceroy's maritime forces on a will-o'-the-wisp hunt for a chimerical French colony in a location where none had ever existed.

To the Spaniards, Wilkinson came to be known as *el gran embustero*, a most infamous liar, and there is little evidence to refute this evaluation. Yet in his prevarication, the wily one played a trick on the Spaniards that they failed to perceive. Had the Englishman been a bit more cunning, had he been adept at their language, he might well have had the jealous protectors of the Spanish realm running circles around themselves. For he was trapped not so much by his own lies as by Spanish refusal to view his stories in any light but that of their own preconceived notions, their own fears and prejudices.

Wilkinson's first stop, after he and other members of the crew of the English frigate *Dark Wanderer* were captured by Captain Mateo Guarín, was the public jail in Havana. There he passed three days, receiving scant notice from his captors. Then an English captain, whom the Spaniards called Juan Felipe de Vera, interceded in his behalf with the governor, and he was given free run of the town. Vera, after winning Wilkinson's release from jail, signed him on his salvage ship for an expedition to Cayo Largo, off the tip of Florida. During the voyage the captain related to the carpenter a rumor he had heard of a sailing from Veracruz to seek a French settlement called San Juan, on the Bay of Ascensión.[1]

Wilkinson then claimed to have been at the place called San Juan, speculating that the Spaniards would pay well for information concerning it. Vera cautioned Wilkinson to say nothing of the matter to Andrés de Munibe, the Spanish governor at Havana;

---

[1] Ralph Wilkinson, "Declaración," Mexico City, November 21, 1687, A.G.I., México, 1685-1688 (61-6-20), p. 201. José Antonio Pichardo (*Pichardo's Treatise on the Limits of Louisiana and Texas*, I, 359) identifies the Bay of Ascensión with Atchafalaya Bay on the Louisiana coast.

first, he suggested, they would go to the French settlement together and make sure of the route, then barter their services to the official.[2]

On reaching port, however, Vera went to the governor himself and disclosed his conversation with Wilkinson. The unwary carpenter was promptly summoned before Munibe to make a statement. His "settlement of San Juan" was interpreted to mean Espíritu Santo Bay. Snared by his first lie, Wilkinson sought to escape by telling others.

The principal question concerning Wilkinson's mendacity is one of motive. Probably he merely wished to ingratiate himself with his captain. It is possible, even, that he had heard of La Salle's venture through the pirate grapevine and scented possibilities for plunder. He may have hoped to win Vera's aid in searching for the prize. In any event, Spanish officials made more of his falsehood then he had bargained for.

In a formal deposition on August 29, 1687, Vera related the story Wilkinson had told him: Four years ago the English carpenter from Jamaica had been in Petit Goâve. There he had met "the French leader from Canada," who, under orders from the king of France, was going to settle the "Bay of Ascensión" on the Gulf of Mexico. He was taking with him ships loaded with French families to form the nucleus of the settlement. Later, on a trading ship, Wilkinson claimed to have found the bay in question and to have spent fourteen months at the French settlement, sixty leagues north of Tampico, at latitude 30°.[3]

Munibe then sent for Wilkinson who, being a Protestant, "swore on the Holy Bible, which is the manner in which those of his religion are accustomed to making oaths."[4] Wilkinson, forty-six years of age, a native of England, and a carpenter by trade, testified that he had lived twenty-three years in Jamaica, whence he had sailed to many different places. Then he repeated what he had told Vera, with embellishments.

Wilkinson claimed to have sailed from Jamaica on a trading vessel, *La Cabrita*. While following the coast north of Tampico in

[2] Wilkinson, "Declaración," Mexico City, pp. 201-202.
[3] Juan Felipe de Vera, "Declaración," Havana, August 29, 1687, A.G.I., México, 1685-1688 (61-6-20), pp. 209-211.
[4] Wilkinson, "Declaración," Havana, August 29, 1687, ibid., p. 211.

pursuit of trade, the ship had happened upon the French settlement fourteen months ago. At the mouth of a river that flowed into a lagoon outlined by cays, he related, he met a Frenchman he had known previously. The Frenchman cautioned him against proceeding farther, lest he be taken captive. His vessel therefore turned back to Jamaica.

After his return to Jamaica, Wilkinson continued, he had learned that the French settlement was being reinforced. This news had been given him six months ago by his brother, a sailor on a sloop that had met two French *pingues* and a warship of twenty-six guns. These vessels, he related, were carrying more families and provisions to the colony on—note the name change— Espíritu Santo Bay.[5]

He would be able to recognize the entrance to the lagoon, Wilkinson claimed; once inside it, he could find the river; on this he would stake his life. But many discrepancies would appear between this statement and his later depositions. On completing his testimony Wilkinson was returned to jail. Placed on the first ship for Veracruz, he arrived there October 20. The following day Admiral Francisco de Navarro ordered the prisoner examined before the royal notary. With sweeping strokes Wilkinson began to alter the picture he had painted previously:

From Newcastle, in northern England, he had come to Jamaica to work as a carpenter in the ship-building trade. As for the port or bay called Espíritu Santo, he knew nothing of it; his knowledge was of the San Juan River, where he had been seventeen months previously on the trading sloop *La Cabrita*. His ship, bound for the port of Apalache, had encountered foul weather and sailed past its destination. When the weather cleared, it anchored "near the cays," which Wilkinson obligingly sketched on a sheet of paper. Short of provisions, they put a launch into the water and, with the help of an Indian passenger from Mosquito Island, sought fish and turtles among the cays. Then appeared the Frenchman La Flora (La Fleur) from the settlement of San Juan (or St. Jean).[6] During his day and a half at the place, Wilkinson related, he was kept in

---

[5] Ibid., pp. 211-214.

[6] Wilkinson's use of this name, coupled with his description of a fort built on an island in the middle of the river and a mention of an Indian from Mosquito Island, suggests the possibility that he was drawing on his memory of a visit to the mouth of the St. John's

the company of an English-speaking German constable called Diego Nicolás. He claimed to have viewed, but without entering, a castle of stone masonry, which stood on an island in the middle of the river.

Wilkinson declared the castle had sixteen artillery pieces, the settlement possibly as many as six hundred men and women; abundant crops of corn were grown, and cattle were brought overland from New France. The settlement was at peace with adjacent Indian tribes, and native women brightened the lives of the unmarried Frenchmen.[7]

After leaving the place, Wilkinson related, the sloop *La Cabrita* reached Tampico in seven days, then proceeded to Veracruz and Tabasco. For a seaman's pay, he agreed, he would be willing to accompany a Spanish force to dislodge the French settlement.[8]

Exactly one month later, on November 21, Wilkinson appeared in Mexico City for a fullscale hearing convened in the Royal Palace by the viceroy. Present were Don Francisco Fernández de Marmolejo, judge of the Royal Audiencia, and *auditor general de guerra*; Captains Andrés de Pez and Juan Enríquez Barroto, both of whom had conducted voyages in search of La Salle's settlement; Father Antonio de Astina of the Compañía de Jesús, himself an Englishman, and John Paule, an English artilleryman in Spanish service, both of whom served as interpreters; and the royal scribe, Sebastián Sánchez.

The viceroy, noting discrepancies and contradictions in Wilkinson's two previous declarations, ordered English translations made and read to the deponent. The first one, Wilkinson claimed, was accurate for the most part, but he admitted that on some points he had not told the whole truth. The Veracruz statement, he said, was true, except for an erroneous name given the London-bound English vessel from which he had been captured. The prisoner was then advised that if he told the truth he would receive appropriate reward; otherwise, he would be severely punished. With his hand on the Protestant Bible, he took the oath.

River. It was on an island in the middle of that river that the French built Fort Caroline in 1564, but this short-lived settlement soon gave way to a Spanish fort called San Mateo.

[7] Wilkinson, "Declaración," Veracruz, October 21, 1687, A.G.I., México, 1685-1688, (61-6-20), pp. 215-217.

[8] Ibid., pp. 218-219.

Wilkinson chronicled his life story, from his birth in Newcastle and his apprenticeship as a ship's carpenter. He detailed his travels from the first time he had sailed from London twenty-five years previously until his capture by Mateo Guarín the Greek off the Florida coast. Sailing far and wide—always on legitimate trading vessels, the way he told it—he had called at most of the ports in the Indies until, six years previously, he had settled down at Jamaica. There he plied his trade on land until, in June, 1686, a five-hundred-tun French vessel with a broken mainmast had reached Negril Point. Captain Juan Rosa—Spanish version of the name—needed a ship's carpenter, and Wilkinson was his man.

The French vessel, having sailed from Martinique, was pressed into service by the French governor at Petit Goâve to carry to San Juan a warning of the Spanish expedition proceeding from Veracruz. Wilkinson, the prisoner related, was persuaded to join the crew, and the ship sailed by way of Cuba's Cabo de San Antonio for the settlement of San Juan. Of the distance Wilkinson was not certain; he knew only that he had been paid a month's wages for the voyage. Captain Rosa, he had heard the pilots say, had anchored at 30°, between the cays and the mainland, ten leagues from the mouth of the river. There the ship had remained twenty-four hours before weighing anchor to negotiate the channel.

Wilkinson's detailed description of the area in question indicates one of two things: either he possessed a vivid imagination or else he was describing a place he actually had seen. In time of storms, he related, the island of sand that bordered the channel was completely erased by the sea. The channel itself was six to seven fathoms deep, according to soundings. It had taken from four o'clock in the morning until sunset to reach the lagoon and drop anchor, and the following day was spent in crossing the lagoon to the mouth of the river. The day after that a canoe bearing three Indians and a Frenchman came down the river. Hailing the ship in French, they showed great relief when answered in the same language. The Frenchman, Jean de la Fleur, sent one of the Indians on board with a quarter of venison for the ship's company and received the warning that a Spanish force was coming to destroy the French colony. So elaborate was Wilkinson's yarn.

Captain Juan Rosa and Wilkinson himself—the prisoner continued—then embarked in the canoe with Monsieur de la Fleur.

Traveling slowly up the river, they spent five days in reaching the French settlement thirty leagues upstream. After four leagues the river flowed fresh water, and at the widest part it was more than a league in breadth, a quarter at the narrowest place.[9]

Five or six days after they reached the settlement, Wilkinson continued, Captain Rosa's ship arrived. The settlement had no large ship of its own, he noted, but there were canoes all around because of the location in midriver. Besides the fleet of canoes, there was only a ruined bark, which had come from Canada, or New France, by way of the river.

Wilkinson never faltered in answering the interpreters' questions. Concerning the dimensions of the island, he said it seemed to him that it was two English miles long (translated by the Spaniards as half a league) and half a mile wide; that it was made up of sand and small stones, that it had no trees except around the castle, where there were orchards and herb gardens, and that the terrain was so low that pilings were used to keep the river in its course. Actually, he qualified, the island was not in the middle of the river but somewhat nearer the south bank than the north. The castle, built in the form of a quadrangle with four bastions of stonemasonry, was situated at the downstream point of the island, looking toward the sea. It had sixteen artillery pieces mounted and another seven that were not, and Wilkinson claimed that he had helped to make carriages for the seven, which fired balls of three, nine, and sixteen libras. Inside the castle were the governor's quarters and barracks for soldiers, which Wilkinson estimated to number fifty or sixty, adding that "when the occasion arises, everyone is a soldier."[10]

Upstream two stones' throw from the castle was a masonry redoubt with eleven pieces of artillery, including six that fired balls of sixteen libras, the others being of smaller caliber. On a wharf farther upstream was a platform with nine pieces of artillery. A drawbridge connected it with the redoubt. The settlement itself was situated across from the castle on the north bank of the river, where there were fields of corn, tobacco, and potatoes. The houses of the settlement were of wood. In the settlement of San

[9] Wilkinson's distances, it is noted, were given in English miles and translated into leagues.
[10] Wilkinson, "Declaración," Mexico City, November 21, 1687, p. 196.

Juan and on the adjacent haciendas were 400 men, women, and children, of whom 250 were capable of bearing arms.

As to the origin and purpose of the settlement, Wilkinson was vague, perhaps with design. He seemed to recall having been told that a Frenchman from Canada had come down the river to the sea; recognizing the island as a suitable place to settle, he had left some of his people there and returned to Canada to bring more colonists and supplies. He seemed to remember that the French leader's name was "Monsieur de Salas," but of this he could not be certain.

In response to further questioning, he said he had been in the settlement from June 20 or 30, 1686, until February 1 of the current year, 1687. (He previously had said he was there 1½ days.) There was a church within the walls of the fort, and he had seen two priests. At the start of the interrogation Wilkinson had declared that, four months after coming to San Juan, he had married a widow named María, a native of the island of Jersey. The woman was a Roman Catholic, and one of the two priests had performed the ceremony. Having spent so many years as a wanderer, and being poor, Wilkinson explained, he had wished to settle down and save for his old age. While on the island he had occupied himself at jobs of carpentry, working one day a week for the fort. His wife owned a hacienda on the mainland and kept two Negro women as her slaves.

No other ships had come to the settlements, but three vessels from France had been expected. He had heard it said that a ship of up to five hundred tuns could navigate the stream, and once in Petit Goâve seven years ago he had seen a ship of twenty-four guns said to have come down the river from Canada to the sea.

The interrogators pressed for explanations. If, as Wilkinson said, he had married to retire and stay in one place, why had he left after only a few months to return to the sea? The prisoner replied that he owned property in London that he wished to liquidate, and that he had planned to return to his wife as soon as the business was finished. After seven months he had left the settlement the first of February on the same ship. The vessel passed through the Yucatán Channel to arrive after twenty-three or twenty-four days at Negril Point, Jamaica. There Wilkinson remained while the French trader proceeded to Petit Goâve. Then came the English frigate *Dark Wanderer* and a brigantine, and he sailed on the former. After collecting a cargo of masts at Laguna de Términos, on the Campeche coast, the two vessels sailed for England. Just before they entered the Bahama Channel, the piragua of Mateo Guarín captured the ships and took them to Havana.

Thus the English carpenter was brought into the clutches of the Spaniards. Whatever his intentions, he had heightened their frustrations with his wild but piquant tales. Was he insane? Or was he perhaps the key to the long-sought French colony? It had been a bad day for the interrogators. After seven continuous hours of probing questions and questionable answers, the session adjourned at midnight.

Next day, after reading over the transcript of testimony, Viceroy Monclova ordered the hearing resumed in the house of Marmolejo. The interrogators now confronted the prisoner with certain discrepancies. Wilkinson performed with agility, and it is difficult to imagine that one whose story was false could come off so well.

The questioning at first concerned the number of persons who lived on the various creeks out from the settlement of San Juan who might assist in the work of the haciendas and plantations. Wilkinson's reply astounded his hearers. To the north, toward Virginia, he said, there were many, because the land was good; on the haciendas of that region, which he had visited, there were perhaps eleven hundred persons. He had heard that a force of fifteen hundred men could be raised from the environs. The figures given the day before, he said, referred only to the settlement proper.

Shown the sketch of the settlement that he had drawn in Veracruz, he acknowledged having made it because he was ordered to, but it was without method or form because he was neither pilot nor draftsman. Whatever he had told differently on the other occasions, he said, was due to fear, since he had sailed on a French vessel, under a French captain, to warn the settlement of San Juan of the Spanish move against it. Since the Lord Viceroy had promised not to punish him if he told the truth, he had done so during this interrogation.

While the Spanish officials in Mexico City pondered the declarations of Ralph Wilkinson, a similar case came to the attention of the governor of Florida. A mulatto slave from St. Augustine had fled to join a pirate vessel. While sailing up the coast to attack the English settlement of St. George, the pirates were captured and taken to St. George as prisoners. The mulatto was freed by a Dutch pirate captain, with whom he sailed for the windward islands to seek a buccaneer crew. Then, looking for Indian guides, they landed on "the coast of New Spain," according to the runaway slave, who gave this account:

While cruising along the coast, they came to a point of land at the entrance to a large bay. Fifteen leagues inside, they found the mouth of a river and, a league and a half upstream, a French settlement of two hundred men, women, children, and slaves. The settlement had a stone redoubt ten feet high overlooking the river, with fourteen artillery pieces. The pirates remained six days, then proceeded along the coast of Apalache to Tampa Bay. The mulatto and six other men went ashore at this point while the sloops went to find Indian guides. The sloops failed to return, and thirty-five days later they were captured by the Spaniards and taken to St. Augustine. The mulatto made his declaration to Governor Diego de Quiroga y Losada.[11]

Before Quiroga's report reached the viceroy, the higher official had overruled his own misgivings to act in the Wilkinson case. The Conde de la Monclova noted the divergence in Wilkinson's three declarations: In the one made in Havana, the English carpenter stated that he had not entered the French settlement of San Juan, because a Frenchman he had met at the mouth of the river had warned him he would be made prisoner. In the declaration made in Mexico City, he claimed to have spent seven months in the settlement and even to have married there. His story was given great credance in Havana, the viceroy reported. There were many in Veracruz and even in Mexico City who believed him also; so hungry were these people for news, Monclova temporized, that they swallowed any that was offered. As for himself, the colonial official wrote to the king, he feared that the Englishman had invented his story, perhaps to delay his being punished for piracy. It made no sense, Monclova believed, for the French to have fortified such a remote outpost; even the windward islands and the

---

[11] Diego de Quiroga y Losada, "Auto sobre el mulato de Arguelles," San Agustín, December 15, 1687, A.G.I., México, 1685-1688 (61-6-20), pp. 220-224.

French settlements on Santo Domingo, so strategically situated, had neither fortification nor artillery.[12]

Wilkinson's claim that he had seen many more people in the area surrounding "Espíritu Santo Bay" rendered it even less credible, in the viceroy's opinion; but it also heightened the urgency for ascertaining the truth. Although less credulous than others, Monclova deemed it unwise to let his doubts cause hesitation.

Therefore, in conference with the general of the windward fleet, Don Jacinto Lope Gijón, he decided to send out a new maritime expedition with Wilkinson as a guide. Captain Andrés de Pez and the pilot, Juan Enríquez Barroto, acquainted with the coast from having been there previously, would take the Englishman and seek the settlement of which he had told them.

The new expedition left from Veracruz on March 8, 1688.[13] Pez and Barroto, on the *Santo Cristo de San Román*, sailed with the full moon. They set a course for Mobile Bay, which was now generally considered to be the elusive Bay of Espíritu Santo. Twenty days later they anchored in the bay, stationed gun crews, and launched the *chalupa* that was carried on board for exploring the shallow coves and inlets. Taking Wilkinson and the English interpreter John Paule in the small boat, Pez explored the coast and took soundings until, on April 5, they reached Cabo de Lodo, the mud cape at the mouth of the Mississippi. As they disembarked on the point of land at the big river's mouth, Pez confronted Wilkinson: From Mobile Bay to the cape they had found only a shallow lagoon and land incapable of supporting any human being because it was so swampy. Where, he demanded, was the port with seven fathoms of water and the French settlement?

At last Wilkinson was cornered. With no retreat open, he confessed that he never had been on this coast, or in the French settlement he had described. He only had heard of it from two Frenchmen at Laguna de Términos. The rest of his story was merely the product of his natural bent for lying; but . . . if they could go back to the laguna and ask the two Frenchmen where they had obtained their information . . .

[12] Viceroy Monclova to the King, March 20, 1688, ibid., pp. 188-189.
[13] Ibid., p. 189.

On the entire voyage, recalled Pez, still incredulous at the whole affair, the English prisoner had held steadfast in what he had declared previously. "He put on many acts for me, sometimes telling how severe was the month of March in that place, or of the large number of piraguas they had at the mouth of the river, all of which was intended to frighten the crew. At the end he had arranged to remain among the Indians, but he did not know that he was being placed in irons first. . . . Having always been negative, he was hopeful that some misfortune would befall the boat, which at that point was a real possibility."[14]

When on April 24 the *Santo Cristo de San Román* returned with her disgruntled crew to Veracruz, Pez delivered the errant Englishman to prison to await orders from the viceroy. Dispatching to the high official his diary and map of the expedition, he sent his assurances—"pledging, unlike the Englishman, with my head"—that no foreign settlement existed on the coast. The area examined, he asseverated, could offer no suitable port, not even for a sloop.[15]

One task remained for the Spaniards before they were finished with the mendacious Englishman: they must try to determine the motive for his falsehoods. Once again, on April 26, a hearing was convened to cross-examine Wilkinson. In response to the new round of questions, he owned to having declared in Mexico City that he had spent seven months in the French settlement and to having offered to take the Spaniards there. His offer to lead the Spaniards to the settlement, he claimed, had been conditional upon their taking him to the mouth of the right river. At Cabo de Lodo, he recalled, they had taken a declaration from him concerning the location of the settlement, but he did not remember telling them he never had been in that region.

He still maintained that he was married and had a wife in the colony. Did he remember leaving the *patache* anchored in Mobile Bay and going with the captain in a boat to look for the settlement? Yes, he had done so, but, not being a pilot, he did not know whether they had approached the vicinity of the French colony.[16]

[14] Andrés de Pez to the Viceroy, Veracruz, April 24, 1688, A.G.I., México, 1685-1688 (61-6-20), pp. 228-229.
[15] Ibid., p. 229.
[16] Wilkinson, "Declaración," Veracruz, April 26, 1688, pp. 232-238.

The time had come to pass judgment, and the deed was done incisively in a letter from Marmolejo the the viceroy. "The conclusions to be drawn from all these declarations, Most excellent lord, is that this English heretic has not spoken a word of truth." He must have invented these lies to avoid punishment, or with the hope of finding opportunity to escape during the voyage just ended.[17]

Marmolejo believed that "he should be considered as guilty in his lies as in his piracy, managing with his contradictions and inconsistencies to increase the punishment he has earned. . . . One should believe that there is no such settlement on all the Mexican coast." Four diligent maritime searches had failed to find it; there was no need for another. All that remained to be done was punishing "this English heretic, of whom I have had for many days information that he has practiced piracy in these seas and was present at the invasion of the Port of Campeche and other windward ports."[18]

It was not Wilkinson's first time to be in a tight place, according to Marmolejo. He had been imprisoned and sentenced to hang for piracy on Curaçao but had escaped. Marmolejo suggested that the viceroy might wish to make further investigation of the circumstances of this incident as well as "other piracies and invasions he has been making all his life." Other French and English pirates in Spanish custody, he had learned, were acquainted with Wilkinson and had sailed with him.[19]

Viceroy Monclova was not surprised at the outcome of the voyage with Wilkinson. "I feel I have nothing else to do in the matter," he wrote to the king, "except to punish this English hoaxter as he deserves and to scorn the credulity with which such news is spread in these regions."[20]

About the time of the *Santo Cristo*'s return with news of the voyage's outcome, Monclova had received Quiroga's report on the runaway slave. The mulatto's claim of having been in a French settlement, he felt, was to be taken in the same light as that of the

[17] Francisco Fernández de Marmolejo to the Viceroy, May 5, 1688, A.G.I., México, 1685-1688 (61-6-20), pp. 234-235.
[18] Ibid., p. 236.
[19] Ibid., p. 237.
[20] Monclova to the King, May 27, 1688, A.G.I., México, 1685-1688 (61-6-20), pp. 226-227.

Englishman: fearing punishment, he had used this method to gain time, hoping for opportunity to escape.

With his letter to the king, the viceroy sent the diary and map of the fourth maritime expedition in the search for La Salle's colony of French intruders. He also sent a copy of his order "to punish the Englishman, who remains prisoner in Veracruz." A similar order was being dispatched to the governor of Florida "so that he may proceed against the mulatto slave."[21]

The fate of the mulatto is not to be found. The *gran embustero*, Ralph Wilkinson, was condemned to a life of slavery in the galleys.[22]

---

[21] Ibid., p. 227.

[22] William Edward Dunn, *Spanish and French Rivalry in the Gulf Region of the United States*, 1678-1702, p. 84.

13. THE DEMENTED FRENCHMAN

They were both Sailors, this Man, who was of *Britany*, was call'd
Ruter; the other, of *Rochelle*, *Grollet*. They had ... so perfectly
enur'd themselves to the Customs of the Natives, that they were
become meer Savages. They were naked, their Faces and Bodies with
Figures wrought on them, like the rest. They had taken several Wives,
been at the Wars and kill'd their Enemies with the Firelocks ... but
having no more Powder nor Ball, their Arms were grown useless, and
they had been forc'd to learn to shoot with Bows and Arrows.

—Henri Joutel
Journal, p. 149

From time to time men had deserted from La Salle's company,
choosing a free life among savages in preference to the tyranny of
their leader. It was a French deserter living among the Indians—
though not definitely linked to La Salle's colony—who next
alarmed the Spaniards.

The Wilkinson episode had served to rouse officials of New
Spain from their complacency and to stir anew their fears of
French intrusion. When the glib stories were proved false, the
leaders might once again have been ready to assure themselves that
no such settlement ever had existed, or ever could exist, but for
the new alarm from the Coahuila frontier. Just a few days after
Captains Pez and Barroto had sailed from Veracruz in search of
Wilkinson's chimera, the viceroy received a letter from Alonso de
León. It told of a Frenchman living among the Indians beyond the
Río Grande and serving as their chief. Like Wilkinson's inventions
concerning the settlement of San Juan, this news wafted like
smoke, betraying the presence of a smouldering fire, with poten-
tial for breaking into raging flames. The firefighter nearest the

scene was General De León, already a veteran of the search for the elusive colony of La Salle.

On July 13, 1687—just a few months after his second expedition in quest of La Salle from Nuevo León—De León had been named governor of Coahuila. Arriving in the province on October 14, he took his residence in the village of San Miguel de Luna, adjacent to the Presidio of San Francisco de Coahuila, the present-day site of Monclova.

From the start De León's meager settlement was beset by Indian troubles, as the intractable Tobosos repeatedly attacked mission settlements and haciendas, driving off horse herds, inciting mission converts to rebellion, and killing settlers. According to the governor's claims—which some historians are inclined to discredit[1] — he generously offered the natives pardon and fair treatment in exchange for a cessation of hostilities and freeing of prisoners. But in all their dealings, he alleged, the Indians acted in bad faith.[2]

In March, 1688, De León was informed that the chieftain known as Don Pedrote was making preparations for an attack on Spanish settlements. The same day alarming news came from the struggling mission of Caldera,[3] where the neophytes were threatening revolt. De León, leaving Captain Diego Ramón in charge, hastened with three men to deal with the mission's difficulty. On April 2, however, he was summoned from Caldera by an urgent appeal from Ramón and hurried back to his presidio to make ready for a fullscale campaign to end the depredations. He dispatched pleas for help to Nuevo León, Parras, Saltillo, and Nueva Vizcaya. When reinforcements arrived from Nuevo León, the governor moved to attack. During a twenty-day campaign, he pursued a policy of taking captives, extracting from them all the information he could get, and, after they had confessed, sending them to the gallows. By his own count sixteen of the rebellious natives

[1] See Vito Alessio Robles, *Coahuila y Texas en la época colonial*, p. 312.
[2] Ibid., p. 307.
[3] At present Candela, Coahuila. Alessio Robles (ibid., p. 371) notes that the Mission San Bernardino de la Candela was founded by Alonso de León in 1690 at the same site as the old Caldera Mission, the name undergoing a transition from Caldera to Candela. Lino Gómez Canedo ("Introducción," *Primeras exploraciones y poblamiento de Texas* [*1686-1694*], p. xiv) says that Fray Damián Massanet had founded the Mission San Salvador in 1689 "near the old Mission of San Bernardino de la Caldera." Massanet was in charge of the Caldera (or San Salvador) mission when De León became governor of Coahuila and Massanet left from there to accompany him to Texas in 1689.

either were killed in the campaign or were captured and then hanged.[4]

On returning to San Francisco de Coahuila in May, De León immediately began preparations for a new campaign. Before he could depart again, however, news came from the north of a threat even more formidable than the Indians. The messenger told of a white man—doubtless a Frenchman—who held sway over the Indian nations beyond the Río Bravo and was organizing them, for what purpose no one knew.

Of how this intelligence came to the governor two different versions are at hand: De León's and that of Father Damián Massanet, who was in charge of the Mission Caldera. Even before De León's arrival in Coahuila, the priest claims to have begun inquiring of native visitors concerning the presence of Frenchmen in the wilds to the north. At last one of his Christian converts had brought word that there was indeed a settlement of white people who looked like the Spaniards. Then came an Indian of the Quems nation with news "that he had been even to the very houses of the French."[5] The people were many, well armed, and in possession of artillery, he reported; and there were women, as well as priests, in the settlement, where corn and other crops were being planted. The native messenger offered his services to Massanet to take him there.

About this time, Massanet relates, De León stopped at the Caldera Mission on his way to assume command of the Presidio of Coahuila. The priest tried to persuade the new governor to undertake an expedition to seek the French colony, but De León wished first to report to the viceroy. He expressed the hope that Massanet could produce more conclusive evidence that the settlement existed.

By the priest's account, he called a captain of the Pacpul nation named Juan, who had seen, in the region of Sierra Sacatsol,[6] the

---

[4] Alessio Robles, *Coahuila y Texas*, pp. 310-311; Alonso de León to the Viceroy, Monterrey, June 21, 1688, in Canedo, *Primeras exploraciones*, p. 72. The latter document also is found in A.G.I., México, 1685-1688 (61-6-20), pp. 244-248.

[5] Fray Damián Massanet to Don Carlos de Sigüenza, 1690, in Herbert Eugene Bolton (ed.), *Spanish Exploration in the Southwest, 1542-1706*, p. 355. This letter is printed in the original Spanish in Canedo, *Primeras exploraciones*, pp. 3-38.

[6] Also called Sierra Yacasol and Sierra Dacate, identified as Anacacho Mountain in southeastern Kinney County, Texas, fifteen miles southeast of Brackettville (Robert S. Weddle, *San Juan Bautista: Gateway to Spanish Texas*, p. 71).

Frenchman who ruled over a number of native tribes. The Indian Juan offered to go again to the *ranchería* to bring the white man back to Caldera; " . . . and that he might the more readily execute his commission I gave him the clothing and the horses which I had with me, for him go give to the chiefs of the place where was the man of whom he spoke."[7]

Twenty leagues beyond the Río Bravo, Juan reached the *ranchería* near the Sierra Sacatsol. Finding the Frenchman, he told him of Father Massanet's desire to see him. Although Juan returned to Caldera without the white man, he informed the priest "that we might without fear go after him."[8] Massanet claims then to have informed De León, who went to look for the foreign intruder.

De León's report on the matter, however, fails to accord any part of it to Massanet—an oversight that may have given the priest his first misgivings toward the military man he later was to regard with rancor. Before going out on his first campaign, the governor claimed, he had sent a Tlaxcalteco Indian from Boca de Leones (present Villadama, Nuevo León) to gather friendly natives to assist in putting down the uprising. The emissary, Agustín de la Cruz, was waiting with his alarming news when the governor ended the campaign. On May 18 he reported to the governor as follows:

Beyond the Río Bravo he had encountered a *ranchería* of one thousand inhabitants, unlike any native village he had ever seen. In the middle was a huge dwelling, fashioned like a drawing room, covered with buffalo skins, and ringed by a cordon of warriors. When Agustín rode into the village, the inhabitants surrounded him, bade him dismount, and took him inside the lodge. He was made to kneel before speaking to the man who was sitting on a dais. This man, he now informed De León, was of good stature and light coloring; he could easily be mistaken for a Spaniard. Adorned in buffalo robes, he appeared to be perhaps fifty years of age. His hair was graying, his face tattooed like those of the Indians who protected him. It was evident the natives regarded him with veneration.

Agustín, in his own native tongue, reverently addressed the man,

---

[7] Massanet to Sigüenza, in Bolton, *Spanish Exploration*, p. 356.
[8] Ibid.

but the honored one did not reply. Agustín's attitude, however, won him the assistance of the natives, who volunteered as interpreters. The man then responded courteously to Agustín's greeting, informing his visitor that he was French, and that he had been in this region for some time, gathering the Indian nations to subdue the tribes who refused to come, and to establish villages among them. On such a mission, the Frenchman declared, he had been sent by God.

Native messengers had been dispatched to Governor De León, he related, to ask the Spanish official to bring a priest to visit him. He had assigned six Indians to go with Agustín to Caldera and to serve as guides to bring De León to the Frenchman's *ranchería*. As Agustín prepared to depart, however, the Indians took his harquebus, which they kept as security for his return.

In Agustín's report the governor saw dire threat; the Frenchman must be planning to use the Indians he was gathering to further an evil design on Spanish territory. De León visualized a French troop standing by, awaiting the summons to join with the native horde in attacking the settlements of northern Mexico. Such a plan was feasible, the governor reasoned, because the frontier forces were so meager. He himself had but twenty-five soldiers and a few citizens who had come to assist in the founding of the new village of Santiago de la Monclova. Bringing adequate reinforcements from Saltillo, Parras, and Nuevo Reino de León was not feasible, because distances were so great, and these neighboring provinces faced the same threat as did the settlements of Coahuila. The Frenchman, therefore, must be captured and brought to Spanish justice, his hold on the native populations broken once and for all. De León reported plans to proceed immediately with eighteen men. He would leave the rest of his soldiers and all able-bodied citizens behind to guard the settlement against attack either by Indians acting independently or by those directed by Frenchmen.[9]

Without delay the governor assembled the eighteen soldiers, three mule drivers, and eighty horses and began the journey northeastward toward the Río Grande. They reached the stream a week later at a point forty-two leagues from Monclova, by De León's reckoning.[10]

[9] Alonso de León, "Auto," San Francisco de Coahuila, May 18, 1688, in Canedo, *Primeras exploraciones*, pp. 74-76; also in A.G.I., México, 1685-1688 (61-6-20), pp. 248-254.
[10] De León, "Derrotero y diario," in Canedo, *Primeras exploraciones*, pp. 81-82.

1. The *armada de barlovento* of the Spanish Indies in action against English pirates, Maracaibo, 1668. (*Historia con las Indias*)

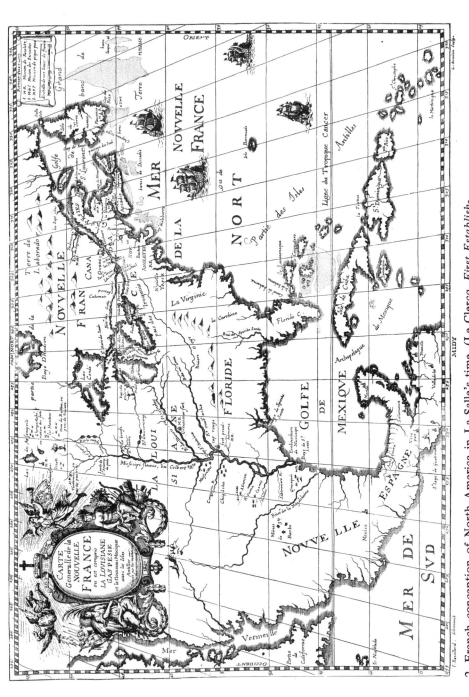

2. French conception of North America in La Salle's time. (Le Clercq, *First Establishment of the Faith in New France*)

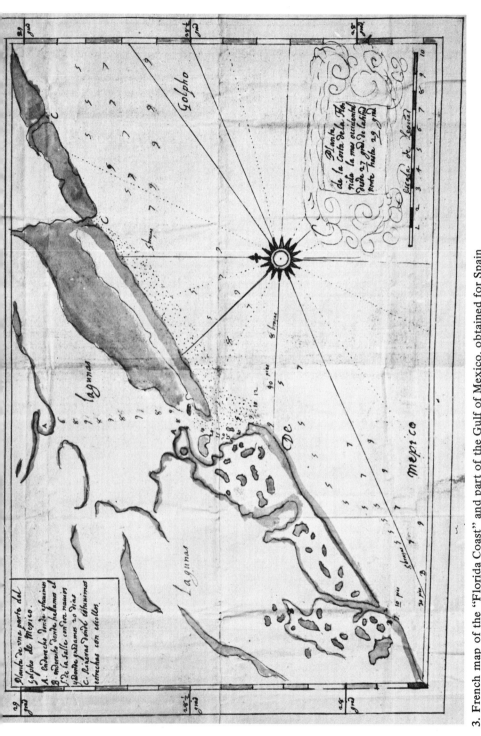

3. French map of the "Florida Coast" and part of the Gulf of Mexico, obtained for Spain by Pedro de Ronquillo. (J. P. Bryan Collection, University of Texas Archives)

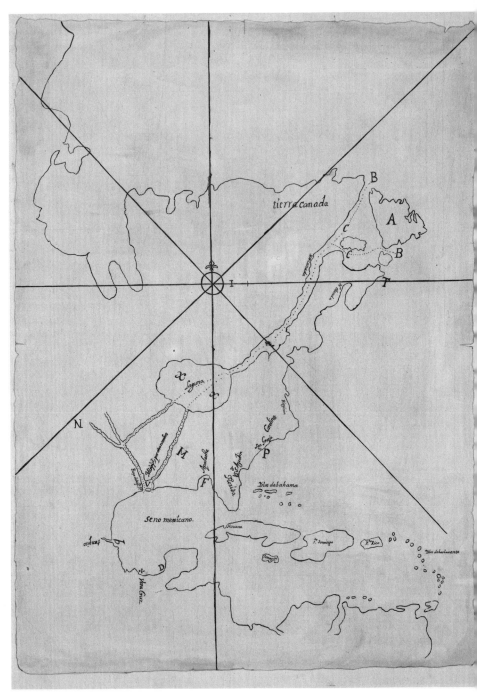

4. Martín de Echagaray's "Map of the Coasts of the Gulf of Mexico and from North America to Newfoundland, with Report on the Location of Espíritu Santo Bay, near the Mississippi, Which is Occupied by the French." (J. P. Bryan Collection, University of Texas Archives)

Journal Du 25e novembre 1684
part an Du petit goüe en
Lille De St Domingue —

Le 25e Dudict a deux heure du matin leuent
est toit suet et nous auont leue lan
cre et en may me ten nous auont mis tu
les voille et nous auont single le cap
a ouest   3 lieus

Jeus que ann Dix que le calle me nous
a pris le tout le sam Dix

Le maime Dudict a midix leuent est
venut ouest et nous auont courut Du
faute De la gounaue et nous auont
single le cap au nordrouest   6 lieus

Jeus que a quatre heure du soir que
nous auont tourne De bord et nous auont
single le cap au sud   5 lieus

Jeus que a sept heure du soir que
a vont tourne De bord et nous auont
single le cap au nord   5 lieus

Jeus que a si heure du soir que nous
auont change De bord et nous auont
single le cap au sud suïrouest   4 lieus

Jeus que a quatre heure du matin
le 26e Dudict le Dimanche que le
vent est uenut et nous auont sin
gle le cap au ouest quard De nord
rouest   5 lieus 2

Jeus que a 10 heure que le vent
say calle me et a continue jeusque
a mi Dix le 26e Dudict le Dimanche

Le 26e Dudict amidix le vent est uenut ouest
suïrouest et nous auont single le cap
au sud quart De suest   13 lieus

Jeus que a dux heure apres midix
que nous auont tourne De bord et nous
auont single le cap au nordrouest   13 lieus

Jeus que a sept heure du soir que
nous auont vire De bord et nous a

. Page from the log of the frigate *La Belle* for November 25, 1684, which was among the papers carried by the Indians to El Parral. (University of Texas Archives)

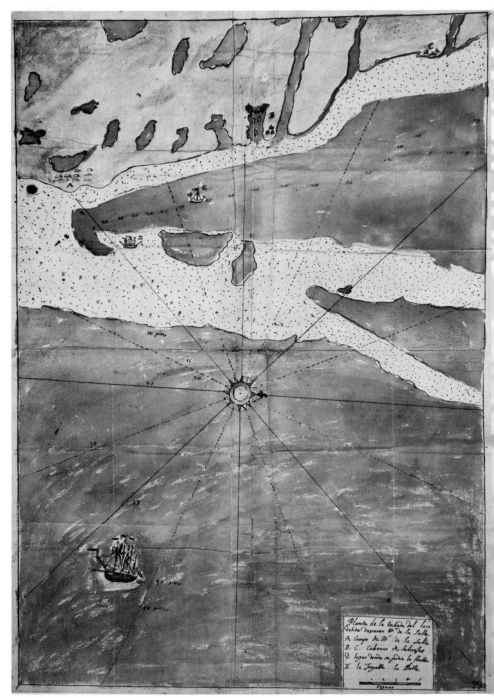

6. Map of the vicinity of La Salle's camp on Matagorda Bay, brought to France by Captain Beaujeu and obtained for Spain by Pedro de Ronquillo: *A*, La Salle's camp; *B*, *C*, Indian camps; *D*, place where *l'Aimable* was lost; *E* the frigate *La Belle*. (J. P. Bryan Collection, University of Texas Archives)

Lavaca Bay, with Sand Point at lower right, the mouth of Garcitas Creek at
per left. Port Lavaca is at left of bay, Point Comfort and ALCOA plant at right.
ASA photograph)

A 24 de Marzo salió el R.ꟸ y hasta A anduvo 8 leg al Nordeste
A 25 de A. a. B 7. leg. al Nordeste
A 26.de B. a. C 6. leg. al Leste
A 27 de C. a. D. 3 leg. al Leste
A 28 de D. a. E. 6. leg. al Nordeste
A 29 de E. a. F. 5. leg. al Nordeste 4ª al Norte
A 30 de F. a. G. 4. leg. al Norte
A o1 de G. a. H. 5. leg. al Norte
A 2 de H. a. I. 1. leg. al Norte y de I. à J. 4 leg al Nordeste
A 3 de J. a. K 5. leg. al Nordeste.
A 4 de K. a. L. 8 leg. al Nordeste
A 5 de L. a M. 5. leg. al Leste, pero rodeando fueron).
A 6 de M. a. N 3. leg. al Nordeste y de N à O 2. leg. al Leste
A 7. de O. a. P 4 leg. al Lest-Sueste
A 8 de P. a. Q 8. leg. al Leste guiñando al Nordeste
A 9 de Q a. R. 5 leg al Nordeste 4ª al Norte
A 11. de R. a. S 6. leg. al Leste y de S. à T. 6. leg. al Nordeste
A 12 de T. a V. 5. leg. al Leste
A 13 de V. a X 6. leg. al Leste guiñando al Nordeste
A 14 de X. a. Y. 6 leg. al Leste 4ª al Nordeste
A 15 de Y. a. Z. 2 leg. al Nordeste
A 16 de Z. a. A. 3. leg. al Norte
A 16 de A. a. B 5. leg. al Norte el Gouernador solo
A 17 de B. a. c. 5 leg. al Norte el Gouernador solo
A 16 de A. a. D 3. leg. al Leste el R.ꟸ solo
A 18 de C. a D Voluio el Gouern.ꟸ al Real
A 21 de D. a E 6. leg. al Lest Nordeste
A 22 de E. a F 3. leg. al Leste. Hallaron la Poblacion
A 23. de F. a S. 5. leg. al Sudueste y de S à H 3 leg. al Leste
A 24. de H. a S. 8 leg. y llegaron rodeando la Bahia hasta 2. leg de la boca

R.º Hondo
R.º Zarco
R. de las Nueces
R. de Ramos
R.º Brauo
R. de las Sabinas
R. de Nadadores
R. de la Caldera
R. de Cuahuila
Cuervos
Cuahuila
LEGVAS
N O
L
M
K
J
I
H
G
F
E
D
C
B
A

el año de 1689 hizo el Gouernador Alonso
e Cuahuila hasta hallar cerca del Laõ de
lugar donde hauian poblado los Franceses ½

R.º de S. Marcos

R.º de Guadalupe

R.º de Francés

C

B

A. D

Z

E F

Lago de
S. Bernardo
2 2

2 2

R.º de Medina

T

V

X Y

R.º del Leon

S

Hauio quebrado
2

3

1 ½
1 ½

2 3

En F. estaba la Poblacion

l. Blanc

P.ta de Culebras

p.ta de S. Francisco

Boquilla

R.º de Flores

SENO

R.º de S. Joseph

MEXÍCANO

20

1689.

R.º Brauo

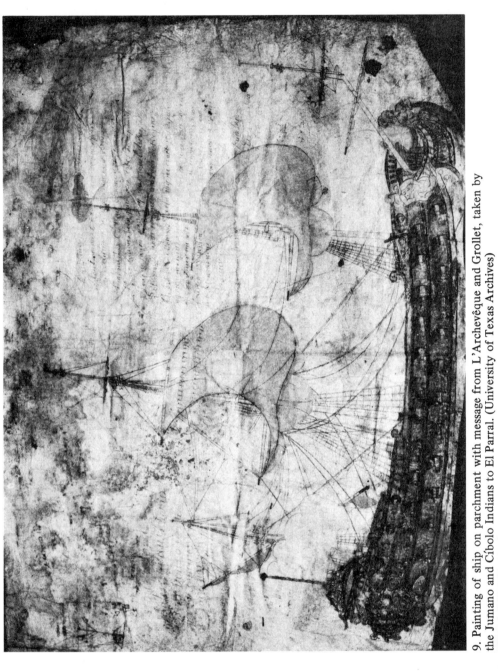

9. Painting of ship on parchment with message from L'Archevêque and Grollet, taken by the Jumano and Cíbolo Indians to El Parral. (University of Texas Archives)

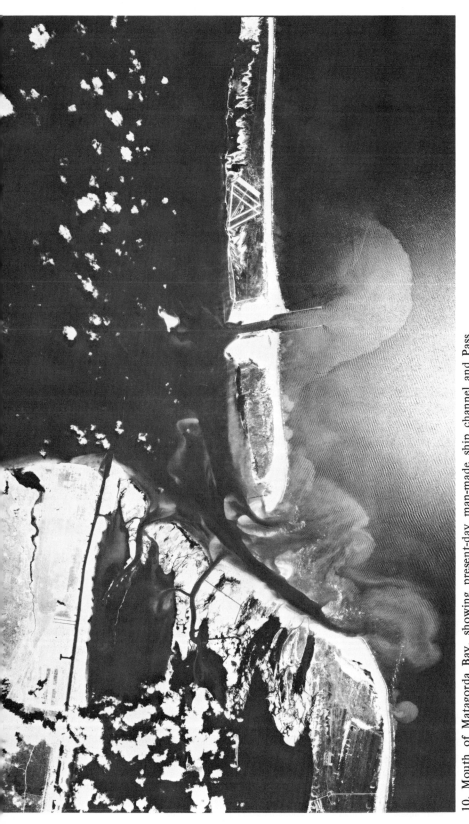

10. Mouth of Matagorda Bay, showing present-day man-made ship channel and Pass Cavallo, the natural entrance where La Salle's ship *l'Aimable* ran aground. (NASA Photograph)

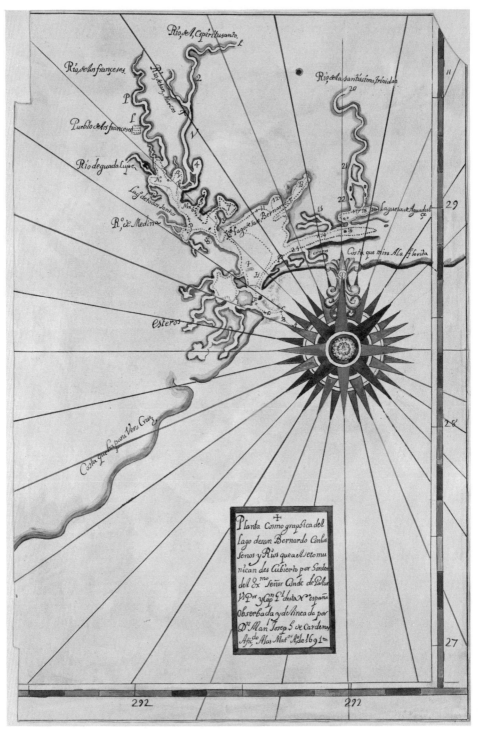

11. Manuel Joseph de Cárdenas's map of San Bernardo Bay, 1690. (J. P. Bryan Collection, University of Texas Archives)

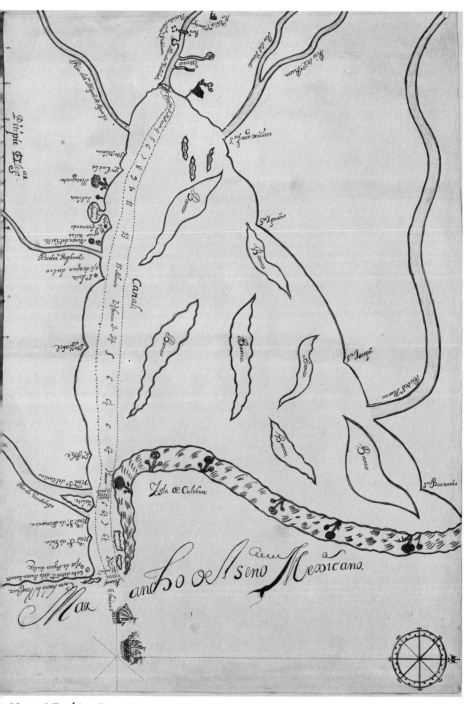

. Map of Espíritu Santo Bay as observed by the Marqués de San Miguel de Aguayo in ril, 1722, showing location of presidio and mission. (J. P. Bryan Collection, University Texas Archives)

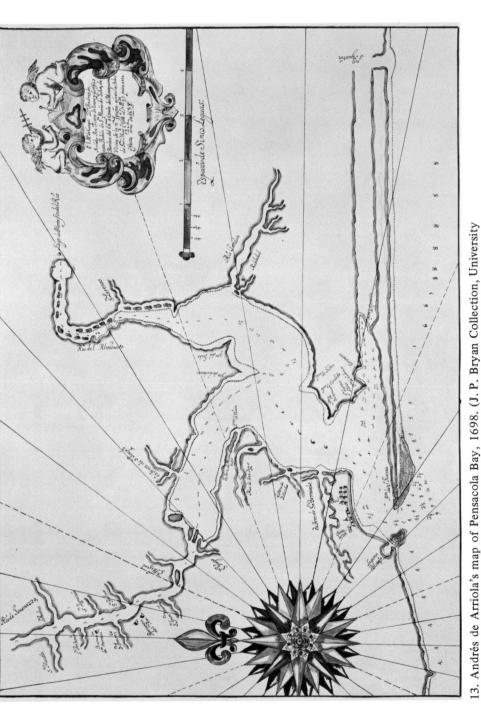

13. Andrés de Arriola's map of Pensacola Bay, 1698. (J. P. Bryan Collection, University of Texas Archives)

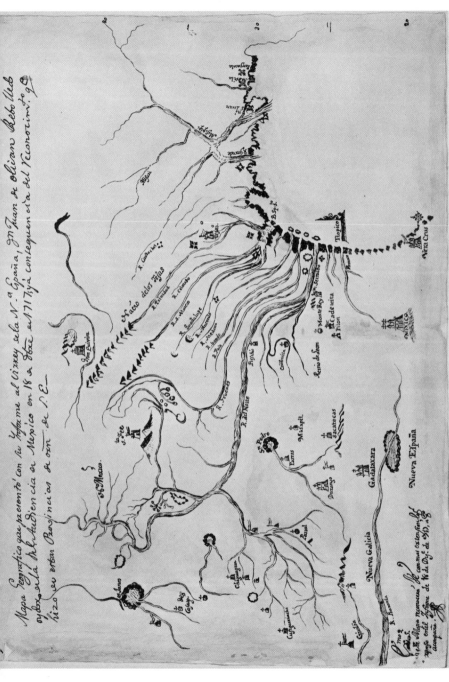

14. Juan de Oliván Rebolledo's map of New Spain, showing coastline from Veracruz to Pensacola, 1717. (J. P. Bryan Collection, University of Texas Archives)

15. La Salle memorial in Indianola State Park looks out over Matagorda Bay, which the great explorer mistook for the mouth of the Mississippi River. (R. S. Weddle photograph)

On Wednesday, May 26, De León left five soldiers at the camp on the Río Grande and crossed with the other thirteen over "a very good and wide ford" with water reaching no higher than the stirrups. The passage was the width of two harquebus shots; according to the governor, it was suitable for crossing an entire army. The ford was Paso de Francia, over which Spanish expeditions to and from Texas would pass for a century and a half.[11]

The land over which De León's small band traveled the next two days, though covered with mesquite brush, was open and well watered. After traversing almost twenty leagues without raising sign of the Indian village described by Agustín, De León kept the soldiers in camp on Friday, May 28, sending out Indian scouts to search for the Frenchman's *ranchería*. When one of the scouts returned the following day without success, De León decided to return to the Río Grande to wait for more precise information. Retracing the previous day's travel, the Spaniards came upon more than five hundred Indians killing buffalo.[12] Through an interpreter they made inquiry for the "Spaniard who was living among them" and learned that they were his subjects, and that his *ranchería* was nearby. "They helped us to kill some of the *cíbolas*, and one of them served as guide to take us to spend the night very near the *ranchería* of said Indians." The stopping place was three leagues from the previous overnight stop.[13]

Next day, Sunday, May 30, the thirteen Spanish soldiers, following their Indian guides, crossed several arroyos in swift current. Three leagues from the day's starting place—six leagues from their meeting with the Indians and twenty from the Río Grande—they spied the *ranchería* with its multitude of Indians, spread out on a ridge with a commanding view. This eminence probably was the Sierra Sacatsol, as related by Father Massanet. The natives, numbering some three hundred, stood in military formation.

[11] One of the major crossings within about five miles of the mission settlement of San Juan Bautista (Guerrero, Coahuila), which served as the point of departure for most of the important expeditions bound for Texas from 1700 on through the Spanish period. Another was El Paso Pacuache (or Paso de los Pacuaches), says Weddle (*San Juan Bautista*, p. 5 n.), identifying Paso de Francia with a ford called Las Islas. Ben E. Pingenot of Eagle Pass, Texas (oral statement, March 7, 1971), more recently has uncovered evidence that the latter two names represent different crossings, Paso de Francia being about one mile upstream from Las Islas Crossing, and that two other nearby fords were used.

[12] De León, "Derrotero y diario," in Canedo, *Primeras exploraciones*, p. 82.

[13] Ibid.

Arriving at the buffalo-skin house, which De León recognized from Agustín's description, the Spaniards found it guarded by forty-two warriors with bows and arrows at the ready. De León, General Martín de Mendiondo, and the expeditionary chaplain, Fray Buenaventura Bonal, on an invitation from the guard, went inside to find themselves in a clean, neatly arranged salon. In front of the door stood three chairs of well-tanned buffalo skin, each with a finely made leather cushion. On the middle chair sat the Frenchman, appearing very much as Agustín had described him. Standing rigidly on either side was an Indian attendant, ready to act upon his slightest whim.

The Frenchman seemed to move from his chair as if automated; falling upon his knees before the padre, he kissed the sleeve of his habit. Courteously he extended his hand, first to General De León, then to Mendiondo. Clasping his hands across his breast, he exclaimed repeatedly, "*Yo francés* [I French] "—which, to De León, was a damning admission. He proceeded with caution:

In the Castillian language he asked me how many of us there were. I told him we were many and that the greater number had remained behind as rearguard nearby, with which news he seemed baffled and confused. At this time, having brought some clothing, petticoats, sack dresses, knives, earrings, beads, rosaries, and tobacco to be divided among the Indians to win them to my devotion, I took out these things and gave them to the Frenchman so that he might distribute them to the Indians himself. Before this he had remarked about the soldiers on horseback, and I realized from his question that the Frenchman knows very well the mother tongue of the Indians who were gathered, because no one had entered the salon but the said religious, myself, and General Mendiondo. I questioned him in the Mexican language by means of an Indian interpreter, through whom I advised him that I must take him to the Río Bravo, where I had left a Frenchman who would talk with him in his own language and we could discuss whatever was appropriate, and that from there he would be returned to his habitation. He strongly resisted this idea, as did his Indian assistants. In view of this resistance, such rashness as bringing him by force was very serious and dangerous. By such a move the entire company might be placed in jeopardy, for he had more than one thousand Indian bowmen who could attack us. By suave manner and courtesy I importuned him, that he should come with me and, always being resisted, we took him with artfulness and ingenuity from the habitation where he was, placing ourselves at known risk, since the Indians stood by him with such obedience, respect, and veneration. They even knelt before him. In his house, which was extensively decorated, they fanned him with plumes and cleansed him of sweat, fumigating the dwelling with fat and other substances unknown to us. With great vigilance we observed the militia like form and disposition of the Indians. We saw in the said dwelling a harquebus which, although broken, was recognized as having been long, like a musket, and a flask of powder, ramrod, and balls. When asked his name, he said Francisco, and that he is Christian, but that in his language he is called Captain Monsieur Yan Jarri and that he was gathering many Indian nations to make them his friends."[14]

His intentions were good, said the Frenchman, for he never would use the natives of his following for destructive ends.

Although it was with considerable reluctance that "Yan Jarry"—or Jean Géry—agreed to accompany the Spaniards, De León managed to persuade him. After a ceremonious parting with his Indians, he mounted a horse. The governor himself went back to reconcile the natives by distributing to them the rest of the gifts he had brought, trying to make them understand that their white chief would suffer no harm in his custody.

The small company of Spanish soldiers, with Jean Géry, arrived at the Presidio of Coahuila on June 6, having traveled sixty-seven leagues to reach the *ranchería* beyond the Río Grande. They had shortened the distance by five leagues on the return.

Next day De León began interrogating Géry, using as interpreter the Christian Indian Ignacio of the Mission Caldera. Ignacio was said to be fluent in both "the Mexican language"—probably meaning that of the Coahuiltecan Indians among whom the Frenchman had been found—and Spanish.

Certain parallels may be seen between the depositions given by Géry and the Englishman Ralph Wilkinson. While it seems doubtful that either ever would have brought ruin to Spain if left unmolested, the captors in each case viewed the activities of the captive as inimical. The Frenchman, on the face of it, offered more reason for Spanish concern than had Wilkinson, for it appeared he was mustering Indians for sinister purposes.

Géry, as did Wilkinson, gave the Spaniards false information. Each told such wildly contrived and imaginative tales as to cause

---

[14] De León, "Auto," in Canedo, *Primeras exploraciones*, p. 78.

one to suspect that he believed them himself. Wilkinson, as his accusers surmised, may have been employing his natural talent for lying to gain time, hoping to find a means of escape. Géry, on the other hand, almost certainly was demented, his memory of his true past lost in the fuzziness of an atrophied mind. When the inquisitive Spaniards pressed him, prying as eagerly for his past activities as for his future intentions, he filled in the blanks with whatever tale he could bring to his lips.

The irony concerning these two historic prevaricators is that one caused the Spaniards to find the French colony they sought, and that it might well have been so with the other. After three years of futile seeking by land and sea, the Spaniards could afford to overlook no possibility; and even though some suspected from the first that Géry, like Wilkinson, was lying, the protectors of New Spain must seek the fire that lay behind the smoke. They pressed hard for answers, some of which were alarming.

In response to their questions, the Frenchman said he was baptized Francisco, but his countrymen called him "Captain Monseiur Yan Jarri [*sic*]"; that he was a native of St. Jean d'Orléans, France, and that he was one of a company of Frenchmen who by order of Monsieur Philippe, governor, had formed a settlement on the banks of a large river. Géry, having learned the language of the Indians, had come to the region where the Spaniards had found him, to gather other nations from the territory surrounding his village. His motive, he candidly—or stupidly—stated, was to reduce all the tribes to the obedience of the king of France.

In the native village, he revealed, he had married and now had a three-year-old daughter. He could not tell his age, but from his appearance the Spaniards believed him to be more than fifty. Finding it necessary at times to resort to signs and gestures, the prisoner estimated that fifteen years had elapsed since the French settlement had been planted on the big river to the east. He recounted the colony's progress as follows:

A French fort, well garrisoned and protected by five pieces of artillery on each of its four walls, had been built on the river. The settlement's four streets were under protection of the guns of the fort, which was defended by six companies of soldiers. There was a church and a monastery for six Capuchin priests. Both the fort and the church, which had six bells, were of stone. Ordinarily, there were three merchant ships in the settlement. Vessels passed to and from France, bringing the necessities of the colony.

In adjacent fields the colonists raised corn, wheat, tobacco, and sugar cane, as well as cattle, sheep, horses, and mules. The crops and livestock were produced with the help of many Indians who had become French subjects. For navigating the river the colonists had seven barks equipped with oars and sail, capable of reaching the sea in one day, whereas three were required on horseback.

Since settling among the Indians, Géry declared, he had not returned to the colony. A year previously sixteen Frenchmen had visited him, and just two months ago another seven had come. He had communicated to them only the success he was having in gathering the Indians. The Frenchman did not sign the deposition, because he could not write. The governor affixed his own signature, as did two witnesses.[15]

De León was convinced by the testimony that a French settlement existed "on the river or bay of Espíritu Santo." He moved quickly to start the prisoner, together with the transcript, on the way to Mexico City, where Viceroy Monclova would determine the appropriate course of action. Under no circumstances, the governor resolved, should this foreign intruder be allowed to return to lead the sundry bands of Coahuiltecan Indians who had pledged him their allegiance.[16]

By June 19 De León had taken the captive to Monterrey. Thence the new governor of Nuevo León, Don Pedro Fernández de la Ventosa, sent the Frenchman on toward Mexico City in the custody of General Mendiondo.[17] The journey had been delayed several days, he wrote to the viceroy, because the prisoner had fallen ill, and it was not wise to risk losing him by making him travel in such a condition. De León considered the information that Géry had given in the Coahuiltecan tongue to be unreliable. Getting him safely to the capital, where a French interpreter could obtain a better understanding of his account than was possible in the Indian dialect, was of vital necessity.

[15] Jean Géry, "Declaración," San Francisco de Coahuila, June 7, 1688, A.G.I., México, 1685-1688 (61-6-20), pp. 254-258.

[16] De León, "Auto," June 7, 1688, ibid., 258-259.

[17] Pedro Fernández de la Ventosa to the Viceroy, Monterrey, June 19, 1688, ibid., p. 263.

The matter was all the more urgent, De León suggested, because the Frenchman had so many Indians at his command. The settlement Géry had described appeared to be fully capable of carrying out its heinous design. Should the French learn of the meager protection of the northern provinces, they might well visit ruin upon them. If action against the French settlement were delayed, the intruders might employ the Indians at their command to take over the settlements and ports of New Spain. "Since I find myself with only twenty-five soldiers and some citizens, the number to resist them is very small. . . . For that reason, Lord, the province of Coahuila needs another twenty-five soldiers, two or three quintales of powder, some harquebuses, and *cueros*.[18] With the prisoner on his way to the capital, the governor prepared to return to Coahuila to dispatch spies in the hope of learning from Géry's Indians the true designs of the French.

On July 12 in Mexico City, Viceroy Monclova convened a hearing similar to the one held for interrogating Ralph Wilkinson the previous November. This time, however, instead of a mendacious Englishman suspected of piracy, the principal witness was "a Frenchman tattooed like a Chichimeco"[19] —Jean Géry, or, as his name now was written into the transcript, "Juan Enrique." Some of the other principals, however, were the same, including the *auditor general*, Don Francisco Fernández de Marmolejo, who conducted the hearing.

Géry, like Ralph Wilkinson, when confronted by the array of viceregal officialdom, gave testimony that varied considerably from his earlier statements. Like Wilkinson, he offered glib explanations, adding or altering details as he went along. In an effort to iron out the discrepancies, the hearing extended to three long sessions, finally ending on July 20.

Now, instead of being a native of St. Jean d'Orléans, Géry was from a place in France called "Xeble," had been baptized in the Church of the Holy Spirit, and as a young man had become a soldier. Then he was captured on the high seas by an English vessel called *Santa María*. He was asked where the English took him, and when he gave no answer, the question was rephrased and ex-

---

[18] De León to the Viceroy, June 21, 1688, in Canedo, *Primeras exploraciones*, p. 73.
[19] Jean Géry, "Declaración del Prisionero," Mexico City, July 12, 1688, A.G.I., México, 1685-1688 (61-6-20), pp. 263-264.

plained. His only reply was a senseless chuckle. He had been sent by Monsieur Philippe to the Indian village where the Spaniards had found him, having left France five years ago (instead of fifteen, as stated previously).

When asked the distance from the *ranchería* where the Spaniards found him to "the French settlement which he said was on Seno Mexicano," he replied that it was three leagues, then amended himself to say three hundred. When questioned further concerning the distance, and confronted with a map, he nervously twisted his handkerchief and shrank from his interrogators, declaring that he knew nothing.

Concerning his marriage to an Indian woman in the *ranchería*, he said a Capuchin priest from the French colony had performed the nuptial ceremony two years previously, that he had a son—not a daughter as had been recorded.

Although the French captive could not read his native language, he was able to identify two pages printed in French as those which he had torn from a book. They were the ones he had given to an Indian (Agustín de la Cruz) to take to Coahuila, hoping to induce the Spaniards to visit him.

He once had returned to the French fort where the Capuchin priests were, traveling on foot. When asked how long the journey had taken, he slapped his breast and fell silent. Pressed for details on how he had first come to the *ranchería* where Governor De León had found him, he gave an imprecise answer. He had come with three ships, of four, six, and ten guns, to a bay, and the party had proceeded up the river in the seven barks mentioned earlier. From the fort he had traveled overland to the Indian village, where he had married, established his authority over the natives, and governed them in such a manner that they accorded him complete obedience.

The attention shifted again to the fort on the big river, which Géry had sketched on the map. It had, the Frenchman said, six companies of twenty-four men each, under command of Monsieur Philippe. It was built of "earth like adobe"—not stone, as he had stated previously. Twenty artillery pieces taken from the three ships and a moat with drawbridge protected it. Seventeen houses of wood stood outside the stockade, under protection of the fort's artillery. Thirty-four horses obtained from the Indians were kept inside. Ships from France supplied the settlement, which had white women and children, as well as soldiers.

Pressed for distances, Géry said travel from the bay to the fort required three days by land or one by river. From the fort to his *rancheria* took much longer; he knew not how long, although he had walked the entire distance. He could not even say whether it was one hundred leagues or three hundred.

The Frenchmen who had come to the *rancheria* to bring him powder, Géry now stated, numbered seven on the first occasion, instead of sixteen. Then had come two, not seven, bringing an Indian who was still in the village when the Spaniards had come to take Géry away.[20] The native since had gone to report Géry's capture to Governor Philippe.

By now it was late at night, and the interrogation was halted until July 16. When the hearing began anew, the Spaniards deftly pinpointed the discrepancies between the declaration made to Alonso de León in Coahuila and the one recorded on July 2: The prisoner had first said that he was a native of St. Jean d'Orléans, then of "Xeble." He had related previously that he had come with Monsieur Philippe fifteen years ago, but now he said it was five. In his earlier declaration he had said the fort was of stone and mortar, but now he changed this to "mud like adobe."

The two declarations, it seems, were consistant in nothing. Where the deponent had a daughter before, now it was a son. While the Capuchin chapel previously had ten bells, it now had two. But for all the variations the Frenchman had a simple explanation: his interrogators in Coahuila had not understood him well; the confusion was theirs, not his. The testimony he was giving here was correct, and it varied from his previous statements only because of the failure of his interrogators to understand him. He never had said, for example, that he came from France fifteen years ago. Actually, his landing on the American continent had been seven years previously, with the three ships mentioned. After spending two years at the fort on the big river, whose name he professed not to know, he had gone five years ago to live among the Indians.

Having been taught by his priest as a youth, Géry could say the

[20] Ibid., pp. 263-267.

Padre Nuestro, the Ave María, the credo, and the blessing in Latin. He was put to the religious test by being asked to repeat the Commandments in French, which he did ably, interposing that he knew it was a sin to break them.

Why, then, had he chosen to marry a pagan and live among the Indians, who were of a different religion and who had such savage customs as going about naked and eating raw meat, with never a priest to hear his confession? Why did he not live with his own people and practice his Catholic religion with the Capuchins?

Such choices, he responded, were not his to make; he had gone among the Indians on order of Governor Philippe. Once with the natives, he had looked upon the Indian woman and found her attractive. She had given her hand, and the priest had performed the marriage ceremony. To please her he had allowed himself to be tattooed in keeping with the native custom. This, and not what he had said previously, was the truth.

The line of questioning turned again to the distance from his *ranchería* to the French fort. Géry now recalled that his journey on foot from the Indian village to the French settlement had taken twelve days over an untrod path so densely wooded that it could not be penetrated on horseback. His governor had sent him neither clothing nor provisions. On three occasions he had received money, which he had sent back to the fort for safekeeping, since it had no utility among the Indians.

Did the prisoner know the way from his village to the French fort and settlement? Having marked the trail, Jean Géry answered, he knew it well.

Asked again about the number of persons in the settlement and the fort's armament, he replied that there were three hundred Frenchmen, comprising six companies. Only two companies lived inside the fort, because there was not room enough for all; the rest lived with their wives in houses outside the compound. Some of the twenty artillery pieces corresponded in size to the crown of his hat, others to his fist. Some of the soldiers used muskets fired with a fuse, others with a spark (flintlock), and most had pistols.[21]

In the final session of the hearing, attention was focused on the Frenchman's life among the Indians. His native followers, Géry

---

[21] Jean Géry, "Segunda Declaración," July 16, 1688, ibid., pp. 268-273.

testified numbered "eleven times a hundred." When they stopped for a while in one place, which was seldom, they built grass-covered huts that looked like haystacks. They moved about as they felt like it, or as forced to by their wars with other tribes. Géry himself had moved with his followers many times, sometimes going one league, sometimes two or three, "according to necessity."[22]

Further questions concerned the nature of the land on the big river and the natives who dwelt along it. On both banks, from the sea to the fort, lived Indians of different tribal affiliations; those on the same side as the fort were friends of the French, coming often to the colony to bring buffalo meat and fruits. But those on the opposite shore were hostile, sometimes fighting the French. After taking captives these savages killed the older ones and made slaves of the younger.

Géry, like Ralph Wilkinson, had been a wanderer, according to his testimony. Having left home when he was nineteen or twenty years of age, he went to war as a foot soldier for seven years. Then he went to sea on a French privateer, sailing he knew not where, with Captains De la Flor (Fleur) and De la Rose[23] (or De la Roche), serving as sergeant, ensign, and lieutenant. At last returning to the "Port of the Virgin Mary," Géry had joined the three ships commanded by Monsieur Philippe, as they proceeded to found the colony on Seno Mexicano. During the voyage he was made a captain and served two years in that capacity at the fort on the great river.

The Indians who came to render obedience to Monsieur Philippe made the governor a present of thirty-four horses and asked the governor for a captain to lead them against their enemies. Géry was chosen. Not knowing the language of the natives among whom he was sent to live, he learned it from his wife. It was recorded that the prisoner now was a little more than forty years of age (instead of fifty) and could not sign his name.[24]

There seemed to be little use in continuing the hearing, for the more the Spaniards questioned, the more confused Géry's answers

---

[22] Juan Géry, "Declaración," July 20, 1686, ibid., p. 274.

[23] By strange coincidence Wilkinson used these same two names in his spurious account (see Chapter 12).

[24] Géry, "Declaración," July 20, 1688, pp. 273-277.

became. By now the officials were thoroughly convinced that the prisoner was demented. "Such flagrant contradictions were perceived in his answers given in Coahuila . . . and those given here were so confused, that certainly they must be attributed to his not being in his right mind," the viceroy later recounted. Regardless of the man's mental state, the count added, two facts stood out as incontrovertible: the man was a Frenchman, and he had been found well within the limits of territory claimed by Spain.[25]

As in the case of Ralph Wilkinson, it seemed unlikely that Géry could have drawn upon his imagination for all the details he had recited concerning the purported French settlement. His testimony, therefore, could no more be ignored than Wilkinson's had been. Like Wilkinson, Géry claimed the ability to lead his captors to the settlement he had described. It was incumbent upon the Spaniards to put him to the test.

As had been the case so many times in the abortive search for La Salle's colony, other factors entered the picture to strengthen viceregal resolve. In May, while Alonso de León was bringing the French prisoner from beyond the Río Grande, Captain Francisco de Cárdenas of Presidio de Cerro Gordo had made a campaign into the region north of Tampico to punish the Pame Indians for their depredations. Returning with prisoners from the vicinity of the Río de las Palmas, he took them to Jalapa for questioning by Father Juan de la Cruz Durango. To this large river, 140 leagues north of Mexico City, the captives said, had come three thousand white men resembling Spaniards. On the river, more than a league from its mouth, the strangers had built a stone quadrangle with tall chimneys and were wooing the native women with gifts of necklaces. Their language was distinctly different from the Spaniards of Cerro Gordo.[26] More smoke to spur the Spaniards onward in search of the fire. The viceroy acted promptly to convene a *junta general*.

The junta, meeting on July 23, considered the letter that De León had written from Monterrey, almost a month previously, reporting on the Indian wars of Coahuila, the capture of Jean

[25] Viceroy Monclova to the King, February 10, 1687, A.G.I., México, 1688-1690 (61-6-20), pp. 21-22.
[26] Juan de la Cruz Durango to the Viceroy, no date, A.G.I., México, 1685-1688 (61-6-20), pp. 277-279.

Géry, and the meager condition of the frontier forces. The council pondered the diverse declarations of the French prisoner, as well as the curious news from Father Juan de la Cruz. "The diversity and confusion of the contents of the reports and declarations made by the prisoner are evident, making it impossible to form either judgment or definite opinion as to the action that should be taken. Nevertheless, the prisoner's statements, as remote, improbable, and apart from all reality as they are, oblige one to take every precaution."[27]

In total accord, the junta called for a new land expedition to be led by Governor Alonso de León, whose knowledge and experience had proved their worth. A hundred men should be placed at his disposal, half of them to be drawn from the presidios of Cerro Gordo, Cuencamé, El Gallo, Conchos, and Casas Grandes, each to provide ten men from its garrison of fifty. The other fifty should be recruited by De León himself from the villages and ranches in Coahuila.

Preparations for the journey, on which the French prisoner would go as a guide, began at once. But the time-consuming task of raising men and supplies was to delay the start until the following April. More immediate action was required, and in order to renew the search at once, the Count of Monclova turned again to his maritime forces.

[27] Juan de Arechaga and others, "Junta," Mexico City, July 23, 1688, ibid., p. 282.

14. SAN BERNARDO REVISITED

... we set forward without *Larcheveque* and *Meunier*, who did not
keep their Word with us, but remain'd among those Barbarians, being
infatuated with the Course of Libertinism they had run themselves
into. Thus there were only seven of us that stuck together to return
to Canada.

—Henri Joutel
Journal, p. 161

Had Spanish officials known the true state of La Salle's meager
forces in Texas, they might have been spared a year's arduous
labor. La Salle himself had been murdered more than a year before
Jean Géry's capture. When the seven members of his last expedition took up the march for the Illinois and Canada, the six men
and boys who remained among the Cenis made plans, not immediately carried out, to return to Fort St. Louis. Left at the fort were
barely more than twenty—men, women, and children—and they
hardly constituted a threat. But the Spaniards could not know.
They continued to fret, during the summer of 1688, over the
testimony of their French captive.

Seldom in the days that followed the interrogations was Jean
Géry far from the consciousness of Viceroy Monclova. Fully aware
of the contradictions in the prisoner's story, and of the confusion
in his mind, the count sought an answer to gnawing questions:
What was a citizen of a foreign nation doing among the savages on
the isolated frontier of New Spain? Where had he really come
from?

Monclova pondered first the possibility that this foreigner, obviously demented, was a fugitive from a labor camp in which the

Viceroy-Archbishop Payo de Rivera (1673-1680) had placed a number of French prisoners during his time. Yet if such were the case, he reasoned, the man would have avoided recapture at all costs, for fear of being put to death. Jean Géry simply did not behave like an escaped criminal. Furthermore, the viceroy had the list checked, and among the few who had fled from this imprisonment, none was found whose age and description corresponded to Géry's.[1]

Perhaps, reasoned Monclova, the captive had been a crewman on the French vessel found wrecked on the bay called San Bernardo, and had drifted inland to find welcome among the natives. This possibility seemed the more likely because of Géry's appearance. The tattoo marks on his face bore similarity to those inflicted on other castaways who had lived among the Indians. The two men from Juan Corso's galley, recently rescued from the Florida coast by Rivas and Iriarte, had their faces marked in the same manner. Having lived such a life, naked among savages and subjected to cruel treatment for a period of years, might well account for the Frenchman's having become insensate. It might even be possible through kind treatment, the viceroy suggested, to restore his faculties so that Géry himself could shed more light on his past. With this thought Monclova had the illiterate and confused prisoner quartered in a room in the viceroy's palace, and ordered him well fed and cared for. As a companion to the captive he assigned a captain who spoke French. In the officer's company, Géry was free to go anywhere he liked in all of Mexico City.[2]

Response, however, was not immediately noticeable. Géry's tales of his life among the Indians remained as confused as ever. As a result the viceroy felt the urgency of sending an expedition to seek the purported French colony. With so much time required to organize a land force, he decided that, in the interim, another maritime expedition should be sent to explore the coastline as far as the "Río de Cíbolas," beyond the bay where the wrecked vessel had been found.

On July 19 the viceroy had sent to Captain Martín de Rivas instructions for dislodging the logwood cutters from Laguna de

---

[1] Viceroy Monclova to the King, February 10, 1689, A.G.I., México, 1688-1690 (61-6-20), p. 22.
[2] Ibid., pp. 22-23.

Términos on the Campeche coast. In the company of a frigate from the windward fleet, Captains Rivas and Andrés de Pez were to take on the mission the two piraguas used for the second maritime search. They were to drive out the poachers and burn the ships that were hauling away valuable timber, to be sold to the shipbuilding industry.[3]

With the instructions, the viceroy sent a request for the opinions of Rivas and Pez concerning Géry and his probable origin.[4] In replying, the two officers reiterated what they had said previously: All the coast of Seno Mexicano afforded no port big enough for a *patache* to enter, excepting Pensacola Bay, which could by no means be the place referred to. It was known that the French explorer La Salle had left a small band of followers in a fortification "between this Kingdom and Canada" and had returned to France to report to the Christian king. Louis XIV then had sent him with ships in search of a port near this fortification, but he had failed to find it, as evidenced by the two wrecked vessels on San Bernardo Bay. "From this we infer that the Frenchman could be one of those who remained in the fortification mentioned, who in the course of seven years, seeing himself cut off from aid from his King, might have penetrated the hundred leagues between the settlement and the place where he was captured. In any event, Lord, it is impossible, in our estimation, that they could have a settlement near to these seas, because of the difficulty of the entries through bars and rivers."[5]

To confirm this assumption, the two captains suggested a new reconnaissance of the Río Bravo, since heavy seas had prevented the piraguas from entering its mouth on the second maritime expedition. (Nor did Pez and Gamarra attempt to enter it on the third voyage, because their vessels were too large and they were

---

[3] According to Henry Powell ("Introduction to the 1893 Edition," in John Esquemeling, *The Buccaneers of America*, p. vi), the logwood cutters of the Yucatán Peninsula and Honduras were wont "to vary the monotony of timber-felling and bullock-driving by an occasional foray upon the Spanish settlements in the immediate neighbourhood. The colony of British Honduras was founded by their descendants, who still carry on the trade in logwood and mahogany." The timber cutters were analagous to the wild-cow hunters of Santo Domingo, whose principal diversion was piracy.

[4] The viceroy's letter of July 19, 1688, is not found. The source here is Andrés de Pez and Martín de Rivas to the Viceroy, July 24, 1688, A.G.I., México, 1688-1690 (61-6-20), pp. 1-3, in which the letter is mentioned.

[5] Ibid., pp. 1-2.

hastening to overtake the previous expedition.) If no settlement or signs of one were found, the new expedition might proceed to San Bernardo Bay, where the lost French vessel had been found, to reconnoiter the bay and mouths of the rivers that empty into it. In the absence of signs here, the voyage should continue to the Río de Cíbolas, where foul weather also had prevented the piraguas from making a thorough search. If no signs of a settlement were found, it would be useless, in the captains' view, to continue the voyage.

None of the available vessels were considered more suitable than the same two piraguas, already manned with fifty men each and with enough supplies and munitions on board to last the voyage. Only a pilot familiar with the coast, a supply of wine and *aguardiente*, and honey with which to regale the Indians were needed.

The viceroy, therefore, decided to postpone the expedition to Laguna de Términos in favor of a new maritime search for the French settlement. With summer growing short, he set the departure date for August 6 to 8. The piraguas should take launches with which to explore the rivers, bays, and lagoons. They should put people ashore to search for signs of a settlement and to interrogate the natives for news of the settlement they sought.[6]

The sea voyage, however, was not to supplant the projected land expedition. To increase the likelihood of success, Alonso de León still should raise his one hundred men and proceed by land to the river of Jean Géry's French fort. Yet, in the viceroy's eyes, the reconnaissance by sea was the most important, and the time most suitable for making it.

On Sunday, August 8, at eight o'clock in the morning, the two piraguas sailed on a southeasterly wind from the port of San Juan de Ulúa. With Captain Rivas in overall command of the two small vessels, they set a course to the northwest, toward Tampico.

Early in the morning of the fourth day, as the piraguas, under oar, moved close to the beach, a large merchant ship from Campeche was sighted, her trimmed sails filled with the land breeze, skirting the outside bar. When the crew of the piraguas hailed her, she lowered her Spanish flag and hove to, her crew scurrying ashore in a launch. This strange maneuver appears to

---

[6] Martín de Rivas to the Viceroy, July 28, 1688, A.G.I., México, 1685-1688, p. 133.

have been a precaution lest the piraguas—the type of vessel often used by pirates—have designs upon her. Three hours later, at eleven o'clock in the morning, the piraguas crossed the bar of Tampico, where the following day was spent taking on water, carrying buckets from the village in launches. A strong wind kept them in port still another day. Then heavy showers inland put the river on a rise, and the current was so swift that Captain Rivas dared not hazard an exit from the harbor until the twentieth.

As the two vessels proceeded on the twenty-first, a sun shot gave them a position of 22° 38', twenty-one leagues from the Río de Maupate. Anchored two leagues offshore, the men fished for food, taking a number of red snapper. The following day a north wind made progress slow and difficult. Beating to windward, the vessels were able to make good thirteen leagues. On the twenty-third some palm trees were sighted on shore and at five in the afternoon the piraguas anchored in front of the bar at the mouth of the Río de Maupate—the river presently known as Soto la Marina, and the one that Pineda had named Río de las Palmas.[7]

The night was spent anchored outside the bar, with little rest, because of the heavy waves pounding the small ships. Next day, August 24—St. Bartholomew's day—the pilots maneuvered the piraguas into the bay, towed by the launches, and dropped anchor. Presently a band of Indians appeared on the coast, and Captain Rivas sent a launch shoreward carrying honey, tobacco, and biscuit. When one of the men from the ship went ashore to present the gifts, the natives instructed him by signs to throw his weapon on the ground, and the Indians did likewise with their bows and arrows. Receiving the honey and biscuit, they made gestures of gratitude and were permitted to go on board the ship. The Spaniards, however, could not understand anything the Indians said.

That afternoon the captain sent the launches for fresh water. Rowing up the river four leagues, the crews found the stream divided by small islands into three channels, the deepest with four fathoms of water. They returned to the ships that night, and next day the galleys traveled upstream seven leagues, still in water four

---

[7] The Count of Monclova (Monclova to the King, p. 25) identifies the Maupate as being the same as the Río de las Palmas. Pedro Fernández Carrasco ("Diario del Viaje," A.G.I., México, 1688-1690 [61-6-20], p. 9) gives the latitude as 23° 03', approximately correct for the south end of the bar at the mouth of Río Soto la Marina.

fathoms deep and a carbine shot wide at the narrowest point. The stream ran bright and clear, with savannas stretching out on one side, the other "lost from view."

Again on Thursday, August 26, the crewmen took the launches to explore farther upstream until the following Sunday, during which time they covered twenty leagues. Natives were seen occasionally, watching from the banks, and when the party went ashore, they found many deer bones, indicating the source of the Indians' sustenance.

When the launches returned, the piraguas proceeded upstream, apparently taking a different arm of the river. After four leagues the water became too shallow to navigate. Along the banks the mariners observed several Indian *rancherías*, but in all the distance they found no sign of European settlement. A sun shot established the latitude as 23° 46'.[8] At five o'clock in the afternoon the searchers started down the river, continuing during the night by lantern light to reach the mouth next morning. Once outside the bar, they set a course to the north-northeast, riding a southwest breeze. At four in the afternoon of September 1, they dropped anchor in five fathoms at the mouth of the Río Bravo, which could not be entered, because of heavy groundswells.

The following day the piraguas entered the mouth of the river under oar, "with the launches by the prow." A large number of Indians appeared on shore, making hostile signs. Captain Rivas sent his emissaries ashore with bread, honey, and tobacco, but the natives took the gifts only to cast them on the ground. "Seeing how hostile they were, the people came back aboard, because they did not wish to agitate them further. That same afternoon the captain ordered that we should go with the two launches to find water for the galleys. We found the river very swift, with many meanders and sand bars. Seeing the little capacity of the river, we came back aboard, since the width was hardly the distance of a stone's throw."[9]

After a conference with his pilots and Captain Antonio de

---

[8] Carrasco, "Diario," p. 10. A marginal note in this source, as well as the viceroy's report (Monclova to the King, p. 25), says that the galleys penetrated upstream twenty leagues, the launches four more, counting all the meanders. The diary itself does not agree.

[9] Carrasco, "Diario," pp. 11-12.

Ybarra, Rivas decided next day to send the two launches, each with nine armed men, to explore farther upstream. Because of the many meanders, it was useless to try to rig sail, and the crews rowed for three days, anchoring each night in the middle of the river for safety against the Indians. By the third day, however, no trace of the natives was to be observed on the banks. Rigging sail the fourth day, they covered two leagues before the wind died, then rowed four more. At midday September 7 they stopped to observe the sun, obtaining a latitude of 26° 24', which would indicate their location near present-day Roma-Los Saenz and Ciudad Mier. From the reduced flow of the river, they believed themselves near its source. Advancing three leagues farther, they stopped often to make computations. Having come thirty-six leagues (about one hundred miles) from the river's mouth, by the diarist Pedro Fernández Carrasco's dead reckoning, the two canoes turned about and headed back downstream. Large numbers of Indians soon appeared on both banks, shooting arrows at the Spaniards. When a soldier aimed a musket at them, they fled with a fearful outcry.

At five o'clock the afternoon of September 9 the eighteen men returned to the piraguas at the mouth of the river. Again no sign of European habitation had been observed. Almost immediately the ships hoisted sail and set a northeasterly course. Favored by a southwest wind, they sailed all night and until three o'clock the second morning before anchoring in four fathoms within sight of land.

A northwest wind brought thunderstorms on Saturday, September 11, and the two small vessels followed the launches through the entrance to Matagorda Bay to anchor in the lee of the shore. When a band of Indians appeared on the coast, the men in the launches rowed shoreward to talk with them. The natives, somewhat more friendly than those encountered on the Río Bravo, gave them some fish but could impart no comprehensible news of foreign poachers.

The next day the mariners sailed to "the other coast"—probably the mainland near present-day Port O'Connor. Later that morning they found nearby the remnants of the lost French ship, *l'Aimable*. Evidently believing it to be the *Belle* (found fully rigged the year before), they noted that time and the ravages of the sea had removed all signs of the vessel except some rotten boards with bolts still in them, some cases of muskets all broken to pieces, and some wrenches covered with rust. Four leagues farther up the coast, probably near Sand Point, they anchored for the night.

After daybreak they began traversing to windward, north-northeast. By four o'clock the explorers, fighting wind and current, had made good no more than three leagues. Anchorage for the night was calculated at twelve leagues from the mouth of the bay—evidently an exaggeration, since no navigable part of the bay is that far from the mouth. The captains and the Indian guides went ashore at this point and observed the short distance "from the bank of the lake to the sea"—about the distance of a cannon shot. Thus it seems that contrary wind had borne them southeastward to Matagorda Peninsula.

On the fourteenth Captain Ybarra and the Indian guides went out in launches to look for the sandbank where the Río de Cíbolas entered the sea. After rowing nine leagues, they reached the river's mouth at eleven o'clock the second day. With the land in the grips of severe drouth, however, the wide channel was virtually dry. Though it seems inconceivable that it should be in such a condition, the stream called Río de Cíbolas must have been the Colorado River. Observing the sun at noon, the crewmen obtained a latitude of 29° 03′—a position obviously in error, since it would place them several miles inland. Turning back on the inland shore of the body of water, they continued to follow the coast west-southwest, always near the sea, until four o'clock the afternoon of the following day. They were nearing "the end of the lake"—probably meaning where it joined the main body of Matagorda Bay. By their reckoning they had traveled thirty-two leagues from the mouth of the bay—again an exaggerated distance.

At seven o'clock the next day they came to a freshwater lake "five leagues long and three wide"—Tres Palacios Bay. They went all around it without finding any outlet except the one by which they had entered. On the following day they killed a buffalo for meat and saw many of the shaggy beasts ranging along the coast. On September 19 they returned to the piraguas. The ships sailed west-northwest "12 leagues," then south "10 leagues" to reach the mouth of San Bernardo.

While the piraguas and the launches had reconnoitered most of

Matagorda Bay proper, they had failed to perceive the entrance to Lavaca Bay. This northwest extension of Matagorda Bay, which could have led them to the long-sought French settlement, lay hidden behind Sand Point (see Plate 7).[10]

Next morning crewmen of the launches, having gone to seek a supply of fresh water, saw more than thirty Indians and sent a messenger ashore to talk with them. In response to the natives' signs, the emissary threw his weapon on the ground, and the savages did likewise with their bows and arrows. But after he had walked toward them the distance of a stone's throw, away from his own weapon, the Indians suddenly picked up their arms and began to shoot at him. Only a miracle saved the man's life, the diarist averred. "Seeing this, our people fired four musket shots over them, because our purpose was not to do them harm but to obtain any information we could."[11]

On the twenty-first the launches examined an estuary "about a league from the mouth" of San Bernardo Bay. Beyond the point at its entrance they found a large lake—Powderhorn—but its shores were low and deemed uninhabitable because they would be subject to flooding.

At dawn Saturday, September 25, the two piraguas began feeling their way around the bar to regain the open sea. At nine o'clock a north wind arose, and the mariners set a southerly course. The wind blew with increased tempo, and the little ships were out of sight of land until early afternoon September 27, when they crossed the Tropic of Cancer and caught sight of the "Sierras de Soto Vento de Mía y Pate [Maupate, near Río Soto la Marina]" off the starboard bow. At midnight the twenty-ninth they dropped anchor at San Juan de Ulúa, completing the fifty-four-day voyage, which, like the previous ones, had failed to find La Salle's settlement.

[10] Francisco de Llanos, in his 1691 diary (Diario y derrota del Viaje que se hecho y Ejecutado a la Bahía de San Bernardo," A.G.I., México, 1688-1690 [61-6-21], pp. 268-269), explains the nature of Sand Point: "It has a reef of sand which extends from the windward point to the southeast [southwest] and crosses almost the entire entrance, leaving a channel on the western side, for which reason its entry has not been found in five expeditions which up to now have been sent to explore this lake." This quotation is translated in Herbert Eugene Bolton, "The Location of La Salle's Colony on the Gulf of Mexico," *Southwestern Historical Quarterly* 27, no. 3 (January, 1924): 180 n.

[11] Carrasco, "Diario," p. 15.

Sometime after the piraguas had sailed on the fifth and final maritime expedition, the Count of Monclova received orders that ended his direct involvement in the prolonged search. He was to take a new post, as viceroy of Peru. When Captain Rivas went ashore at Veracruz the morning of September 30, he found that Monclova's successor, Conde de Galve, had just arrived from Spain. He delivered to him the diary of the expedition, then dispatched a copy to Monclova, still in Mexico City.[12]

When the Count of Galve reached the capital, Monclova discussed with him the plans to send Alonso de León from Coahuila to seek the French settlement. Galve ordered that the new land expedition be made as planned. As the out-going official wrote to the king on February 10, he pledged himself to reserve judgment on fruits the new *entrada* might bear until his return:

> But I cannot wait to say I am convinced of the impossibility that on all Seno Mexicano, or in the interior, there is either port or river possessed or inhabited by Europeans, and therefore there are no settlements adjacent to its sea. The explorations have left no room to think otherwise. Although I assuredly have a propensity for doubting the rumors being spread in these extended dominions, I have not been remiss in investigating them, as Your Majesty recognizes from the repeated efforts I have made to that end. I have been honored to have these endeavors approved by Your Majesty, which is that to which my zeal in Your Majesty's Royal service will always aspire.[13]

Indeed Monclova, while suppressing his skepticism, had done everything possible to get at the basis of the rumors, the doubtful stories, and the outright falsehoods concerning the elusive French settlement. But in his eagerness to put his doubts on record, he transcribed his miscalculation for posterity.

[12] Monclova to the King, p. 25.
[13] Ibid., pp. 25-26.

15. DEATH IN THE WILDERNESS

At length they found a more friendly band and learned much touch-
ing the Spaniards. . . . It would be easy, said their informants, to
gather a host of warriors and lead them over the Rio Grande; but La
Salle was in no condition for attempting conquests. . . . The invasion
of New Biscay must be postponed to a more propitious day. Still
advancing, he came to a large river . . . and, building a fort of pali-
sades, he left here several of his men. The fate of these unfortunates
does not appear.

—Francis Parkman
La Salle, pp. 291-292

From many sources news had come to Spanish officials of a
French settlement in Spanish territory on the shore of the Mexican gulf: from a pirate vessel captured in the Bay of Campeche,
from an English warship overhauled in the Bahama Channel, from
Indian messengers who had encountered Frenchmen in the wilds
of Texas. Three years after the first report, the Spaniards still
lacked definite proof that such a settlement existed. The retiring
viceroy remained convinced that the whole matter was the crea-
tion of rumor mongers. If the stories had even a scintilla of truth,
Monclova believed, that single spark was being fanned to raging
flames by "sinister imaginations."

Five maritime expeditions and four by land had failed to provide concrete evidence that the Sieur de la Salle actually had succeeded in planting his colony on any part of the coast of Seno
Mexicano. But as Alonso de León prepared to make one last
search by land to prove or disprove the muddled account of the

demented Frenchman Jean Géry, distressing rumors wafted elsewhere. To still another advanced Spanish outpost came word that
foreigners had settled on the Texas coast and were carrying on
trade among the Indians of the Hasinai Confederacy (the Tejas).
Such was the news that reached La Junta de los Ríos, and ultimately the Presidio of San Francisco de Conchos and the mining
camp of El Parral.

In the autumn of 1687 Indians of the Cíbolo and Jumano nations came during their annual migration to the Franciscan missions at La Junta de los Ríos—the juncture of the Río Grande and
the Río de Conchos, at present-day Presidio, Texas, and Ojinaga,
Chihuahua. They asked Fray Agustín de Colina for a letter to take
to "the Spaniards who were coming and going among the Tejas."
The padre, not being sufficiently oriented politically to be alarmed
at the request, countered with a suggestion of his own: First bring
him a letter from "the other Spaniards"; then he would reply to it.
The natives agreed, and Father Colina evidently put the matter out
of his mind until the nomadic tribes returned to the junction of
the rivers approximately a year later.

In September, 1688, five of the Cíbolos, just returned from
their journey to East Texas, came again to La Junta. Through an
interpreter they told Father Colina that a "Moor" was living
among a tribe near the Tejas. This man, who carried a broken
harquebus and wore helmet and armor, was said to have fled from
other white men in the Tejas land to escape a plot against his life.
The outcast had gained a position of leadership over his adopted
tribe and was leading them in warfare. They already had destroyed
half the Michi nation.

In such terms the missionaries at La Junta de los Ríos were told
by the Cíbolos of the activities of the Frenchman Jean Géry
among the Coahuiltecans of the Texas hill country.[1] Then came
others of the same tribe, bringing word of the foreigners among
the Tejas—La Salle's men. These Frenchman also had armor and
long harquebuses. They were said to be trading clothing and axes

---

[1] Jean de Saliases, "Declaración," A.G.I., Guadalajara, 1683-1687 (67-4-11), p. 157,
indicates that the foreigner was coming with a band of Cíbolos to La Junta de los Ríos.
Actually, Jean Géry had been taken to Coahuila by Alonso de León the previous June.
Also, it is well to keep in mind that any movement of the French up the Río Grande
would have been somewhat prior to the first reporting of the Cíbolos in September,
1687.

to the Tejas for horses and fruits of the land and courting the native womem with ribbons and beads. They lived on the water in "wooden houses," one of which had been sunk, it was reported.[2]

The foreign intruders were trying to convince the Indians of the evil intent of the Spaniards of Parral and sought the natives' support in a move to occupy that region. Already they had made thrusts up the Río del Norte, evidently seeking the route by which they would come. Still other Indians were said to be approaching La Junta, bringing letters from these audacious ones. Father Colina reported all this to Governor Juan Isidro de Pardiñas Villar de Francos at El Parral.

Pardiñas, like Alonso de León in Coahuila, had his hands full of other problems. Since he had become governor fifteen months previously, one of the richest mineral deposits of the entire region had been discovered. Repeated Indian attacks, however, impeded both the working of the mines and the settlement of the province. With settlers being killed and horse herds driven off, Pardiñas was faced with the necessity of making constant war upon the bellicose natives. So far his forces had been successful in subduing only the Pimas, "after many deaths had occurred on both sides."[3] He was still campaigning against other hostiles in an effort to end their depredations.

Such was the situation at El Parral when the news came from Father Colina of the activities of the French in Texas. Pardiñas was aware of the numerous expeditions already made in search of La Salle's colony. He doubtless knew also of plans for the forth-

[2] Father Anastasius Douay (in Christian Le Clercq, *First Establishment of the Faith in New France*, II, 243-244) recounts that, on La Salle's expedition in the spring and summer of 1686, there were found among the Cenis (Tejas) "some ambassadors from the Choumans [Jumanos] who paid us a visit." He found them well instructed in the Christian religion, but says they spoke ill of the Spanish soldiers' cruel butchery of the Indians and offered to join the French in conquering them. These natives, says Douay, drew for La Salle maps of their country and the Mississippi on pieces of bark.

[3] Juan Isidro de Pardiñas to the King, Parral, November 21, 1688, in Charles Wilson Hackett (ed.), *Historical Documents Relating to New Mexico, Nueva Vizcaya, and Approaches Thereto, to 1773*, II, 231. Documents cited in this chapter are printed side by side in Spanish and English. They are found also in A.G.I., Guadalajara, 1683-1687 (67-4-11), pp. 155-195. For an account of the Indian warfare mentioned here see Jack D. Forbes, *Apache, Navaho, and Spaniard*, pp. 209-211. Captain Juan Fernández de la Fuente of the Presidio of Casas Grandes subdued the Pima revolt in September, 1688, but the Jocomes, Sumas, and Tobosos refused to accept the peace, and the Chisos soon joined them in raiding Spanish ranches and villages.

coming *entrada* to be headed by De León, since troops from the Presidio de Conchos had been asked to join it. Even so, the news from La Junta gave Pardiñas his first real sense of involvement in the matter.

All efforts at defensive warfare, meanwhile, failed to stem the tide of Indian depredations. Members of the Chiso nation—"declared to be the most pernicious enemies which this kingdom has"[4]—had formed an alliance with the Tobosos, Salineros, Cabezas, Chichitames, and Cholemes (Cholomes). Attacking pueblos of peaceful natives, they threatened to disrupt the missionary effort at La Junta. The Spaniards' only recourse seemed to be to move offensively, seeking the hostiles in their own land. To carry out this campaign and to search for the French intruders, Pardiñas decided to send a single expedition. On November 3 an order was drawn directing General Juan de Retana of the Presidio de Conchos to head it. Placed at his disposal were ninety Spanish harquebusiers including the provincial campaign company, soldiers of his own presidio, and citizens, along with whatever number of Indian auxiliaries he chose to take. His purpose was to deal with the hostiles by making "offensive war on them until they are reduced or punished so that through fear they may desire peace." Then proceeding to La Junta de los Ríos, he should cross the Río del Norte (Río Grande) and arrange a pact with the numerous tribes of that vicinity to preclude any alliance with the threatening Frenchmen. His orders further stipulated: ". . . he will take possession, in the royal name, of the lands which he may discover in that region. In sign of this claim he shall raise and erect the form of the holy cross in all places that may seem proper to him, drawing up the legal *auto* or *autos* that are ordered by the royal laws in cases of this sort."[5] As chaplain, Fray Juan de Jumeta, a Franciscan who was well versed in Indian languages, would take possession of the conquered lands on behalf of "our holy mother Church."

Proceeding from La Junta, Retana was to reconnoiter "the place toward which the foreigners are proceeding up the river, and the place whence they came." Every effort should be made to take a captive from among the Frenchmen from whom information

---

[4] Pardiñas, "*Autos* promulgated by the governor on receipt of the first notices," in Hackett, *Historical Documents*, II, 249.

[5] Pardiñas, "Order for an expedition to reconnoitre the Río del Norte," ibid., p. 251.

could be obtained, and caution should be exercised to prevent the friendly Indians from spreading the word of his coming.

"Also he shall reconnoiter the port or Bay of Espíritu Santo, or any other port that they may learn that any foreign nation is settled at; he shall endeavor to obtain through spies good and reliable information concerning the fortifications they may have made and the number of men they appear to have where they are settled."[6] Among other things he was to determine whether the Río Grande emptied into Espíritu Santo Bay, as some believed. He should make careful record of various landmarks, the route followed, the terrain, and rivers, and of any factors that might affect the outcome of a later expedition to dislodge the intruders. He must bring back a complete report that would guide the viceroy and the king in planning appropriate action "concerning a matter which threatens such evil consequences to all these kingdoms."[7] Both phases of the campaign were expected to last more than a hundred days. The governor provided provisions and munitions accordingly, as well as a mule train to carry them.

Start of the expedition had been planned for November 15, but unforeseen circumstances intervened. Indian depredations in the vicinity of La Junta worsened, and the two missionaries were ordered by their superiors to withdraw. Fathers Colina and Joaquín de Hinojosa reached the Mission of San Pedro de Conchos, adjacent to Retana's presidio, two days before that date. Father Colina reported to Retana and Pardiñas the conditions that had caused his superiors to order the withdrawal.

The missions at La Junta had been founded five years previously, in 1683, by Father Nicolás López. Although the natives were of the most docile disposition, Father Colina observed, "many enemy nations surround the country and they unite more readily with one another than with their ministers." This same circumstance had been experienced by two religious who had served at La Junta previously, he recalled. "These, being maltreated, left, and fortunately escaped, but lost the sacred ornaments."[8] Still the holy custody had insisted on sending ministers; but in the present instance the prelate was obliged to withdraw

[6] Ibid., p. 253.
[7] Ibid., p. 255.
[8] Fray Agustín de Colina to Pardiñas, November 18, 1688, ibid., p. 247.

them because the Suma Indians were "in tumult," and the religous could not be protected.

On November 21 General Retana began taking depositions from the Indians who had come with the two priests from La Junta, and who had informed the missionaries that Frenchmen had settled to the east. Then he dispatched to La Junta two Indian messengers. These were to advise the Indian chiefs of Retana's forthcoming expedition to chastise the hostiles who were harassing them and to pledge the peaceful nations his protection. On November 23 Retana took down the testimony of Fathers Colina and Hinojosa. Shortly thereafter he must have set out upon the expedition, though the date of departure is not found.

A few days after beginning his journey, Retana learned that some of the hostiles who had been attacking the settlements were encamped at the Sierra Guapagua. Although this mountain range lay off his projected course, he went to Guapagua and found three of the offending nations in a single camp: the Cocotomes, the Hijos de las Piedras, and the Gavilanes. Retana engaged them in a battle, of which he reports only, "I defeated and routed them, killing many."[9] His soldiers recovered a large number of horses bearing brands of well-known citizens of Nueva Vizcaya and took a number of prisoners.

After spending several days in pursuit of the hostiles, Retana resumed the journey toward the Río del Norte, mindful of the second phase of his campaign. On reaching La Junta he sent out native scouts to reconnoiter the route he should follow—and that which might be used later should a force be sent to dislodge the French invaders. The report that the foreigners had pledged themselves to invade El Parral persisted among the Indians he met, increasing Retana's anxiety.

A few days later the scouts returned with interesting news: a "governor" of the Indian nations of La Junta was returning from the Tejas country, bringing "letters" from the Frenchmen who dwelt among the Tejas. Retana decided to go meet this messenger at once. After four days' travel the Spanish force met the native governor on the Río Salado—the Pecos—and found him to be Don Juan Xaviata (or Sabeata), the principal chief of the Cíbolo and

[9] Juan de Retana to Pardiñas, March 3, 1689, ibid., p. 257.

Jumano nations. It was Xaviata who in 1683 had led Indian delegations to El Paso to ask for missionaries and Spanish help in protecting his people from the Apaches.[10] The result of this plea was the Mendoza-López expedition into the Edwards Plateau region of Texas, and the founding of missions at La Junta de los Ríos.[11]

Xaviata bore interesting news indeed: The Moors—the term the Indians still applied to the Frenchmen—already were dead, attacked and destroyed by the natives who lived in the country surrounding their settlement. Not a soul was left alive in the colony; only the four or five still in hiding among the Tejas survived. The chieftain himself had ascertained the truth of this report, having seen among the coastal Indians the spoils they had taken from their victims. These same natives had given him some papers and a ship painted on parchment, on which a message was written by hand in French (see Plate 9 in the picture section). He carried these items with him, wrapped in a neckcloth of wide lace.

Xaviata's report left Retana in a state of indecision. It was now March 3, 1689, and several months had elapsed since his departure from Presidio de Conchos. With a large number of Indian auxiliaries in his company, his supplies had dwindled. With the French colony already destroyed, there hardly seemed reason for him to continue. Still the road ahead beckoned. Toward the land of the Tejas the route stretched out over level country, cut by occasional rivers and watered by copious springs. Buffalo covered the plains, offering the means to provision his company. From what Xaviata had told him, Retana surmised that the Tejas villages could be reached from the Pecos in eighteen days' travel, since no mountains stood in the way.

All factors considered, however, he decided to send his report to

[10] Herbert Eugene Bolton (ed.), *Spanish Exploration in the Southwest, 1542-1706*, p. 315.

[11] A translation of the diary of this expedition is contained in ibid., pp. 320-343. Mendoza and Fray López, after founding missions at La Junta, penetrated to the Concho River at present San Angelo, Texas, and spent approximately six weeks among the natives at an unknown site on the Edwards Plateau, then returned to Mexico to urge establishment of missions in the area to the viceroy, Conde de Paredes (Marqués de la Laguna). The preoccupation with the La Salle episode at the time precluded consideration of such a proposal (Robert S. Weddle, *The San Sabá Mission: Spanish Pivot in Texas*, pp. 7-8). Memorials of López and Mendoza are found in Cesareo Fernández Duro, *Don Diego de Peñalosa y su descubrimiento del reino de Quivira*, pp. 67-77.

Pardiñas and to wait on the Pecos for the governor's orders. He recorded the information obtained from Xaviata and his companions in a message to the official at El Parral. Returning the French papers to the Indian leader, he asked him to deliver them to Pardiñas. The natives departed for El Parral with a number of Retana's own men who conducted the prisoners and the horses captured at Sierra Guapagua. "Your Lordship will recognize, because of the time that has passed [he wrote], the condition I am in for provisions. Therefore, I have decided to await at this place the orders of Your Lordship as to what I am to do, and whether, with this news, it seems feasible that I should proceed to occupy the place which the Frenchmen have lost, and whether I should be provisioned for keeping the people. I am ready . . . to penetrate as far as necessary."[1][2]

Juan Xaviata and his companions reached Presidio de Conchos on March 30, 1689, and sent Retana's letter on to Governor Pardiñas at El Parral. Not until April 10 did the chieftains of the Cíbolos and Jumanos reach El Parral to relate through an interpreter the dramatic account of the fate of La Salle's colony in Texas.

In addition, the four Indians revealed the sinister designs of the French invaders for capturing the mines of El Parral, their probing expeditions up the Río Grande, and their efforts to elicit intelligence from the natives and to turn their allegiance to the Frenchmen's own purposes. From the testimony of these untutored savages is gleaned the best information available on the activities of La Salle's men as they explored the region west of their settlement in 1685-1686.

It was a long time ago, testified one of the un-Christianized Cíbolo Indians, that some strange white men had come to his village on the other side of the Río del Norte, seven days' journey below La Junta.[1][3] These white men, who carried harquebuses and

---

[1][2] Retana to Pardiñas, in Hackett, *Historical Documents*, II, 258.

[1][3] The Spaniards estimated the distance from La Junta at 67 leagues, or about 175 miles. If the Indians traveled this distance by the most direct overland route, it would place the village to which the Frenchmen came above present-day Langtry, Texas. Forbes (*Apache, Navaho, and Spaniard*, p. 216) concludes that the village was the one where Alonso de León had found Jean Géry in May, 1688. It does seem doubtful that La Salle's men could have ascended the river as far as the natives indicated, on three occasions, without word of their presence having been carried by Indians to the settlements of Coahuila. Yet there seems little reason to suppose that the village was Géry's. It is to be recalled that the Marqués de Aguayo (Aguayo to the Viceroy, June 15, 1686,

wore doublets of steel, had ascended the river in a canoe on three occasions. With them had come an Indian who addressed the Cíbolos in their own language and translated the words of the foreign visitors.

With gestures of friendship the white men told the natives they would be their kinsmen. As tokens of their good will they gave them axes, knives, some copper ladles, and ribbons. To the women they gave beads. Then the Indians and the foreign visitors ate and danced together. During all the festivities the strangers showed no sign of hostility and made no move to do the Cíbolos harm. The natives observed that their appearance was like that of the Spaniards, with whom they were on friendly terms. The visitors, therefore, were accorded the hospitality with which the American Indian customarily greeted the European on first contact.

According to this "heathen" Indian called Cuis Benive, the Frenchmen had come back up the Río Grande for a second visit at the Cíbolo village two moons after the first. Later, this native reporter related the incidents to Don Miguel, captain of the Cíbolos. Miguel accompanied Cuis Benive to his village, hoping for a chance to view the mysterious white men.

Three moons after the second visit the Frenchmen returned. Six of them came up the river in a canoe, and shortly thereafter four others arrived by land, bringing the customary gifts. With them came their Indian interpreter, and through him Miguel conversed with the white men. Cuis Benive was not present for the conversation, because he went with one of the visitors to the river to see their canoe.

The Frenchmen, on learning that Miguel was a Christian and knew the Spaniards of El Parral, plied him with questions. They wanted to know the distance to the settlement, the condition of the road, the number of rivers to cross, and the number of Spaniards in the region where the silver was being mined. Miguel naively answered all their inquiries. Then the Frenchmen told him and the other natives present that the Spaniards were evil. It

---

A.G.I., México, 1685-1688 [61-6-20], pp. 79-80) was informed by a Pelón Indian that white men had been seen on the lower Río Grande by the Blanco and Pajarito Indians. Allowing for several months' delay in the word to Aguayo, this report would coincide with La Salle's westward trek the previous year. Henry Folmer (*Franco-Spanish Rivalry in North America, 1524-1763*, p. 163) concludes that the first visit was in the summer of 1685, the second in the fall. He does not mention the third.

would be to the advantage of the Indians, they said, to ally themselves with these visitors, who would treat them as brothers. Instead of going to El Parral to trade, they should deal instead with the French, who would return with wagons loaded with provisions and would continue on to El Parral to occupy that region. They would bring with them fine goods with which to clothe the Indians. As a token of these promises, they gave the chiefs some shirts. After three days the strangers set out on their return down the river, leaving the Cíbolos with great show of friendship.

At this point in his narration, Miguel was asked if the natives had not recognized that the strangers were the enemies of the Spaniards. He replied that they had not; since the foreigners were like other Spaniards in color, the Indians took them to be the same. Furthermore, the visitors carried rosaries and spoke to them of God, the same as the padres at La Junta de los Ríos and San Pedro de Conchos. And since the intruders took nothing from the Indians, they believed them to be good people. The only questionable feature that Miguel had observed was that some of the visitors wore steel doublets.[14]

After their departure on this third visit, the Frenchmen came no more. "A little while" after his meeting with the white foreigners Miguel went to La Junta and told the missionary priests what he had seen and heard. No clue is found to fix the exact dates of these events. From the accounts of Fathers Colina and Hinojosa, it appears that Miguel brought the news to La Junta in the autumn of 1687. His meeting with the white foreigners at the Cíbolo village must have been almost two years prior to that time.

The Frenchmen who visited among the Cíbolos may have been a splinter from La Salle's main camp, either deserters or members of a small band left by La Salle early in 1686 at a crude fort they had built on a large river. The Abbé Cavelier (La Salle's brother) relates that La Salle's men on February 10, 1686, found a river that they believed to be the Mississippi: "Immediately my brother had a little fort of stakes built, in which he left 18 men." The fate of this group is not known. According to Cavelier, La Salle was ab-

---

[14] Pardiñas, "Declaration of Miguel, captain of the Cíbolos," April 11, 1689, in Hackett, *Historical Documents*, II, 269-273.

sent from Fort St. Louis eight months on this expedition, returning March 30, 1686.[15]

The visitors also could have been La Salle's force itself. According to the Indians, the visits to the Cíbolo village spanned about five months. La Salle's trusted lieutenant, Henri Joutel—contrary to Cavelier—indicates that La Salle was not absent from the vicinity of the settlement that long.[16] Yet who could the native interpreter have been if not La Salle's servant Nika?

When Miguel gave his news to the priests at La Junta, they asked that he and Juan Xaviata go to the Frenchmen's main settlement and bring back a report. Undertaking the mission, they did not go directly to the French settlement, because Father Colina had warned that the foreigners might deal treacherously with them. Also, it appears that the Indian emissaries waited to begin their journey so their arrival would coincide with the start of the annual trade fairs.

"Many moons" after Miguel's visit with the Frenchmen, the two Indian emissaries arrived at the village of Cuis Benive. On learning that the white men had come no more, they decided to go on to the fairs and to find the French habitation. With them went Cuis Benive, another "heathen" Cíbolo named Muygisofac, and some others who were better acquainted with the country than were Miguel and Xaviata.

Seeking information, they went from one *ranchería* to another, without learning anything of the French colony until they reached a small Tejas encampment. There they were told that the settlement had been destroyed, its inhabitants killed by "the Indians who live in the mountains and on the seacoast [the Karankawas]."[17] None was left alive, the Tejas reported, except for five who had been spared only because they were absent from their

---

[15] Jean Cavelier, *The Journal of Jean Cavelier: The Account of a Survivor of La Salle's Texas Expedition, 1684-1688*, p. 65; Francis Parkman, *La Salle and the Discovery of the Great West*, pp. 291-292.

[16] Henri Joutel (*Joutel's Journal of La Salle's Last Voyage, 1684-7*, pp. 99-109), while indicating that La Salle departed from Fort St. Louis in November, 1685, recounts that he remained in the bay region until January before setting out westward. His return was in March.

[17] Pardiñas, "Declaracion de otro yndio gentil," in Hackett, *Historical Documents*, II, 278.

fort when the attack occurred, having gone to the Tejas country to trade. Actually, however, those among the Tejas were members of La Salle's final expedition, some of whom were implicated in their leader's murder.

From this first Tejas village, Juan Xaviata and the Cíbolos advanced to a larger *ranchería*. There they met the surviving Frenchmen, who verified the massacre of their countrymen, a number of whose bodies they had found and buried at Fort St. Louis. When the white men expressed curiosity concerning the land inhabited by the Spaniards and a desire to return to the white man's civilization, Miguel offered to take them to the settlements of Nueva Vizcaya. His offer was accepted, and the band of Europeans and natives started out. During three days of travel, however, the Frenchmen had misgivings. The journey was proving longer than they had expected, and along the way they stood to encounter many hostile tribes, of whose savagery they already had seen enough. They turned back again to seek refuge among the Tejas.

Sometime later an Indian messenger from the Frenchmen overtook Xaviata and his band with a request from the white men. Since they had remained behind, they desired the natives to tell the Spaniards of their presence. They wished the Spaniards to come and conduct them to their settlements. By the irony of fate, when the La Salle party had landed in Spanish territory, their greatest fear was discovery by the Spaniards. Now this miserable remnant of the abortive French colony saw in France's major colonial rival their only hope of survival.

Somewhere along the way, before he saw the Frenchmen for the last time, Don Juan Xaviata acquired the packet of French papers that he took to Pardiñas. According to Xaviata himself the papers were given him by a chief of a *ranchería* near the Tejas. Others thought he got them from the natives who were responsible for the massacre, and Miguel had the impression they were given him by the Frenchmen in the Tejas village. In any event, two of the Frenchmen, knowing that the Indians would carry the papers to the Spaniards, wrote notes to them on the margins of the parchment containing the painting of a ship. The messages were lost to Pardiñas because he could not read French.

As the Jumano and Cibolo Indians withdrew from the land of the Tejas, they visited among other nations and found them holding dances in celebration of their massacre of the colony of foreigners. In many of the villages of the Karankawas they saw plunder taken from the French settlement. At one they saw a cape, which they recognized as a religious habit because it resembled the raiment of the Franciscans at La Junta and San Pedro.

In one of the villages they met an Indian Chief who spoke Spanish, called himself Don Tomás, and said he was from Coahuila. This native probably was the same Yerbipiame chieftain who several years later led attacks on Monclova and the infant settlement of San Juan Bautista.[18] Don Tomás manifested great curiosity concerning the papers Xaviata carried. By the light of a campfire that night, he took all the documents from their wrapping to examine them. He contrived to keep more of the papers than he returned to Xaviata.

While Xaviata and Miguel visited among the coastal Indians, Cuis Benive and Muygisofac decided to view the scene of the massacre, which was not far distant. When they reached the crude log stockade, they found it "abandoned and almost in ruins."[19] Not a living thing stirred about the desolate structure except some pigs running loose in the fields. Inside the palisade were many broken chests and "some very large harquebuses"—their way of describing the artillery pieces. The smoke from Indian fires wafted above the surrounding hills, but not a soul stirred to offer greeting or challenge. Departing the eerie place, they hastened to overtake Xaviata and Miguel.

At last the Indians reached the Pecos River, where they met General Retana and reported to him before proceeding to El Parral to give an accounting to Governor Pardiñas. Juan Xaviata handed over to Pardiñas the papers he had brought with him: "two sheets of paper which appear to be from some book written by hand, apparently in the French language, and a frigate painted on a parchment, with some written annotations."[20] Had any of the frontier Spaniards been able to read French, they would have recognized the sheets of paper as being of the log from La Salle's ship *La Belle*, on its voyage to the Texas coast (see Plate 5 in the

[18] See Robert S. Weddle, *San Juan Bautista: Gateway to Spanish Texas*, pp. 41-42.
[19] Pardiñas, "Declaration of a heathen Indian [Cuis Benive]," in Hackett, *Historical Documents*, II, 275.
[20] Pardiñas, "Autos," ibid., p. 260.

picture section). They would have read on the margins of the painting a desperate plea from two of the survivors, who, having cast their lot among savages, wanted nothing so much as to return to civilization.

The two "heathen" Indians, Cuis Benive and Muygisofac, gave to Governor Pardiñas in El Parral an eye-witness description of the ruins of La Salle's colony on April 11, 1689—eleven days before a Spanish expedition from another quarter at last reached the elusive settlement.[21]

From the account of the four Indians, Pardiñas concluded that the urgency for sending an expedition to find the French colony had abated; the settlement had been destroyed by "the barbarous Indians of that country." Furthermore, the time for making such a journey was inauspicious, because the spring rains were at hand, and rivers in the intervening territory were likely to be at flood stage. So reliable were these vernal floods that the Cíbolos and Jumanos customarily made the trip only if they could begin it when the trees were starting to bud and return when the leaves were falling. Thus it appeared to Pardiñas that, should Retana undertake the expedition, "the weather would compel him to delay longer than would be advisable."[22]

With hostile natives still ravaging the settlements of Nueva Vizcaya, Retana's services were needed in the province. Accordingly, Pardiñas on April 12 dispatched an order for Retana to return to his presidio on the Conchos. Juan Xaviata was asked to deliver the order. Pardiñas himself compensated Xaviata and his followers for their services by giving them supplies and provisions, thus encouraging them to continue in the service of the Spaniards.

Meanwhile, the remnant of the ill-fated settlement of La Salle waited anxiously among the Tejas, hopeful that the message they had entrusted to the Indians from the west would being about their return to civilization. Their time of waiting would not be long, for on April 2 Alonso de León had crossed the Río Grande from Coahuila and was approaching the ravaged French settlement on the wilderness shores of Espíritu Santo Bay.

As for the appeals that two Frenchmen had written on the

---

[21] Hackett, "Introduction," ibid., p. 56.
[22] Pardiñas, "Declaration of a heathen Indian," ibid., p. 277.

margins of the parchment given the Indians, they were to pass unnoticed for two and a half centuries before a researcher discovered them in a musty Spanish archive. One of the messages, signed by Jacques Grollet, could not be made out in its entirety. The other, signed by one of the conspirators in the murder of La Salle, contained a pathetic plea:

Sir:

I do not know what sort of people you are. We are French. We are among the savages. We would like very much to be among Christians such as we are. We know well that you are Spaniards. We do not know whether you will attack us . . . we are sorely grieved to be among the beasts like these who believe neither in God nor in anything. Gentlemen, if you are willing to take us away, you have only to send a message, as we have but little or nothing to do. As soon as we see the note we will deliver ourselves up to you.

Sir, I am your very humble and obedient servant,

Jean Larcheveque [sic]
of Bayonne[23]

La Salle was dead, his valiant spirit departed, his flesh picked by vultures, and his bones scattered by beasts in a trackless wilderness. But already his murderers, who by killing him had canceled whatever chance they might have had of seeing their homeland again as free men, earnestly longed for a Spanish prison in preference to life among the Indians.

[23] J. F. Jameson, "Appendix," ibid., pp. 471-472.

16. FORT ST. LOUIS

Those who remained at the settlement when La Salle undertook the journey on which he was killed, reports Jean-Baptiste Talon, who was among them, were no more than 20 or 25 persons, including the women, a *prestre*, and two religious of the order of St. Francis, all of whom were massacred by the savages called Clamcoëts, who had made war on them because, when La Salle landed, he took their canoes to ascend the river and establish a settlement.
—Interrogations faites à Pierre et Jean Talon
Margry, *Découvertes*, III, 613-614

Following the capture of the Frenchman Jean Géry among the Coahuiltecan Indians in Texas, Captains Martín de Rivas and Andrés de Pez once again had explored the coast from Tampico to San Bernardo Bay and had returned. Preparations for a new land expedition had remained in the discussion stage; the latest maritime search had achieved nothing to preclude it.

The junta of July 23, 1688, had assigned Alonso de León to command the new land exploration. Immediately afterward Viceroy Monclova asked General Martín de Mendiondo to draw a list of supplies needed to sustain a force of one hundred men on the wilderness trek to the elusive Espíritu Santo Bay. Mendiondo submitted his list on July 30 and amended it August 4 to include gifts for the Indians. Three days later he received authorization for purchase of the supplies: eighty mule loads of flour, two hundred beeves, five hundred pounds of chocolate with sugar, three loads of salt for seasoning the meat, twenty mules to carry the meat, two dozen large knives for clearing paths through the wilderness, twenty dozen knives for gifts to the Indians, two dozen axes, a quantity of beads and rosaries, two hundred blankets, and three mule loads of tobacco.

These details behind him, Mendiondo took the French prisoner Jean Géry and headed north for Monterrey, probably a few days after Captains Rivas and Pez had sailed from Veracruz. General Mendiondo carried the viceroy's orders with him. From Monterrey they were dispatched to the commandants of the Nueva Vizcaya presidios, each of which was asked to supply ten men. At Mendiondo's suggestion, Governor Ventosa of Nuevo León was instructed to supply the other fifty instead of taking them from Coahuila, as previously ordered.[1] Because the orders had to be carried great distances through wild and difficult country, weeks, or even months, were required for them to reach their destination. Because each of the presidios of Nueva Vizcaya, beset by Indian warfare, had its own set of problems, response to the orders was not immediate. Not until March of the following year were all the supplies and the men from the western presidios gathered at San Francisco de Coahuila, ready to begin the journey.

Some months previously De León had received orders from the new viceroy, Conde de Galve, informing him that the expedition was to be made as planned, despite the change of administration. On Wednesday, March 23, the troops from Nueva Vizcaya and Coahuila moved out from the Presidio de San Francisco (Monclova) to make camp one league down the Coahuila River. The following day Governor De León—just promoted to general—left the presidio to overtake the camp, and the march was continued down the Coahuila toward its juncture with the Nadadores River. The following Sunday, March 27, they reached the confluence of the Nadadores and the Río de Sabinas and crossed to the north bank of the Sabinas (see Plate 8 in the picture section).

The Nuevo León troops, meanwhile, had set out from Monterrey, bringing the French prisoner Géry, who was to serve as guide. They followed the road northward to Boca de Leones (present-day Villadama), where the previous year Fathers Francisco Estévez and Francisco Hidalgo had established a mission among the Alasapa Indians, in the shadow of the Sierra de Gomas. North of Boca de

---

[1] Viceroy Monclova, "Decreto," August 9, 1688, A.G.I., México, 1685-1688 (61-6-20), p. 286; Juan de Arechaga and others, "Junta," July 23, 1688, ibid., p. 282.

Leones they struck the headwaters of the Río de la Caldera (Candela). Following it to its juncture with the Sabinas, they passed near the site of present-day Lampazos, where Fathers Diego de Salazar and Hidalgo would found a mission in 1698.[2] Crossing the Sabinas, they marched upstream to the rendezvous with De León. Meeting in the vicinity of present Don Martín Dam, below the juncture of the Nadadores and the Sabinas, the two forces greeted each other by firing a salute.

After traveling three leagues downstream, the expedition halted and De León held muster, listing all the people of the entourage and inventorying the supplies. He counted eighty-five soldiers. Included were General De León himself; two of his kinsmen, Miguel de León, a sergeant, and Alonso de León III, a captain; the historian of the expedition, Juan Bautista Chapa; Francisco Martínez, who besides being the general's mainstay, was to prove his worth as a French interpreter. In addition were the Frenchman Jean Géry; two priests, Toribio García de Sierra, curate and vicar of the province of Coahuila, and Fray Damián Massanet of the mission at Caldera, who served the expedition as chaplain; twelve mule drivers, most of whom bore arms; and thirteen servants—making a total of 113 men, plus a number of Indians whom De León neglects to mention. There were 720 horses and mules and eighty-five mule loads of provisions.

According to Father Massanet, the expedition was made up of forty men from the presidios of Nueva Vizcaya and another forty from Nuevo León. Five officers from Coahuila rounded out the total of eighty-five military men. The force was divided into three companies, headed by Tomás de la Garza, Lorenzo de la Garza, and Alonso de León III. Nicolás de Medina served the troop as *sargento mayor*; Martínez, a discharged sergeant who had just finished his term of service in Flanders, as the *alférez real*.[3]

The two priests evidently came with the general from Coahuila, though Massanet's account gives a different date (March 26) for

[2] Robert S. Weddle, *San Juan Bautista: Gateway to Spanish Texas*, pp. 12, 19-20. In colonial times the river now called Salado after it enters the state of Nuevo León was known as the Sabinas, a name that applies today only to that portion of the river in Coahuila (ibid., p. 21 n.).

[3] Fray Damián Massanet to Don Carlos de Sigüenza, 1690, in Herbert Eugene Bolton (ed.), *Spanish Exploration in the Southwest, 1542-1706*, p. 357.

the departure. According to Massanet the expedition proceeded with an Indian guide named Juan, or Juanillo, captain of the Pacpul nation, who the priest says first brought him news of a white man [Jean Géry] dwelling among the Indians beyond the Río Grande.[4]

After two days' travel toward the northeast, the troop turned north the morning of the thirtieth. De León, on being informed by the French prisoner that a native village of his acquaintance was near, permitted him to send out an Indian "of his following" to advise the village of the Spaniards' coming.[5] A league short of the Indian habitation more than seventy natives, many of them armed, came out to meet the troop, which they accompanied to the village. The natives had made special arrangements to receive their old friend, Jean Géry. With a great display of affection, they placed the Frenchman in a hut covered with buffalo skins.

In front of the hut, on a post four varas high, sixteen dried human skulls were suspended from pegs. These had belonged to enemies killed in war by the very Indians who now surrounded the Spaniards. The village's inhabitants numbered 490 persons of all ages. The Frenchman said they represented five nations, and De León recorded the names: "Hapes, Jumenes, Xiabu, Mescale, and another"; Chapa lists them as Apes, Mescales, Jumanes, and Ijiaba.[6] Eighty-eight huts were counted in the village, to whose inhabitants the Spaniards distributed clothing, blankets, beads, rosaries, knives, and flour. The natives manifested pleasure with the gifts, and five beeves were killed so that the entire village might feast.

This village was located about ten miles from the Río Grande at the nearest point (see Plate 8), but the Spaniards took a longer route to reach the stream. After a day's rest at a nearby creek, the troop continued its course to the north over low hills whose slopes

---

[4] See Chapter 13 of this study.

[5] Alonso de León, "Diario," in Lino Gómez Canedo (ed.), *Primeras exploraciones y poblamiento de Texas (1686-1694)*, p. 90. The diary as printed in Spanish contains two lines omitted in the translation contained in Bolton, *Spanish Exploration*, p. 389. This portion contains the start of a new day and a course change (from northeast to north), an omission that may have influenced previous chroniclers of the expedition in fixing the point at which the Rio Grande was crossed. Such an error also would account for the tendency to place De León's course across Texas too far to the south.

[6] De León, "Diario," in Canedo, *Primeras exploraciones*, p. 91; Juan Bautista Chapa in Alonso de León, *Historia de Nuevo León*, p. 210.

were watered by numerous springs. It traveled thirteen miles to reach the river, to arrive at Paso de Francia (Passage from France, or French Crossing), which is said to have carried the name from that day forward.[7] The ford is five miles southeast of present-day Guerrero, Coahuila, which in 1700 became the site of the mission settlement of San Juan Bautista. De León found it to be a suitable crossing, about a musket shot in width. The troop negotiated it next day without difficulty.

Either Géry was proving worthless as a guide or the Spaniards were wary of placing too much trust in him. On reaching the Río Grande, says Massanet, "I sent for the Indian who knew the country and had been among the Frenchmen, whom I call Quems, because he belonged to the Indian nation of that name.[8] De León, however, says, "Already we carried in our company as a guide a trustworthy Indian, who assured us that he knew the whole country and would take us to where some men like ourselves were settled with six or seven houses. He said that these people, who had women and children, were some six days' journey from the Río Bravo. This Indian is untamed, but we were able to understand something from what he said through another Indian, [though he was a] poor interpreter."[9]

After crossing the Río Grande on Saturday, April 2, the Spanish troop traveled one league north to get around the heads of gullies that bordered the flood plain. Then the course was directed to the northeast. After five leagues the march was halted at some pools, where more than three thousand crows flew in to roost at nightfall. Because of the plethora of the big black birds, De León gave the place its name: Paraje de los Cuervos. Throughout the colonial period it was to serve as the first night's campground beyond the Río Grande for expeditions proceeding into Texas.

Out across the grassy plains De León's troop advanced at a rapid pace, its royal standard bearing the image of the Lady of Guada-

[7] Weddle, *San Juan Bautista*, p. 14. So exactly do the distances and directions given in De León's diary lead to this point on the Río Grande that there hardly seems room to doubt that he crossed here. Unfortunately, however, the diary of the journey as it proceeded into Texas does not lead to such precise conclusions.

[8] Massanet to Sigüenza, in Bolton, *Spanish Exploration*, p. 358. Carlos Eduardo Castañeda (*Our Catholic Heritage in Texas*, I, 334) ignores this statement to assume that the Quems Indian joined the band at the village of Jean Géry's friends.

[9] De León, "Diario," in Canedo, *Primeras exploraciones*, p. 91.

lupe fluttering in the breeze. The mule drivers and servants pushed the pack animals, the *caballada*, and the cattle along briskly. On Palm Sunday, April 3, a number of mesquite thickets punctuated the otherwise open land, impeding progress of the march. Halting at a creek, which he named Arroyo de Ramos, De León observed the sun with his defective astrolabe and, using out-of-date tables, obtained an erroneous latitude. This was the first of three such observations recorded on the expedition, all of which prove useless for establishing its route. Not only are all in error, but they also are inconsistent with each other. This one was off two degrees.

On Monday the troop covered almost double the customary day's march—eight leagues, or twenty-one miles, by De León's estimate—to reach the Nueces River, passing up an intermediate stop utilized by later expeditions, at Arroyo de Caramanchel (possibly a corruption of Carabanchel, a town in the Madrid province of Spain). Mesquite thickets, including one three leagues long, made travel difficult.

Beyond the Nueces the course lay through open country for several miles before mesquite thickets and a dense growth of prickly pear again frustrated progress. Forced to dismount, the soldiers used their cutlasses and axes to carve a path through the thorny tangle. Nevertheless, they logged seven leagues for the day, reaching a stream of blue water, which the general named Río Sarco—probably Jahuey Creek.[10]

Traveling over level, grassy plains, dotted with clumps of live oaks, the troop came the following day to a river with a deep channel, which the general named Río Hondo, probably the present Frio. As the soldiers approached the stream they observed a phenomenon that De León—like historians of a later period—was at a loss to explain: some crosses "and other figures artificially made with great skill, apparently a long time ago."[11] Marching down the

---

[10] Ibid., p. 93. Slight variations are seen in the route as described in other sources (cf. Castañeda, *Our Catholic Heritage*, I, 334-336).

[11] De León, "Diario," in Canedo, *Primeras exploraciones*, p. 93. Expeditions that might have left such figures include those of Juan de la Garza or Fernando de Azcué, who led Indian campaigns north from Monterrey and Saltillo in the early 1660's; Brother Manuel de la Cruz or Father Peñasco de Lozano, who made missionary *entradas* from Coahuila in 1674; and Father Juan Larios and Fernando del Bosque, who headed a similar expedition a year later. It seems unlikely, however, that any of the missionary expeditions penetrated this far east (see Weddle, *San Juan Bautista*, pp. 4-9).

stream the following day, De León reflected upon the fact that many Indian signs had been observed along the way but not a single native had been encountered since "the village of the Five Nations."

De León's force proceeded across Texas on a course approximating 61 or 62 degrees. Unfortunately, both the directions he recorded and his latitude reckonings are in error, and any attempt to fix the route exactly only can be guesswork.[12]

Two events made the Saturday night camp of April 9 memorable, and one can but speculate upon the relation between the two. First, De León permitted a cask of wine to be opened, and the creek on which camp was made was named in honor of the occasion: Arroyo del Vino—probably a tributary of the Atascosa River near present Christine. Then at nine o'clock that night the horse herd stampeded, although fifteen men were supposed to be on guard. All of Easter Sunday was spent rounding up the 102 horses that got away. A sun shot with the damaged astrolabe indicated a latitude of 27° 55', almost a degree off. Crossing the stream next day, the Spaniards soon found themselves in a pecan and oak wood five leagues across. Traveling twelve leagues east and northeast, they came to a large river, which was named Río de Medina—most likely the San Antonio, near Panna Maria.

All this way the Spaniards had been following the lead of the Quems Indian, apparently with confidence that he was guiding them correctly.[13] On April 12, however, when they reached a dry stream at the end of four leagues' travel, De León suspected the guide of having mistaken the direction. A league farther on they

---

[12] Castañeda (*Our Catholic Heritage*, I, 334-336) makes such an attempt, but it seems liberty is taken with some of the distances, and undoubtedly the troop meandered more than he indicates. These meanders probably took the expedition several miles farther north than he supposes. By orienting the direction of the Río Grande on De León's map (Plate 8) with that shown on modern maps, it is found that his "north" actually was almost 30°. This explains much of the confusion suffered by those who have tried to reconcile directions of travel given in the diary with the point at which he arrived. The map, as evidenced by the signature, was prepared by Don Carlos de Sigüenza y Góngora from data given him by both De León and the maritime leaders, and it includes place names supplied by the navigators.

[13] Chapa (in De León, *Historia*, p. 212) says that the Quems Indian was looking for his wife, who had been carried off by some enemy tribe, implying that the troop made many meanders to accommodate his search.

struck a stream of good water, which was named Arroyo del León because a dead lion was found nearby.[14]

Two more days' travel, each of six leagues to the east-northeast, brought the searchers to the banks of the Guadalupe. As they approached the river, they again had to clear timber to make a path for the caravan. They killed six buffalo, the first seen in a hundred leagues.[15] The river was named for the saint whose likeness the troop carried on its royal standard. After crossing the river a league downstream and marching one league farther, De León convened a council of war. It was decided to move the camp to a better location next day, then send out a reconnaissance party of sixty soldiers. On Saturday, April 16, the march was begun after mass had been sung to the Lady of Guadalupe.

After three leagues the rearguard caught sight of an Indian in the timber and induced him to come out. Through the two native guides De León was able to understand that the Indian's village was nearby and that four Frenchmen lived there. Ordering the main camp to remain where the Indian had been found, De León and the sixty men hastened with the new-found guide to seek the village, which belonged to the Emet and Cava branches of the Tonkawas. As the Spaniards approached the Indian encampment, however, they could see its inhabitants disappearing into the woods, followed by eight or ten dogs laden with buffalo hides. The guide called to his tribesmen that the strangers were friendly, and thus he induced them to come out of hiding. As the Indians advanced to meet the Spaniards, a number of the natives repeated the word *techas*, which was translated to mean "friends." Popular legend has it that this is how Texas got its name, but it must be remembered that the name Tejas, or Texas, was applied to the Indians of this region and the region itself long before this incident occurred.[16]

---

[14] Bolton (*Spanish Exploration*, p. 394 n.) identifies this stream as the San Antonio; Castañeda, (*Our Catholic Heritage*, I, 335) as Coleto Creek. It appears to have been a stream between the San Antonio and the Coleto, perhaps in the vicinity of Nordheim, DeWitt County.

[15] The fact that they had seen no buffalo probably was coincidental, since the Indians had advised Juan de Retana and Governor Pardiñas (see Chapter 15) that the beasts were to be found all along the way from La Junta to the land of the Tejas.

[16] Institute of Texan Cultures (*The Indian Texans*, p. 8) relates: "In 1541 the Caddo

One young Indian brave came wearing a garment that Father Massanet recognized as a Recollect friar's cloak. The chaplain tactfully gave the Indian a blanket and took the cloak from him. Massanet identifies these natives as the Emet and Lavas.[17]

De León now found the Frenchman Jean Géry useful as an interpreter. Through him the general learned that the four Frenchmen had left the village four days previously to go to the Tejas. With gifts of tobacco, knives, and trinkets, the general recruited as guides two of the natives who claimed knowledge that the Frenchmen could be found in a *rancheria* two days' journey beyond. Pushing northward, the Spaniards reached an encampment of more than 250 Indians, identified as Toxo and Toaa (Toho and Tohaha, of the Tonkawas). From this village they received their first news of the fate of the French colony on the bay: that the coastal tribes had attacked the village three months previously, killing all its occupants. The Tonkawas also reported that an epidemic of smallpox had decimated the settlement before the massacre, a statement for which no reliable verification is found.

Later some of the natives brought to the Spaniards' camp near the village some French books and a Bible. One of the Indians wore French clothing. De León obtained the books to send to the viceroy.[18]

Five leagues farther north the troop came next day to a habitation of natives known to the French prisoner Géry.[19] Still the four survivors of the French settlement, traveling on horseback, were said to have passed four days before, now being on the north bank of the Colorado, which was flooding and could not be crossed. Further pursuit appeared futile, and De León decided to try to contact the Frenchmen by letter. Francisco Martínez, the *alférez real* who knew French, composed the message. The Spaniards, he told them, had learned of their escape following the massacre of the Christians who had lived on the coast. The French-

Indians, living at the bend of the Red River, greeted the Spanish explorer Luis de Moscoso with the word *Tayshas* or *Teyas*, signifying friendship. The Spanish soon applied the term to all East Texas Indians. The word *Tejas* was then used to designate the province, and finally the state, of "Texas."

[17] Massanet to Sigüenza, in Bolton, *Spanish Exploration*, p. 359.
[18] Chapa in De León, *Historia*, pp. 212-213.
[19] Massanet (Massanet to Sigüenza, in Bolton, *Spanish Exploration*, p. 360) identifies them as belonging to the Emet nation.

men were invited to join the Spanish force, which could be found in three or four days at the Indian village from which they recently had departed. De León and Massanet signed the letter, to which the priest appended a postscript in Latin, in the event that one of the four might be a religious. Paper for a reply was sent, and an Indian was promised a horse for carrying the letter. From this point ten leagues north of the main camp the Spaniards turned back.

De León quickened the pace next day, after a messenger reached him with bad news. The horse herd at the camp had stampeded the night before, scattering more than a hundred animals over the countryside, and thirty-six still were missing. On reaching the camp the general learned that a soldier, Juan de Charles, had become lost in searching for the horses. Two days were spent looking for the man and the animals before Charles rode into camp on the morning of April 20 to relate his strange adventure.[20]

At this campsite, which Massanet describes as being five miles beyond the Guadalupe River, De León again righted his broken astrolabe to observe the sun and compute a latitude of 28° 41'. This time the result may have been nearly correct, for it would place the Spaniards about eight miles southeast of present-day Victoria, near State Highway 185. The general's entry the following day reads: "Thursday, the 21st, we went with the camp in the direction of east, at times a quarter to the north, traveling over large, treeless plains, marching eight leagues to a creek of good water. Here the guide told us that the French settlement was nearby, on the bank of this creek. All the land was very pleasant and we encountered many buffalo."[21]

"Now the old Frenchman who accompanied us," writes Father Massanet, "took occasion to say that the settlement of the Frenchmen was not in the place to which the two Indian guides were taking us. On the way this Frenchman tried several times, by means of an Indian of the Cava nation whom he had with him, to make our two Indians dessert us, or say that it was very far, and that we should not be able to cross the rivers which were on the

---

[20] Massanet (ibid.) relates the incident in detail.
[21] De León, "Diario," in Canedo, *Primeras exploraciones*, p. 98.

way." Then, as the searchers drew near to the fort, Jean Géry changed his tune, saying, "Sir, I know very well, yea, very well, that the houses are on this little river."[22] The priest became angry at the Frenchman's conduct, but De León reassured him.

The morning of the twenty-second dawned bleak and rainy as the Spaniards took up the march down Garcitas Creek. After three leagues they came, at eleven o'clock in the morning, to the ruins of the French settlement. It stood silhouetted against the gray sky on a high point overlooking the creek from the southwest bank. De León halted his troop the distance of a harquebus shot away. No sign of life stirred in the fort. The general or his scribe at this point began a report with the words that officials in Mexico City had waited almost four years to read:

> By the will of God and the prompt dispatch which has been made, we have arrived today near the French settlement. I have ordered that the camp be established nearby. It is on a deep creek, which according to our observations enters the bay, since the water appears to be salty and it rises and falls with the tide. From this camp we have not seen any people in the settlement, by which fact the rumor that is widespread among the Indians we have seen and talked with . . . is recognized as certainty: that the Indians from the seacoast have killed the inhabitants of the settlement."[23]

Because he must make a detailed report to the viceroy on the condition of the settlement as he found it, said the report, De León had ordered that no officer or soldier should go near it until he himself had examined it. Then, with the major and the captain and other company officers, he proceeded to the fort itself.

Before entering the settlement, De León observed from the outside that there were six buildings. The one nearest the creek, solidly built from the hulk of a wrecked vessel, was the fort. It had five rooms, including one in an upper story that served as a storeroom and another at the lower level that had been used as a chapel. Standing four varas high, the fort had a gabled roof of planking designed to turn the heavy rainfall of the region. Among

[22] Massanet to Sigüenza, in Bolton, *Spanish Exploration*, p. 361.
[23] De León, "Autos y diligencias," April 22, 1689, A.G.I., México, 1685-1688 (61-6-20), p. 294. A translation of this document is found in Walter J. O'Donnell, *La Salle's Occupation of Texas*, pp. 13-15.

the other houses, Father Massanet observed, was a larger one where pigs were fattened. The buildings apart from the fort were "not very large, built of poles, plastered with mud, and roofed over with buffalo hides."[24]

Except for the fort, De León noted, the houses were useless for defense. On the frame of the fort's main gate was inscribed the year the voyage was undertaken—1684—and below it was what evidently was intended to be the date the settlement was abandoned: "168_."[25] But when the end came no one in the settlement had time for completing the inscription. Signs of the French disaster lay at every hand.

All the houses were sacked, chests and bottle cases broken open, furniture smashed and ruined. Pots, drawers, bottles, and tables were smashed to bits. Many manuscripts and more than two hundred books in the French language, many with expensive bindings, had been torn apart and scattered around the patios. The paper already was disintegrating from recent rains. What the perpetrators of the massacre could use they had divided among themselves; what they did not care for they had sought to destroy. "Not a single thing did we find that was of any use."[26]

Arms as well as books and furnishings were rendered useless. "Scattered around the fort and the houses were eight iron cannons [five- or six-pounders]; and three very old swivel guns, which lacked their bases. In the patios we found a hundred broken stocks of harquebuses from which the barrels and locks had been removed by those who had stormed the settlement. At the fort and the houses we saw also thirty-two iron cannon balls—some of eight and ten pounds, others larger." There were some large nails and some iron rods, or bars. Broken wine casks lay about, their contents spilled on the ground.[27]

As De León and his assistants completed this inventory, they came upon the bodies of three victims of the massacre. One of them, as evidenced by the dress that still clung to the skeleton, was a woman, shot in the back with an arrow as she attempted to

[24] Massanet to Sigüenza, in Bolton, *Spanish Exploration*, p. 362.

[25] Drawing reproduced in De León, *Historia*, facing p. 216.

[26] De León, "Autos," p. 294.

[27] The spilled contents, however, were not wine, as disclosed by Henri Joutel (*Joutel's Journal of La Salle's Last Voyage, 1684-7*, p. 116), who tells of toasting "Twelve-Day" with water.

flee the savage onslaught. Her flesh, as that of the others, appeared to have been gnawed away by wild beasts. The sight provoked much feeling among the soldiers, most of whom were veterans of the Indian wars in their own provinces, and some of whom may well have lost loved ones to hostile natives.

Failing to find other corpses, De León concluded that they had been thrown into the creek to be eaten by alligators, of which there were many. The three skeletons were gathered up and placed in a common grave. After Father Massanet had sung mass, the soldiers covered them with the black earth, and a cross was erected over the burial site.

The fate of the fort's human inhabitants was shared by its livestock. Many dead pigs were found.

Through all the devastation, De León was able to perceive the natural beauty of the site. On the highest point of the creek bank, it afforded a commanding view of the stream. Although the terrain dropped off sharply toward the Garcitas, the land stretched out in a broad, level expanse in the opposite direction. The French settlers had enclosed with a picket fence four hundred varas[28] of ground where they had planted corn and had a herb garden, with endive and asparagus bed. The stalks of corn standing in the enclosure reminded Juan Bautista Chapa of those found at the mouth of the Río Grande in 1686. He was convinced that the cornstalks seen on that first De León expedition in search of La Salle had come from this settlement, carried into the bay by the waters of the creek, swept out to sea by storm, and washed ashore at the mouth of the Río Grande by a gulf current.[29]

Massanet, perhaps through subjective reaction, was inclined to disparage the site: "This place affords no advantages as to situation, for good drinking-water is very far off, and timber still farther. The water of the stream is very brackish, so much so that in five days during which the camp was pitched there all the horses sickened."[30]

In his diary entry for the day De León computed the distance traveled from the Presidio of San Francisco de Coahuila to reach

<hr/>

[28] De León, "Autos," p. 294. O'Donnell (*La Salle's Occupation of Texas*, p. 15) erroneously transcribes the area as two hundred varas.

[29] Chapa in De León, *Historia*, p. 215.

[30] Massanet to Sigüenza, in Bolton, *Spanish Exploration*, p. 362.

the settlement: 136 leagues. That evening in camp the general busied himself with completing his report on the reconnaissance of the moribund French colony, with these words: "I attest to all these facts. I ordered that all the iron be gathered up in order to take it to Coahuila. As for the eight artillery pieces and swivel guns, they will be disposed of in an appropriate manner."[31]

While the leader completed this routine chore, other members of the expedition, in the light of flickering campfires, pondered events of the day. One anonymous soldier composed a verse commemorating the ravaged French colony and the Christian people who had died there:

> Sad and fateful site
>   where prevails the dark of night
>   because misfortune's whim
>   brought thy people death so grim,
>   here alone I contemplate
>   thou epitome of fate,
>   of the inconstancy of life;
>   since in the fierceness of the strife
>   the cruel enemy pressed
>   his heartless hand upon thy breast,
>   upon thy innocence so mild,
>   sparing not the smallest child.
>
> O beautiful French maiden fair
>   who pressed sweet roses to your hair
>   and with thy snow-white hand
>   briefly touched the lily of the land
>   and with thy art perfection brought
>   Greek ladies now in profile wrought;
>   thy needlework made bright
>   the miseries of thy plight;
>   and now so cold, so dead,
>   these woods look down upon thy head;
>   but thou witherest not in vain,
>   art seen in death, but not in pain.
>
> And thou, cadaver, oh, so cold,
>   who for a time did make so bold
>   and now consumed by wildest beasts

[31] De León, "Autos," p. 294.

which upon thee made their feasts,
tearfully I behold thee right;
thou art example bright,
for everlasting glory won,
transient from this life hast gone
for celestial dwelling bound
though pierced with such a wound.
Pray thee to the God eternal,
spare us from the hell infernal.[32]

Though the Spanish author of these verses will, most probably, remain forever anonymous, there is strong suspicion that it was Chapa. In any event this writer offers a rationalization of the horrible devastation visited upon the ill-fated French colony, implicit in the last stanza of the elegy:

These are judgments of God, which we cannot investigate, but it seems also that [events of the massacre] are an admonition that Christians should not go directly against the bulls and mandates of the pontiffs. In that issued by Alexander VI in the year 1494 in favor of the King, Don Ferdinand, and Doña Isabella, he granted them all that the Spaniards had discovered in the West Indies, and all they were yet to discover, with prohibition against their occupation by any other king under penalty of excommunication. It could be that because they [the French] had broken this precept, God visited this punishment upon them.[33]

[32] Chapa in De León, *Historia*, pp. 218-219. My translation.
[33] Ibid., p. 219.

17. THE FRENCH SURVIVORS

"There were four ships in charge of Monsieur de Salle . . . they came by order of the King of France to people these parts. . . . Of all the people who were aboard only six escaped. With some two hundred and fifty persons, more or less, Monsieur de Salle peopled the spot on which we discovered the fort and the houses. He landed eight or nine cannons and three or four swivel guns. . . . They must have had three hundred large guns; and each man had two carbines.

—Alonso de León (from Jean L'Archevêque)
O'Donnell, *La Salle's Occupation*, pp. 16-17

On April 23 De León set out with thirty men to explore the bay south of Fort St. Louis, taking the French prisoner Jean Géry as a guide. Géry, who had used every ruse to steer the Spaniards away from the ravaged fort, now professed extensive knowledge of the area, claiming he had been all over the bay in a bark. Instead of leading the soldiers down the Garcitas, which he said had no crossing, he took them five leagues on a southwesterly course. After skirting the heads of two creeks, they turned east three leagues to reach the shore of what is known today as Lavaca Bay. Probably near the site of old Indianola, night overtook them, and they made camp.

By such explicit knowledge of the bay area, Géry appears to have revealed himself. Were he not a deserter from La Salle's colony, how would he have possessed such knowledge? Desertions from the colony had begun almost immediately after the landing; Géry, therefore, may well have taken his leave before making the acquaintance of members of the colony who had come on other ships. The word of other survivors that they never before had seen the man does not warrant ruling out the possibility that he came with La Salle.

After an early start next day, De León's men found the going difficult over the flat, open terrain that appeared deceptively easy at a distance. Marshy land and salt-water lagoons blocked their passage, the horses quickly sinking to their knees in the muck. For long stretches the soldiers trudged on foot, leading their mounts. As they plodded southeastward along the west side of Matagorda Bay—La Bahía del Espíritu Santo—De León and his companions formed this picture of the large body of water: "The one arm of the sea which seemed to us the largest extends toward the north, another small one to the south, and the smallest toward the settlement referred to in this diary."[1]

From the explorers' vantage point, near the lower end of the bay, they looked northward across its main body. To the southeast they would have seen the island that lies across the bay's mouth, or possibly the body of water that on present-day maps is labeled Espíritu Santo Bay. "The smallest," extending toward the French fort, would have been Lavaca Bay.[2]

They followed the shore eight long leagues—more than twenty miles—apparently going completely around Powderhorn Lake, a five-mile-long projection from the bay's west side. At various places along the way they found fragments from a large ship, which evidently had run upon the coast and broken up under force of wind and waves. There were masts, a capstan, some barrel staves, and assorted ship's timbers. At last the paths of the various searchers for La Salle were about to meet; De León's soldiers were looking upon the pieces of the three-hundred-tun *l'Aimable*, which had carried all the effects thought necessary for the French settlement.[3] It was the same wreckage viewed by the mariners sailing under Captains Rivas and Iriarte in 1687 and Rivas and Pez in 1688.

The soldiers came at last within view of the mouth of the bay.

---

[1] Alonso de León, "Diario," in Lino Gómez Canedo (ed.), *Primeras exploraciones y poblamiento de Texas (1686-1694)*, pp. 100-101.

[2] The name Espíritu Santo Bay as applied by De León signified what is known today as Matagorda Bay, the same as the name San Bernardo Bay bestowed by Martín de Rivas and Pedro de Iriarte. Today the name Espíritu Santo Bay signifies the narrow stretch of water between Matagorda Island and the mainland, near the mouth of Matagorda Bay.

[3] Henri Joutel, *Joutel's Journal of La Salle's Last Voyage, 1684-7*, p. 55.

Enclosed by low-lying bars, it lay an estimated two leagues to the south of the farthest point the Spaniards were able to reach on horseback, the site of present Port O'Connor. An opening that appeared to be two leagues wide gaped between the bars, revealing the open sea beyond. Overjoyed at the discovery, the explorers signaled their triumph by firing their harquebuses.

Jean Géry, recently so knowledgeable of the area to which the Quems Indian had brought them, now affirmed that this was indeed the mouth of the harbor he had entered when he came to this coast with "Monsieur Felipe de la Gala."[4] When De León suggested it, he affirmed that the Guadalupe River ran into the southward extension of the bay, but the Frenchman pretended knowledge he did not possess.

To the north the bay was so wide the Spaniards could not see land on the other side. De León observed that the bar on the side of the entrance toward Veracruz was closer to the mainland than the one on the side toward Florida. He was looking upon the scene of La Salle's first great misfortune on the Texas shore: the loss of *l'Aimable*. It was on this bar to the west of the shallow entrance that Captain Aigron, heedless of La Salle's orders, had run the heavily laden ship aground. With the valuable cargo looted by the Indians and spoiled by the sea, the ship itself had broken up on the shore, her pieces scattered over the beach that De León had just traversed.

From the mouth of the bay the explorers turned to go back the way they had come. They made camp for the night on the bank of a creek, the site of an abandoned Indian village whose inhabitants evidently had taken part in the French massacre. In testimony thereof the Spaniards found a book in the French language, a broken bottle case, and other European artifacts. In the brackish water of the creek were two canoes from which the stream took the name "Arroyo de las Canoas."

While De León explored near the mouth of the bay, the Indian messengers reached the land of the Tejas with the letter written by Martínez several days previously. There a number of Frenchmen who had escaped the massacre—if the source is credible[5]—gathered

---

[4] Juan Bautista Chapa in Alonso de León, *Historia de Nuevo León*, p. 215.

[5] José Antonio Pichardo, *Pichardo's Treatise on the Limits of Louisiana and Texas*, I, 184. Pierre Talon ("Interrogations faites à Pierre et Jean Talon," in Pierre Margry

to read the missive. It provoked considerable debate. On one side of the argument were Hiens and Ruter, the buccaneer and the white savage. Hiens himself had been involved in the murder of La Salle and those closest to him; he and Ruter together were the slayers of the real murderers, Duhaut and Liotot. They drew back from the Spaniards' offer to return them to civilization, unconvinced that the Indians were really responsible for the massacre at Fort St. Louis; the real culprits in their eyes were the Spaniards themselves. It stood to reason, they argued, that should they surrender themselves to such a cruel enemy, the same fate awaited them.

Succumbing to this argument was Pierre Meunier, and at his side was the small lad of thirteen, Pierre Talon. Taking the opposing view were Jean L'Archevêque—who as a servant of the late Duhaut perhaps had more to fear from Hiens and Ruter than from the Spaniards—and Jacques Grollet, who had deserted La Salle's company the year before the leader's death and rejoined the survivors afterward. These were the two who, by means of a message written on the margins of the painting of a ship, had attempted to communicate to Juan de Retana and Governor Pardiñas of Nueva Vizcaya their deep longing to escape their savage environment and live again among Christians.

Had the Spaniards murdered the French colonists, they reasoned, the Indians of the vicinity would have fled, spreading the news. The natives who had brought the letter would have known it. Furthermore, the Spaniards could do no worse than send them as prisoners to Mexico. And how much better to live among Christians, even as slaves, than among these "barbarians"! But at last, L'Archevêque and Grollet had to resolve their course independently.[6]

Returning to the camp near Fort St. Louis on the twenty-fifth, after fifty-two leagues of travel in three days, De León found a reply to Martínez's letter to the Frenchmen. Written in red ochre upon the paper that had been sent with the letter, the reply bore but one signature: that of Jean L'Archevệque of Bayonne. The thick lines of the crudely formed characters spelled out a nostalgic

[ed.], *Découvertes et établissements des Français dans l'Ouest et dans le Sud de l'Amérique septentrionale,* III, 610-612) gives an account that conflicts with this.
[6] Pichardo, *Treatise*, pp. 184-185.

message from the penitent heart of one whose circumstances permitted him only one hope: to live again among civilized people. As he formed the words, the dingy red color upon the paper might have seemed to the writer symbolic of the bloodshed that had exiled him forever from his native land:

> ...I have received your letter informing us that you are near to where we are. We pray that you may have the kindness to wait for us two days more, since we are separated from each other ... As soon as [the others] have come, we shall not spurn your aid. Your coming does honor to the Christian European. We will not be kept from reuniting ourselves with Christians. It is such a long time that we have been among barbarians, who are not even social people. I am satisfied, lord, with everything expressed in your letter. I will not permit separating [ourselves] to go and look for the others, lord. Gentlemen, I am your most humble and obedient servant.
>
> L'Archevêque of Bayonne[7]

As promised, De León rewarded the Indian who had brought the message with a horse.

The following day the main camp moved three leagues up the Garcitas to the site of the overnight stop of April 21. The move was necessary because the water in the creek near the French settlement was brackish; all the horses that drank it sickened. As the Spaniards withdrew they left the buildings of Fort St. Louis intact. Massanet later was to complain of De León's negligence in not putting the fort to the torch.

On the twenty-sixth De León rode out from the Garcitas with twenty men to seek a river that, according to Géry, lay to the north and flowed into the bay. After three leagues they found it and followed the right bank "to where some lagoons form an impediment."[8] This point was a short distance southeast of present Vanderbilt, Jackson County. The river appeared larger than the Río Bravo, of sufficient size for a small vessel to navigate. Wishing to see where it emptied into the bay, the general led his men around the lakes, to a hill that afforded a view of the river's mouth three quarters of a league beyond, having traveled fifteen leagues that day.

---

[7] Chapa in De León, *Historia*, pp. 216-217.
[8] De León, "Diario," in Canedo, *Primeras exploraciones*, p. 102.

De León's observations at this point—especially in the light of those made in his earlier exploration of the bay—should put at rest forever any notion that La Salle's settlement was on the Lavaca River instead of Garcitas Creek.[9] There can be no doubt that he now stood on the banks of the Lavaca—which he named San Marcos, because the discovery was made the day following the saint's feast day. "It appeared to us," he wrote, "that it was about a league and a half from the mouth of the San Marcos to the mouth of the creek [the Garcitas] on which the Frenchmen had lived, and the same distance from the mouth of the creek to the settlement (see Plate 8).[10]

After the reconnaissance party of twenty rejoined the main force, the camp advanced on the twenty-eighth to the Guadalupe and De León again went to look for the Frenchmen who had escaped the massacre. Aside from wishing to arrest the trespassers, the general now was motivated by curiosity as well. Having viewed the ravaged settlement on the Garcitas, he wished to know the circumstances of the massacre.

Ranging northward twenty-five leagues (sixty-five miles), the thirty troopers followed a native guide, probably the same one who had brought the message from L'Archevêque. On the Colorado River, in the Smithville-La Grange area, they arrived at a Tohaha (Tonkawa) Indian village where a chief of the Tejas and a number of his people were visiting. With the Tejas were two of the Frenchmen whom De León sought, L'Archevêque and Grollet.

[9] Robert Carlton Clark (*The Beginnings of Texas, 1684-1718*, p. 18) mistakenly places La Salle's settlement on the Lavaca, an error decisively rectified by Herbert Eugene Bolton ("The Location of La Salle's Colony on the Gulf of Mexico," *Southwestern Historical Quarterly* 27, no. 3 [January, 1924]: 171-189). On December 26, 1969, through the courtesy of John Keeran, the owner, I inspected this site, on which the Spanish Presidio of Nuestra Señora de Loreto de la Bahía was erected in 1721. No visible evidence of either the French or the Spanish settlement remains, since the site was excavated in 1950 for the Texas Memorial Museum. Some of the artifacts uncovered in the excavation may be seen at the museum. Glen L. Evans ("Notes on Fort St. Louis Excavation") says, "The size of the site and the nature of the materials that have been found leave no doubt that the site was that of Fort St. Louis." He fails, however, to offer supporting evidence, such as definitely identified French artifacts of the period. Mrs. Kathleen Gilmore of Southern Methodist University, during 1971, was making an extensive restudy of the archeological data compiled from the 1950 excavation.

[10] De León, "Diario," in Canedo, *Primeras exploraciones*, p. 102. With his defective astrolabe De León computed the latitude at the mouth of the Lavaca at 26°03'. Chapa (in De León, *Historia*, p. 218) gives it as 29°03'. Actually it is about 28°42'. Latitude of the Fort St. Louis site is 28°45'45".

Dressed only in antelope or buffalo skins, they presented an awesome sight to the Spaniards. They were painted, or tattooed, after the fashion of the Indians they have lived among, their faces, arms, and breasts marked with grotesque streaks."[11]

De León returned to the main camp on the Guadalupe on May 1 at vespers. After feeding and clothing the two captives, he lost no time in extracting through his interpreter an account of the life and death of the French settlement, taking formal declarations from the two.[12] The summary of their testimony given in the De León diary, however, includes information that the depositions do not:

> They gave an account of the death of their people [the diary relates], the first saying that an epidemic of smallpox had killed more than a hundred persons;[13] that the rest had been on friendly terms with the Indians of all that region, and had no suspicion of them; that a little more than a month before, five Indians had come to their settlement under pretext of telling them something and had stopped at the most remote house in the settlement; that the Frenchmen, having no suspicions, all went to the house unarmed to see them; that another party of Indians came in from the creek at the same time, and killed them all, including two religious and a priest, with daggers and sticks, and sacked all the houses;[14] that they were not there at the time, having gone to the Tejas; but that when they heard the news of this occurence, [the] four of them came, and, finding their companions dead, they buried the fourteen they found.[15]

[11] Fray Damián Massanet to Don Carlos de Sigüenza in Herbert Eugene Bolton (ed.), *Spanish Exploration in the Southwest, 1542-1706*, p. 303. Joutel (*Journal*, p. 150) says that Grollet, who had lived among the Indians prior to La Salle's death, had not consented to have his face marked "like the other," that is, Ruter, with whom he had been associated.

[12] Alonso de León, "Declaración," Guadalupe River, May 1, 1689, A.G.I., México, 1685-1688 (61-6-20), pp. 295-301; printed in Canedo, *Primeras exploraciones*, pp. 107-112, and translated in Walter J. O'Donnell, *La Salle's Occupation of Texas*, pp. 15-20.

[13] The epidemic is refuted by L'Archevêque (see O'Donnell, *La Salle's Occupation of Texas*, p. 23), who says most of the people died of overwork. No French source at hand mentions an outbreak of smallpox, though Pierre Meunier (Declaration, August 19, 1690, A.G.I., México, 1688-1690 [61-6-21], p. 198) mentions "pestilence" as a cause of some of the deaths. De León appears to have jumped to a conclusion.

[14] How L'Archevêque and Grollet might have obtained this information is not revealed, since they were not in the settlement and had not talked with any of the survivors.

[15] De León, "Diary," in Bolton, *Spanish Exploration*, p. 403. This version is at variance with a later declaration, which says they looked in to see how the settlement was doing.

In taking the formal depositions from the two captives, Martínez served as interpreter. With each taking the Christian oath, the first statement was given by L'Archevêque, described by Joutel as "a native of the city of Bayonne, whom the Sieur Duhaut had taken on at Petit-Goâve."[16] Duhaut was the actual murderer of La Salle, L'Archevêque an accomplice. The latter had set out in January, 1687, with the La Salle party headed for Fort St. Louis of the Illinois, and thence to Canada. After La Salle's death, March 19, 1687, he had remained with the party of Joutel and the Abbé Cavelier for some two months. Having planned to accompany them on the rest of the journey, he failed to show up at the appointed time. Because of his involvement in La Salle's death, L'Archevêque naturally was guarded in his answers.

According to his testimony, he had come to this region "about five years ago," with La Salle's four ships, sailing under orders of the French king to settle the gulf region. La Salle's intention, he claimed, was to enter the mouth of the big river he had previously discovered and proceed to the settlement already established, that is, Fort St. Louis of the Illinois. After a three-month search, the French party had been unable to find the river and had planted the colony where De León had found it. The witness chronicled the vicissitudes of the settlement: the loss of the ships, the death of many of the people from La Salle's harsh treatment, the various expeditions in search of the Mississippi, the murder of La Salle. "On account of differences that an English gunner had with Monsieur de Salle," he related, "the Englishman killed him."[17] This English gunner was James Hiens, a German by birth, then a buccaneer on an English ship, whom La Salle had taken on for the expedition at Petit Goâve. Of all the accomplices in La Salle's death, L'Archevêque may have singled out Hiens for motive of vengeance; it was he who, in a falling-out among the assassins, had slain Duhaut, and who had spared L'Archevêque only at the insistence of the Abbé Cavelier and Father Anastasius Douay.[18]

[16] J. F. Jamison, "Appendix," in Charles Wilson Hackett (ed.), *Historical Documents Relating to New Mexico, Nueva Vizcaya, and Approaches Thereto, to 1773*, II, 473, Margry, *Découvertes et établissements*, III, 323.

[17] De León, "Declaración," in Canedo, *Primeras exploraciones*, p. 109.

[18] This is Joutel's version (*Journal*, pp. 154-155). Pierre Talon, as indicated in n. 5 above, gives a different version of the deaths that followed La Salle's.

A number of the ill-fated party, he related, had gone on toward Canada and, if they were successful in reaching it, would advise the king of France to send help for the destitute settlers on the Texas coast. The purpose in founding this settlement, he declared, was to traffic in buffalo hides, tallow, lard, and Brazilwood. Asked what had happened to the colonists, he said most of them had died from overwork; the Indian massacre "four or five months ago" had killed the rest. Having remained among the Tejas when he became ill while on the way to Canada, he had returned to the settlement on the coast only after the massacre, and he and his companion had buried the victims and burned the powder.

To this summation Grollet, a sailor from La Rochelle, added certain facts. Having deserted from La Salle's earlier expedition to the Tejas to live among the Indians, he and another deserter (Ruter) had joined members of the Canada-bound expedition after La Salle's death. The two men were nearly naked, wearing only breechclout and turkey-feather adornments about the head and feet. Each had taken several Indian wives and aided the Tejas in their wars. Grollet briefly had considered accompanying the group to Canada but finally had decided against it. The way Grollet told it, he, like L'Archevêque, had been one of the seventeen who started out for Canada and, having become ill, was left among the natives. Of 250 persons who had come with La Salle,[19] he said, there remained three men and a boy among the Tejas, and some children captured by the coastal Indians who had perpetrated the massacre. There had been two girls and three boys among the Karankawas, but he had heard that the natives had killed one of the girls. Rumor had it that the party bound for Canada had met death at the hands of hostile natives, though this report later proved to be erroneous.

From a sailor's viewpoint he chronicled the loss of *l'Aimable* on a reef at the entrance of the bay, and the salvage operation, including the removal of her cannon for later use at the fort, where De León had found them; he told also of the loss of the *Belle* in a storm. Afterward he himself had taken soundings of the bay, which he said was twenty leagues long and fourteen wide and

---

[19] Joutel (*Journal*, p. 54) says 280 persons, including the ships' crews, left France. He accounts (p. 90) for 180 in the colony after Beaujeu's departure for France and after a number of desertions had occurred.

contained many reefs. The bay was found to be so shallow that only a galley or a very small frigate could navigate it; four rivers, or sizable streams, emptied into it.

L'Archevêque gave his age as twenty-eight, Grollet as twenty-nine.[20] Grollet did not sign his deposition, because he could not write—a fact indicating that L'Archevêque must have written for him the message to the Spaniards of Nueva Vizcaya.[21]

On De León's return to the main camp on the Guadalupe, he had brought with him the Tejas chief and his eight men with whom the Frenchmen had been traveling. "Although untamed," De León said of the chief, "he was an Indian in whom we recognized capacity."[22] He had in the vicinity an oratory with several images of the saints. The general gave him generously of the clothing, knives, blankets, and beads he had brought along. Responding graciously, the chief promised to come to Coahuila with some of his people for a visit.

Father Massanet was even more impressed with the Tejas chief than was the general: ". . . I tried my utmost to show all possible consideration to [him], giving him two horses, and the blanket in which I slept, for I had nothing else which I could give him."[23] Using one of the Frenchmen as an interpreter, Massanet conversed with the chief at length, exhorting him to become a Christian and have priests come and baptize his people. The chief willingly offered to take Massanet to his country, and the padre promised that he would return the following year at planting time, bringing other priests with him. Before returning to their home country, the Tejas attended a mass with the Spaniards, celebrating the Feast of the Invention of the Holy Cross.

On Tuesday, March 3, the troop took up the march for Coahuila. After passing the Nueces River, De León, Martínez, and the two French captives went on ahead of the main force to reach San Francisco de Coahuila May 13. The governor set to work to complete his report, while the *alférez*, Martínez, prepared to journey

[20] Jamison ("Appendix," in Hackett, *Historical Documents*, II, 472) and Adolph Bandelier (*The Gilded Man*, p. 296) indicate that L'Archevêque was only eighteen at the time, saying that he was born in 1671. The birth date probably is in error.

[21] See Chapter 15 of this study.

[22] De León, "Diario," in Canedo, *Primeras exploraciones*, p. 104.

[23] Massanet to Sigüenza, in Bolton, *Spanish Exploration*, p. 363.

on to Mexico City to carry reports of the expedition and to conduct the two survivors of the La Salle colony.

To the diary, the depositions of the two Frenchmen, and other reports, De León added a letter to the viceroy:

Most Excellent Lord:

Already, thanks to God, we have returned from the journey with every satisfaction, since we have managed to discover Espíritu Santo Bay and the settlement of the Frenchmen, although we found it destroyed. Great numbers died in a severe epidemic of smallpox. Feigning friendship, the Indians killed those who remained, including two Recollect religious[24] and a secular priest, sacking and destroying what was had in the settlement, which we saw in the destruction of books and papers throughout the patios, broken chests and bottle cases, and more than a hundred broken harquebuses, the barrels and locks of which they carried off. We found also eight pieces of artillery, which I left buried in the area indicated, and three swivel guns, although without chambers, two of which I have also brought with me. I found some iron cannonballs, which, with your Excellency's permission, we shall use for nails, bolts, and latches for the church that is just being finished for the village of Santiago de la Monclova.

I send herewith the declarations of two Frenchmen, taken by the *alférez real*, Francisco Martínez, interpreter; the "Diario y Derrotero" that we kept, and the map of the entire route and of Espíritu Santo Bay, showing in detail all that we traveled over and have knowledge of.

The land is plains, with many hardwoods and very fertile. The climate is good, buffalo and all kinds of game abundant. One of the two Frenchmen we are bringing is a sailor and has coasted the entire bay and the ports around it. We found them with the governor of the Tejas, who is an Indian of great faculty, and he had cared for them well. Therefore, I made him many gifts and brought him to where our camp was and gave him clothing, knives, rosaries, and two horses. He asked me to furnish him an Indian guide, saying that he would come with his brother and six other Tejas Indians to this province, because they wished to communicate with Christians, and that they greatly desired to know the evangelical law.[25]

---

[24] Popular in France, Recollect Franciscans, of whom there were three on the La Salle expedition, had established the order in Canada. They have been mistakenly called Capuchins because their habit and life style were similar (Canedo, *Primeras exploraciones*, p. 113 n.).

[25] Alonso de León to the Viceroy, Coahuila, May 16, 1689, in Canedo, *Primeras exploraciones*, pp. 113-114.

On his return to Coahuila, De León found that Captain Diego Ramón had waged successful warfare against the Cabeza and Toboso Indians. The province was calm, and natives recently settled in the missions were proceeding with the planting. The village of Santiago de la Monclova was just completing its founding, with the roof being put on the church.

The soldiers from Parral and Nuevo León had rendered laudable service during the expedition to Texas, as had Jean Géry: "The first Frenchman served well during the entire expedition and remains in this province.... If your Excellency prefers that he should be sent to that Court, I will do so when I have your reply."[26]

When Martínez reached the capital and presented the sheaf of papers to the viceroy, Conde de Galve, a new interrogation of the French survivors was ordered. Officiating in the hearing on June 10 was Don Francisco Fernández de Marmolejo, the *auditor general* who previously had presided over the questioning of Ralph Wilkinson and Jean Géry. Martínez served as interpreter. Present were two personages who had played an important part in the search for the French colony by sea: Captains Andrés de Pez and Juan Enríquez Barroto.

L'Archevêque, again questioned first, revealed few facts not already known to the Spaniards. He told of the capture of the *St. François* off Santo Domingo, where she had anchored after having sprung a leak. "The enemy"—whose identity the deponent professed not to know—had captured the ship, then attached a cable and towed her away with her cargo of wine, brandy, flour, and clothing. The crew of the *St. François*, he said, had consisted of only eight men and their captain. Asked about the reported deaths of large numbers of persons in an epidemic, L'Archevêque said he knew of no such illness. Some had suffered from "hemorrhages"— probably dysentery—and others had died at the hands of the Indians before Captain Beaujeu had returned with the large ship to France. Later many persons had succumbed to La Salle's harsh treatment— from overwork and long exposure in the water.[27]

When the questioning turned to the death of La Salle, or to the

[26] Ibid., p. 115.
[27] Jean L'Archevêque, Declaration, Mexico City, June 10, 1689, in O'Donnell, *La Salle's Occupation of Texas*, p. 23.

reasons for L'Archevêque and his companions' having been found among the Indians, the prisoner was less than candid. They had remained with the Tejas, he claimed, because the road back to Fort St. Louis, a hundred leagues distant, lay through the country of hostile savages. To please their hosts, who cared for them and fed them, the Frenchmen allowed their faces to be tattooed. At last their return to the settlement came about in an unusual way. The Tejas wished to take them to visit the Jumano Indians, among whom they said a Spanish priest was living. In the company of a number of the Tejas, the four Frenchmen set out to seek the friar, "moved by their Catholic instincts."[28] When the party came to the road to Fort St. Louis, the Frenchmen asked leave to go there to see how their countrymen fared. Thus they came upon the scene of the massacre. With their countrymen dead, they then had no recourse but to return to dwell among the Indians. With knowledge that there were Spaniards among the Jumanos, said L'Archevêque, he wrote two letters (his and Grollet's) "to Coahuila," in which he informed the Spaniards of their presence and asked to be rescued, that they again might live among civilized people of their own religion.

From the witness the Spaniards sought the answer to the mystery of Jean Géry. Did L'Archevêque know him? Was he a part of the La Salle settlement? How had he happened to come to the territory where he had been found living among the Indians? The witness replied that he had met the man but neither he nor his companion knew any more of him than the name of the town he came from.

He had told them that he was from Xeblu in France. Since they have never heard of any such place in France, they regard it as certain that this place is in New France, and that it is the first settlement which Monsieur de Salle established and which he later was unable to find. To this Frenchman, whose name is Juan Xeri, the same thing must have happened that befell both this witness and his companion. He must have left his settlement, which then was destroyed as ours was, and after wandering among various Indian nations, have come into the territory in which the Spaniards discovered him.[29]

[28] Ibid., p. 25
[29] Ibid., p. 26.

L'Archevêque's deposition was read to Grollet, who said he had nothing to add or to subtract.

The viceroy asked Captains Pez and Barroto, both of whom had reconnoitered Espíritu Santo Bay, to give their opinion of De León's diary dealing with his discovery of the French settlement on the Gulf of Mexico, and of the declarations taken from the two Frenchmen. At last the trails of the searchers by land and by sea had come to a focal point, having cut through false rumors and wild tales to fix the location of the bold attempt by the French to colonize Spanish territory.

"The bay that they [L'Archevêque and Grollet] say they called St. Louis, and that Governor Alonso de León judged to be Espíritu Santo [said the two maritime officers], is the one we called San Bernardo on the discovery we made from Veracruz in 1687."[30] The mouth of the bay, the two officers noted, was at 28° 23′ north latitude, the northernmost part at 29°. The accuracy of the first reading, coupled with the miscalculation of the second, appears to indicate their failure to explore the body of water to its full extent; the northern limit was but a guess. Four leagues northeast of the mouth, members of the Rivas-Iriarte expedition, which Barroto had served as a pilot, had found the wreckage of the small vessel, said to have been of fifty or sixty tuns (the *Belle*) on April 4, 1687. Soundings at the mouth of the bay had borne out depths given by the Frenchmen. At the entrance the water was two fathoms, or more than eleven French feet. Inside the bay it was four and five feet, shallower near the shore, and the rest of it was too shallow for navigation except by small vessels or barks.

While exploring in two canoes captured on the Río de Flores— near San Antonio Bay—the 1687 expedition had found fragments of the larger ship of 259 tuns and inferred that it had been lost at the mouth of San Bernardo Bay because a ship of such size could not possibly enter there. This assumption now was verified. The coastal Indians evidently had picked up in their canoes some of the merchandise from the wreck of the *Aimable* and carried it "through the channels that connect these lakes with the Río de Flores."[31]

[30] Andrés de Pez and Juan Enriquez Barroto, "Paracer de Pez y Barroto," A.G.I., México, 1685-1688 (61-6-20), p. 311.
[31] Ibid.

The four-year search for the elusive French colony at last had ended; the mystery was solved. While the Spaniards searched, the forces of the hostile environment had elminated any threat offered by the daring intruders. The hazard had been removed with the swish of a Karankawa arrow, the strike of a rattlesnake, the snap of an alligator's jaws, the unbearable heat and torture attendant to the effort to carve a foothold on the wilderness shore. It had ended with the hate and avarice of Frenchman toward Frenchman, with sinister murder that begat more bloodshed. No longer was there cause for Spanish alarm at the threat posed by the intrepid La Salle or his followers. Yet by the episode Spanish leaders had been dealt a warning; never again would they dare to sleep so soundly. They must move to protect their territory, lest another attempt be made to snatch from Spain her rightful possessions.

Such a step was not long in coming. Already General Alonso de León and Father Damián Massanet were advocating a plan. Before the year 1689 drew to a close, machinery was in motion to take the adelantados back into the region so recently claimed by the French. They must occupy and settle it, before it was lost to another power.

18. MISSION TO THE TEJAS

Learning now, for the first time ... of the death of his beloved friend and chief ... that war had again been declared against Spain, Tonti decided to rescue, if possible, the remaining members of La Salle's party on the Gulf coast; and, by making them the nucleus of a small army, to cross the Rio Grande, and thus win a new province for France. ... he pushed on ... finding, upon reaching the village where he had expected to find them, that they had been killed.

—Henry Reed Stiles
Joutel, *Journal*, p. 202 n.

With La Salle's ill-fated colony found, two tasks remained for the Spaniards: to find the invaders' remnants among the Texas Indians and to erect barriers against another intrusion. Less than complete success was to attend their efforts in the first task, complete failure the second; having strained at a gnat, the Spaniards now would swallow a camel.

Four years of intense effort had gone into the search for La Salle's settlement, which was impotent to begin with, moribund by the time the Spaniards found it. Despite the determination with which they rose to this nebulous threat, and the resources expended to remove it, the real menace, when it came, would find them inert. While the French drove a wedge between Florida and Texas with settlements at Biloxi and Mobile Bay, the Spaniards floundered in perplexity.

With more poachers upon their territory than they had resources to combat, the ultimate choice of an invader was between French Catholics and British Protestants. The primary obligation of the Spanish sovereigns, a junta was to observe, was "to keep the

Catholic faith pure and undefiled in the new world which had been granted them by the pope."[1] In this choice, as well as in the vicissitudes of the La Salle colony itself, the fate of Spain in America and much of the future of the North American continent were determined.

Had La Salle planted his colony at the mouth of the Mississippi, as he had intended, the Spaniards eventually would have found the settlement and perhaps destroyed it. Their reaction then would have been the same as it was on finding the ruined settlement on the Texas coast: to settle the area where the threat had arisen so that it might not come again. One only can imagine how early Spanish control of such a strategic spot might have shaped the course of history. But instead of reacting to a threat at the mouth of the Mississippi, the Spaniards rose to an affront on an obscure, unnavigable bay on the Texas coast.

Unbridled optimism greeted the news that General Alonso de León had brought back to Mexico from the bay now called Espíritu Santo. As viceregal authorities of New Spain viewed this happy deliverance from longstanding peril, their religious zeal quickened, and they gave thanks to the Diety "for the renewed proof of His devine aid and favor."[2] The viceroy, Conde de Galve, focused his attention upon that portion of De León's May 16 letter which dealt with the Tejas Indians, and the news that these people claimed that their ancestors had received religious instruction from "the Lady in Blue."[3] "They had in the area where I saw the Indian governor a chapel, beautifully and neatly adorned with many flowers. It has an altar; four images of the saints and a cross with a painted Santo Cristo; a rosary upon the altar; musical in-

[1] William Edward Dunn, *Spanish and French Rivalry in the Gulf Region of the United States, 1678-1702*, p. 211.
[2] Ibid., p. 110.
[3] Between 1621 and 1629 the Jumano Indians of West Texas repeatedly brought to Fray Alonso de Benavides, in New Mexico, reports of a woman dressed in blue having appeared to them, teaching them the Christian faith. When Benavides returned to Spain in 1631, he heard of the claims of María de Jesús de Agreda, a nun born in 1602, that her spirit had left a Spanish convent on many occasions to go among the Indians in the American Southwest, taking them the divine message. After visiting her, Father Benavides was convinced that it was she whom the Indians had seen (Walter Prescott Webb [ed.], *The Handbook of Texas*, I, 11; Carlos Eduardo Castañeda, *Our Catholic Heritage in Texas*, I, 195-198).

struments with which they honor the saints; and an altar light that burns night and day in front of the door of the chapel in order to give light within, which they replenish with deer tallow every morning."[4]

De León's letter also contains a description of the habits and customs of this people—not considered altogether accurate in the light of later knowledge, but of decided influence upon forthcoming events. He related their desire for missionaries, and the enthusiasm with which one of the mission chaplains of his expedition responded to this wish.

> They say they have nine settlements of wood houses, and plant corn, beans, pumpkins, watermelons, and muskmelons. They are a people who are sedentary in their villages. They have political organization and government like the Mexicans.[5] They asked me for ministers to teach them. I told them that I would report to Your Excellency in order that appropriate measures might be taken. An apostolic religious of the Colegio de la Cruz, Fray Damián Mazanet [*sic*], who was one of the chaplains I took, very zealous in God's service and in the conversion of souls, has proposed to me that if it is arranged for ministers to go, he will bring from the Colegio de la Cruz companions who are fervently dedicated to this enterprise. It is certain, Most Excellent Lord, that with any kind of encouragement much can be done in that region toward winning the souls of those poor infidels.[6]

The viceroy had this portion of the letter extracted, referred it first to his advisers, then called a junta. Members of the July 5 gathering saw in the entire La Salle episode the workings of divine providence; God had used the French settlement as a means of opening the way for extension of the gospel and the saving of "pagan" souls. Father Massanet's offer to work among the Tejas should be accepted, and all supplies furnished at royal expense. And to the viceroy the junta gave its eloquent blessing: "May the grace of divine love dwell in your Excellency's heart and fill it with spiritual consolation, granting you the health and strength

[4] Alonso de León to the Viceroy, Coahuila, May 16, 1689, in Lino Gómez Canedo (ed.), *Primeras exploraciones y poblamiento de Texas (1686-1694)*, p. 114.

[5] This description is quite contrary to those contained in reports of priests who entered the East Texas mission field in 1716 (see Robert S. Weddle, *San Juan Bautista: Gateway to Spanish Texas*, p. 142).

[6] De León to the Viceroy, May 16, 1689, in Canedo, *Primeras exploraciones*, pp. 114-115.

needed for success in all your undertakings, to the glory and honor of God our Lord, and the conversion of the souls of the many heathens now living in darkness."[7]

While accepting Father Massanet's offer to head the missionary enterprise among the Tejas, the junta asked De León to recommend procedure for carrying out the conversion. His report, dated August 12, presented the military point of view, based on his long experience in dealing with natives on the northern frontier. For protection against Indian uprising and French invasion, he suggested, forts should be built at four locations: on the Río Grande, on the Río Zarco (Jahuey Creek or the Frio River), on the Guadalupe, and in the principal village of the Tejas. These strongholds would form a line of communication between the Coahuila settlements and the new missions.[8]

The value of this advice was not to be recognized in De León's lifetime, or before costly blunders had resulted from the lack of following it. Idealistic officials in Mexico City insisted the "heathens" were to be converted not by force of arms but by the light of the gospel: the presence in their land of large numbers of soldiers would only make settling them more difficult. The projected enterprise was viewed almost wholly as religious rather than military in nature.

This view was not altered by the arrival from Coahuila of a new De León report dated sixteen days later, despite the alarming news it contained. A Mescal Indian just back from Tejas country claimed that shortly after the Spaniards' departure eighteen Frenchmen had entered that region from a great river to the east. They had begun, with the help of the Tejas, to form a settlement twelve miles east of the village where L'Archevêque and Grollet had been captured. Although the Tejas remained steadfast in their friendship for the Spaniards, the Mescal claimed, the French were determined to form a settlement among them. The Tejas chief had sent word that some of his people were soon to visit Coahuila in the hope that priests would come and live among them.[9]

[7] Dunn, *Spanish and French Rivalry*, p. 111.
[8] De León to the Viceroy, Monclova, August 12, 1689, in Canedo, *Primeras exploraciones*, p. 124.
[9] Alonso de León to Viceroy Monclova, August 28, 1689, A.G.I., México, 1688-1690 (61-6-21), pp. 75-77.

Having kept the demented Frenchman Jean Géry in Coahuila rather than sending him with the others to the capital, De León was making use of him. He had sent Géry to the Río Grande to await the Tejas visitors.[10] This is the last mention found of the prevaricating foreigner; he does not reappear on the expedition to found missions among the Tejas. Given the opportunity, he may have returned to live among the Coahuiltecan Indians, as he was doing when De León found him; or he may have fallen ill and died or been killed by some enemy tribe. Evidently the Spaniards, after the first *entrada*, had decided that he was harmless and gave little heed to his failure to return.

Undoubtedly the facts related by the Mescal Indian were magnified, but there can be no doubt that they were soundly based. In September, 1687, the party of Joutel and the Abbé Cavelier had reached Fort St. Louis on the Illinois. The following March, having concealed the fact of La Salle's death from the great explorer's faithful servant Henri de Tonti, as from all others, the small band departed for Canada and thence proceeded to France. Tonti, who in 1686 had journeyed to the mouth of the Mississippi in search of La Salle's settlement and left six men in a log hut at the mouth of the Arkansas, undertook a new expedition in 1689. This time he penetrated to the country of the Tejas. It was news of this expedition that the Mescal Indian now brought to De León.[11]

In Mexico City officials viewed the report in the light of developments on the international scene: France and Spain were again at war, the flimsy Truce of Ratisbon having ruptured the previous April. Viceregal advisers regarded with grave apprehension the vague reports of new French incursions in Texas. While still resisting any idea of attempting to convert the natives by show of military might, they instructed De León to return to the Tejas country with whatever troops he deemed necessary to investigate fully the activities of the French. The intruders should be arrested and brought to Coahuila for interrogation.[12]

[10] Ibid., p. 76.

[11] Henri Joutel, *Joutel's Journal of La Salle's Last Voyage, 1684-7*, pp. 202-203 n.; José Antonio Pichardo, *Pichardo's Treatise on the Limits of Louisiana and Texas*, I, 183-184.

[12] Benito de Novóa y Salgado, "Parecer," September 9, 1689, A.G.I., México, 1688-1690 (61-6-21), p. 78; Dunn, *Spanish and French Rivalry*, p. 116.

Father Massanet looked upon the latest De León report in quite a different manner. The letter was to become the source of misunderstanding between the priest and the governor. To the padre it appeared as an effort by De León to make the forthcoming expedition a military one, at the expense of the religious aspect. Massanet, rankled by this conviction, soon begain seizing upon every opportunity to disparage De León and to arrogate unto himself all possible credit. The priest's jealous behavior and the reaction to it—in this instance and others—were to have far-reaching effects upon the outcome of the venture.

With 110 soldiers and 4 priests, the expedition crossed the Río Grande at Paso de Francia on April 2. Guided again by the Quems Indian, it proceeded by much the same route as the *entrada* of the year before to the crossing on the Guadalupe. From that point twenty men pressed on to Fort St. Louis, which they found on April 26, much as they had left it. Father Massanet himself put the torch to the wooden structure, built largely of the timbers from the ill-fated ship, *l'Aimable*. A brisk breeze from the gulf fanned the flames, and in half an hour the fort was in embers. The French artillery pieces still lay buried where De León had left them in 1689, and so they were left again.[13]

The twenty Spaniards then crossed the Garcitas and proceeded to the mouth of the San Marcos River—the Lavaca—where De León made a mistaken observation that was to cause him much grief later on. In the mouth of the river he saw what appeared to be two buoys situated as if marking the channel. Since he had no boat, he could record in his report only what he was able to observe from the shore. Viceregal officials, perhaps inspired by Massanet's carping criticism of the military leader, were to regard him with disfavor for this failure. Not until after De León's death was the true nature of the objects determined; they were found to be nothing more than upended logs held fast by the silt deposited where the river disembogued.

After returning to the camp on the Guadalupe the following day, De León set out to the northeast, seeking Indians who could help him locate the French remnants. After crossing the Colorado

---

[13] Alonso de León, "Diario," March 26-July 11, 1690, in Canedo, *Primeras exploraciones,* p. 138.

on May 9 he learned from the Tonkawa nations of Emet, Toho, and Tohaha that two French boys were living in nearby *rancherías*. The following day the Spaniards met a band of natives with whom was a fourteen-year-old lad named Pierre Talon. Two days later three Indians came to their camp bringing another young Frenchman, Pierre Meunier, age twenty.[14]

In the meantime De León had summoned up the main camp. As the company pressed the search for the French survivors, he gleaned reports from the natives that other Frenchmen were to be found near the mouth of Espíritu Santo Bay.

On May 22 the expedition came to the first *ranchería*, of the Tejas, near the Neches River, and soon thereafter began the various steps in the founding of the first East Texas mission, San Francisco de los Tejas. While looking for a suitable site for the mission, the Spaniards were shown by the Indians "two dead bodies of Frenchmen who had shot each other with carbines."[15] These unfortunates appear to have been Hiens and Ruter, who after binding together to slay Duhaut and Liotot eventually had a falling-out between themselves.[16] The Spaniards placed a cross upon a tree to mark the burial place.

During the stay among the Tejas, De León probed diligently for information concerning the visits of Frenchmen to the region. From the Indian governor he learned that, on the day he had received news that the Spaniards were approaching on their return, a message had come also from four other white men, who had stopped at a *ranchería* three days' journey in the opposite direction. These strange visitors, doubtless members of Tonti's party, were seeking the friendship of the Tejas. The chief had sent them word that he could not receive them because his friends, the Spaniards, were on their way to see him. With this news the Frenchmen had withdrawn, promising to return later to establish a settlement and asking that the Spaniards not be informed of their visit. Three of the visitors were said to be members of the French party that

[14] Ibid., pp. 141-142.
[15] Fray Damián Massanet to Carlos de Sigüenza, 1690, in Herbert Eugene Bolton (ed.), *Spanish Exploration in the Southwest, 1542-1706*, p. 379. De León ("Diario," in Canedo, *Primeras exploraciones*, p. 145) says they were shown the graves of the two Frenchmen, without mentioning how they had died.
[16] See Francis Parkman, *La Salle and the Discovery of the Great West*, p. 333.

had set out for Canada (not so), while the other had only one hand—a description that fit Henri de Tonti himself. On their departure the strangers had gone to the east, crossed one large river and continued to another, where, as the Indian told it, they had a settlement. They had crossed the Red River and proceeded to the Mississippi, on which stream Tonti, during his expedition of 1686, had left the first few settlers at a place later to be known as Arkansas Post.[17]

Tonti had left Fort St. Louis on the Illinois in the latter part of 1689, on his second attempt to find the survivors of La Salle's gulf coast colony. He reached the Natchitoches village on the Red River and pushed on to one of the villages of the Nabedaches, of the Hasinai, or Tejas, confederacy. It was at this village, three days' travel from the nascent Mission San Francisco de los Tejas, that he had sought Indian guides. Meeting refusal and learning of the approach of the Spaniards, he turned back toward Arkansas Post.[18]

From the Tejas governor's report, it appeared that the French had established a settlement somewhere to the east, and that they still entertained hopes of establishing themselves in Texas. The new Spanish mission, De León believed, could serve as a listening post and would report any French efforts in that direction. De León, therefore, made no effort to pursue the retreating Frenchmen or to find the settlement to the east.

With appropriate ceremony De León gave possession of the new mission to the priests and began preparations for the return to Coahuila. His plans to leave a garrison of fifty men to guard the mission met strong opposition from Father Massanet. Therefore, only three soldiers remained, along with the three priests, Miguel de Fontcuberta, Antonio Bordoy, and Francisco Casañas de Jesús María.

Returning along the same route by which they had come, De León and Massanet reached the Colorado on June 17 and were informed by the Tonkawas[19] that three French children were captives of the coastal Indians. While the main force marched on

---

[17] Dunn, *Spanish and French Rivalry*, p. 117.
[18] Webb, *Handbook of Texas*, II, 789; Castañeda, *Our Catholic Heritage*, I, 354-355.
[19] Emat, Toho, Tohaha, and Cavas, says Massanet (Massanet to Sigüenza, in Bolton, *Spanish Exploration*, p. 384).

toward the Guadalupe, De León and sixteen soldiers split off to search for them. Traveling south, they came on June 20 to the Arroyo de las Canoas—the creek near the mouth of Espíritu Santo Bay where they had found Indian canoes the previous year. Still marching south next day, they met two Indians of the Cascossi (Karankawa) nation. Accompanying the natives to their village, they found Robert and Marie Madelaine Talon. De León, after giving gifts all around, began bargaining for the children's ransom. The Indians, meanwhile, sent to a neighboring village to get the third child, Lucien Talon. On their return the natives made demands that De León considered exorbitant, and several appeared in battle dress. Massanet, who now had become quite critical of the military leader and his followers, claimed the incident was provoked by soldiers who began to enter the Indian dwellings, "peering with too much curiosity into their belongings, and committing other acts so that the Indians became resentful . . . and distrustful."[20] The natives then threatened, said De León, that if their demands were not met they would kill the Spaniards, and they immediately set about proving their point by loosing a shower or arrows upon them, wounding two horses.[21] Two arrows struck De León, but since he wore mail he was not hurt. De León's men launched a counterattack, their harquebuses more effective than arrows, and the Indians took flight. Leaving four Karankawas dead and three wounded, the Spaniards took the three French children and put four leagues between themselves and the native village before nightfall. On the twenty-third they overtook the main camp at the ford of the Guadalupe.

By the evening campfire the three French children huddled together in silence, their tattooed faces marked with fear. Not even their countryman, Pierre Meunier, or their older brother, Pierre Talon, seemed able to engage the boys in conversation, as they hung close to their older sister. At last the reason became clear: "The two boys, having been taken from the settlement only a little more than a year ago . . . , cannot speak their own language but only that of the Indians."[22]

Reaching the Río Grande on July 4, the Spaniards found the

[20] Ibid.
[21] De León, "Diario," in Canedo, *Primeras exploraciones*, p. 149.
[22] De León to the Viceroy, Río Grande, July 12, 1690, in ibid., p. 157.

river at flood stage, the facile crossing they had become accustomed to transformed into a raging torrent half a mile wide. They waited for the flood to abate until July 12, the day the governor finished writing his report to the viceroy. Then De León, feeling the urgency of getting the report of the journey's outcome to the capital, swam his horse across the river, though the stream still was on a rise and extremely dangerous. Father Massanet, Captain Gregorio de Salinas Varona, the young Frenchman Pierre Meunier, and three soldiers followed. Salinas, taking Meunier with him, proceeded to Mexico City with the dispatches. The others reached Monclova on the fifteenth.

In the report that Captain Salinas carried, De León dwelt at length upon the many attributes of the land he had explored, as well as those of the Tejas people. In the combination the governor saw a wealth of opportunity, but if the Spaniards did not move in force, he believed, it would be lost. "This is a very affable and cordial people," he said of the East Texas natives, "highly competitive with each other."[23] So abundant were the cornfields that there was no need for thievery. The natives also raised beans, squash, and watermelons, which they cultivated with wooden hoes. In their round houses of wood and thatch, they had bins for storing corn, beans, and acorns throughout the year. They ground their corn on mortars to make *atole* and tamales. Their houses were well furnished with wooden benches and raised beds with canopies.

The first fruits of the harvest each year always had been given to the Indian designated as minister of the tribe as their offering to God. The native minister had a chapel, containing saints' images and a large cross, where the divine offerings were made. As the chief pledged his people's obedience to the Spanish crown, the spiritual leader promised that thenceforth the offerings would be given to the Franciscan religious, whom he now acknowledged as the true ministers of his people.[24]

In the villages he had seen, De León claimed, there were more than four thousand persons. The Indian governor and the two Frenchmen had informed him that many other pueblos lay in the

[23] Ibid., p. 154.
[24] Ibid., pp. 154-155.

surrounding country: to the north and northeast were the large villages of the Cadodachos, who raised crops and managed their produce to make it last all year. Five days' hard travel to the north, it was said, two religious like those who had come with the Spaniards were teaching Christianity and baptizing the natives, but no one could say whence they had come.

Also to be considered were the four Frenchmen who had approached the Tejas country from the east at the same time De León had entered from the opposite direction. These interlopers had sought to convince the Indians that the Spaniards were an evil people, who would steal their women and children and all their possessions.[25]

In the coastal region the Spaniards had been told that a ship had entered the bay to take on wood and water, then departed. This news was but another indication that foreign invaders still threatened, and that failure to counter the threat could result in great loss for Spain.

If settlements are not made among the Tejas, as well as on the Guadalupe River and the port of Espíritu Santo Bay, [De León reasoned], it will not be possible to go to and from the province of the Tejas, or to settle the great number of infidels in those regions. [All the various Indian nations were asking for ministers] in imitation of the Tejas [he claimed]. With the French already having reconnoitered this land and the port of the bay, where they enter to get meat, water, and wood, they will be able to seize the port as well as the province of the Tejas, which is of great consequence and could cause great damage to all of New Spain. In order to pursue the settlement of the infidels and new conversions, many ministers are needed in different regions because of the ferver with which all the Indians are asking for them. The Reverend Father Commissary Fray Damián Mazanet [*sic*] will report to Your Excellency in greater detail when, God willing, he arrives at that court with the nephew of the governor of the Tejas and another kinsmen of his.

Besides the two Frenchmen [Pierre Meunier and Pierre Talon] whom I captured first [he related], I took two boys of seven and eight years old and a little French girl of twelve or fourteeen from among the Indians of the coast. . . . The two boys, it having been little more than one year since they were taken from the settlement, when it was attacked, could not speak their own language but only that of the Indians. They are

[25] Ibid.

brothers of the little French girl and of one of the two whom I captured first, the smallest.[26]

The reunion of the Talon children was less than complete, for a brother and another boy still remained among the savages of the coastal country. Pierre, who had been fearful of joining the Spaniards the year before, now was impressed by the kindness shown them. He expressed the hope that his captors would seek out the other children still among the Indians.[27]

In relating the capture of the French children, De León, though a hardened veteran of the frontier, reveals himself as a man of compassion. The fear-stricken little faces, streaked with indelible tattoos, touched him deeply. He vowed he would give them a home until the viceroy made other provision.

This tough old soldier, who in the Indian wars had allowed his captives to confess, then hanged them, expressed feeling also for the departed Jean Géry: "On this journey I sorely missed the old Frenchman, because of his knowledge of all the Indian languages of the region. He was always found faithful. Only with his help would it have been possible . . . to discover the settlement he came from, which I judge is where the Frenchmen now have come from to the Tejas."[28]

Along the trail from the Guadalupe to the Río Grande the Spanish force had left many horses, some dead from the rigors of the journey, others reduced to walking skeletons. The animals had been in poor condition to start with, as a result of the Indian campaigns and a snow that had covered the Coahuila countryside the winter before. De León himself appears also to have suffered during the *entrada*. He was now fifty-three years old and failing.

[26] Ibid., p. 157. Cyprian Tanguay (*Dictionnaire Généalogique des Familles Canadiennes depuis la Fondation de la Colonie Jusqu'à nos Jours*, I, 558) gives the birthdates of the children of Lucien Talon and Isabelle Marchand Talon: Marie Madelaine, November 3, 1673; Marie Elizabeth, September 10, 1672; Pierre, March 20, 1676; and Jean-Baptiste, May 26, 1679. Lucien, and possibly Robert, was born after the family left Canada, hence no record.

[27] Robert Carlton Clark, *The Beginnings of Texas, 1684-1718*, p. 26; Pierre Margry (ed.), *Découvertes et établissements des Français dans l'Ouest et dans le Sud de l'Amérique septentrionale*, III, 617. These sources indicate that it was Pierre Talon and not the Tonkawas who had first informed De León that his sister and three brothers dwelt among the Karankawas.

[28] De León to the Viceroy, July 12, 1690, in Canedo, *Primeras exploraciones*, p. 157.

Probably as a result of poor health, he had relaxed the discipline of his soldiers and thus incurred Father Massanet's bitter criticism. Through his vindictiveness the priest achieved results that he neither expected nor desired.

When Massanet made his own recommendations to the viceroy, they were at odds on many points with those of De León. He saw no need for either presidio or Spanish settlement in the Tejas country, but instead urged a "captain protector" who would govern Spanish tradesmen sent to aid the missions while defending the Indians from Spanish cupidity. Reinforcements should be sent for the ministers already working "in the vineyard of the Lord, winning souls to the society of our Holy Mother Church," he added, suggesting a need for fourteen priests and seven lay brothers to work among the Tejas and the Cadodachos. He believed that the only settlement needed was one on the Guadalupe, which would serve as a halfway station between the Tejas missions and Coahuila while protecting the coastal region from a new French invasion.[29]

Even before Massanet's letter was received, however, the viceroy had called a *junta general* to consider the facts contained in De León's diary and report. The officials' attention focused on the diary reference to the "buoys" near the mouth of the Río de San Marcos (Lavaca River). As if the fate of the kingdom depended on it, they ordered immediate steps to see that the objects were removed. De León was at fault, they believed, in not having removed them himself; likewise, he was held culpable for failure to ascertain the whereabouts of the French settlement to the east of the Tejas country. Captain Salinas Varona, questioned along with the French prisoner, Meunier, attempted to defend De León's decisions. The buoys were a long way from shore and could be reached only in a substantial boat, which was not available. The settlement said to lie to the east was possibly as far as a hundred leagues beyond Tejas country. Despite such alibis, the governor was placed under a cloud from which he would never emerge.

---

[29] Fray Damián Massanet to the Viceroy, in ibid., p. 162.

19. THE PREMATURE THRUST

I then decided to undertake our retreat secretly, and we left the twenty-fifth day of October this last year of 1693. I was able to take only the chalices, chrismatories, and other silver ornaments. Everything of iron and copper, along with the swivel guns, was left buried, the bells in their place. On our departure the mission was burned. We proceeded with great care, by day and by night, and after four days' travel, we realized that a throng of [Indians] was following us.

—Fray Damián Massanet
Canedo, *Primeras exploraciones*, p. 319

Following the testimony of Captain Salinas Varona, the *auditor general*, Marmolejo, had him bring in the French prisoner from the Río Grande. With the captain serving as interpreter, Pierre Meunier (Pedro Muñi) related lucidly the events surrounding the voyage from France and the life and death of the French colony. His is one of the most complete firsthand accounts, for all its conciseness, to be found except for that of Joutel. While Meunier may be judged in error on some points, it is to be remembered that he was but a lad of fifteen when the voyage began; he lacked Joutel's vantage point as a member of La Salle's inner circle. From his forthright relation it is readily understandable that he was chosen by La Salle to learn the Tejas language, and by the Spaniards to accompany the next expedition to Texas as interpreter.

Meunier, from Paris, called himself Sieur de Preville. His father, Louis Meunier, had held the same title. He was a Roman Catholic. Having traveled from Paris to La Rochelle as a companion to La Salle, he had sailed on *l'Aimable*, a bark of two hundred tuns burthen, in company with the flagship *Le Joly* and the other two vessels. Approaching Santo Domingo, the small fleet had encountered a storm, and four piraguas of unspecified nationality had sailed out from the island to capture the ketch (*St. François*).[1]

During the expedition's stay at Petit Goâve, says Meunier, "one of the pirates found in that port with a large ship, many people, and very good armament sought to persuade Monsieur de Salas that he should come with him to this kingdom. To this [La Salle] replied that he had no order from the king of France."[2] Thus appears a refutation, consistently ignored, of the oft-repeated theory that La Salle expected to receive reinforcements from the Santo Domingo buccaneers to assist him in an invasion of Mexico.

With plans to find the settlement La Salle had established on the Mississippi previously, Meunier relates, the expedition reached the coast of Seno Mexicano after fifteen days underway. The pilots insisted from the beginning that their landfall was too far west. La Salle, however, kept his own counsel. At his insistence the ships traversed westward, seeking the marker he had left at the mouth of the Mississippi. At the entrance to the bay later to be called Espíritu Santo, La Salle was convinced he had found the place he was seeking because the latitude was the same.

Over Captain Beaujeu's protests, he proceeded to sound the bay. The channel was marked and *La Belle* taken inside. In anticipation of entering with *l'Aimable*, part of the larger ship's cargo was transferred to the *chaloupes* and launches to lighten her. In attempting to enter under sail (rather than waiting for a tow), she managed to get outside the buoys, and a sudden wind carried her into a sandbar. She split open under force of heavy waves. The night was spent unloading people and cargo.

---

[1] Pierre Meunier, Declaration, August 19, 1690, A.G.I., México, 1688-1690 (61-6-21), p. 193. Henri Joutel (*Joutel's Journal of La Salle's Last Voyage, 1684-7*, p. 61) says two piraguas. It is to be remembered, however, that the *Joly*, on which Joutel sailed, had gone on ahead of the other vessels. Meunier, on the *Aimable*, may have been an eye witness to the capture.

[2] Meunier, Declaration, p. 193. Meunier here is recorded as saying that his ship was in Petit Goâve twenty-two days. By Joutel's version (*Journal*, pp. 59-62) the *Joly* arrived September 27, the *Aimable* October 2, and both departed November 25. Joutel's account is borne out by pages from the log of the *Belle* brought to Parral by Indians (J. F. Jamison, "Appendix," in Charles Wilson Hackett [ed.], *Historical Documents Relating to New Mexico, Nueva Vizcaya, and Approaches Thereto, to 1773*, II, 474, 479-480).

Competing with the Frenchmen for the salvage were the Cauquesi (Karankawa) Indians, with whom La Salle had already had a friendly exchange by means of his Indian servant, Nika, and from whom he had obtained some canoes. To recover kegs of wine and bundles of merchandise from these natives the leader sent some sailors and soldiers in one the the *chaloupes* to their camp. The goods were retrieved, but at a cost the French could ill afford. That night as the sentry slept at his post the natives fell upon the camp, killing two soldiers and wounding two. La Salle put his encampment under arms, but the Indians had fled to the interior.[3]

Loss of the two soldiers occasioned more bitterness between La Salle and Beaujeu. The naval captain charged the explorer with having deceived the king by accepting money for the enterprise, only to sacrifice his followers to his own mismanagement. Beaujeu was determined to set sail for France forthwith, taking with him the crew of the wrecked ship.

With the departure of *Le Joly*, La Salle had a wooden fort erected on the "south"—actually west—shore of the bay, where his three hundred men were encamped.[4] He then began a systematic exploration of the bay area, landing first at Arroyo de las Canoas, where a buffalo was killed and eight men were left to continue the reconnaissance. Then he put a party of woodcutters ashore between Arroyo de los Franceses (Garcitas Creek) and Río de San Marcos (Lavaca River) to fell trees for building the more permanent settlement at the place Alonso de León was to find it. In three Indian canoes the supplies and provisions were transported from the first fort, which was abandoned, and planking from the wreck of *l'Aimable* was brought for building a warehouse that doubled as a fort. Dwellings also were constructed and covered with buffalo skins.

Constantly plagued by the "Caucosi" Indians, La Salle then set out to make war on them. He engaged four *rancherías* near the

[3] Meunier, Declaration, pp. 194-195. Since Meunier is cryptic in his relation, it appears somewhat different from that given in greater detail by Joutel (*Journal*, pp. 79-87), who indicates that the events from landing to Indian attack extended over the period February 13 to March 5.
[4] Meunier, Declaration, p. 195. Joutel (*Journal*, p. 90) indicates there were about 180 persons in the colony after the *Joly* had departed. Jacques Grollet ("Declaration of Jaques Grole" in Walter J. O'Donnell, *La Salle's Occupation of Texas*, p. 19) says that La Salle had peopled the settlement with 250 persons.

mouth of the Guadalupe River, where they had retreated in canoes. Four Indians were killed.[5]

Meunier, unfortunately, sheds no light on the explorations La Salle made during the winter of 1685-1686. This failure is understandable, since Joutel, a trusted lieutenant, lacked explicit knowledge in this area, and the leader's brother, the Abbé Cavelier, who accompanied him, writes obscurely of the journey.[6] Only the word of various native bands, as recorded by the Spaniards, relates that La Salle or some of his men traveled a considerable distance up the Río Grande. Meunier describes events of this period in the following manner: La Salle spent the winter sounding and reconnoitering the bay area, and in bringing the frigate *Belle* farther inside the bay. This vessel finally was caught by a sudden wind and wrecked upon "the north shore." La Salle, his brother, and fifteen men, carrying provisions on their backs, went out to explore the country northeast of the settlement and were gone six months. Meunier evidently believed that the six-month journey did not extend beyond "the bay area."[7]

La Salle then undertook another exploration to the north, with twenty men and one of the Recollect friars (Father Anastasius Douay), penetrating to the province of the Tejas. Returning after six months, they brought five horses loaded with corn and beans, for which they had traded their axes. Only five of the twenty men came back, the others having died or deserted. The deserters, says Meunier, were presumed to have eaten each other.

A third journey, also toward the Tejas land, was undertaken with the intention of proceeding to La Salle's previous settlement on the Mississippi. On a river identified by Meunier as Espíritu Santo, La Salle was murdered by "Monsieur de V.," who, feeling himself cheated and wishing to avenge the loss of his brother, shot La Salle dead.[8] The night before the surgeon (Liotot) had slain the

---

[5] Meunier (Declaration, p. 196) relates an incident that Joutel (*Journal*, p. 100) says occurred in November, 1685.

[6] Jean Cavelier, *The Journal of Jean Cavelier: The Account of a Survivor of La Salle's Texas Expedition, 1684-1688*, pp. 63, 65.

[7] Meunier, Declaration, pp. 196-197. "The north shore" where the *Belle* was wrecked evidently refers to the north side of Matagorda Peninsula, which encloses Matagorda Bay. See Plate 8, which shows a *navio quebrado* (shipwreck) at this location.

[8] Meunier, Declaration, p. 197. The use of such a name is in keeping with an apparent

Indian interpreter (Nika), a lackey of La Salle (Saget), and a lieutenant (Moranget).

Meunier himself was on La Salle's final expedition. When the cleric (Cavelier) and the others proceeded toward the land of the Cadodachos, he remained behind because of illness, along with three others. The Indians grew fond of the Frenchmen, who lived among the natives until the Spaniards brought L'Archevêque and Grollet the previous year and, on the more recent journey, Meunier and "another who is coming behind [Pierre Talon]."

While he was ill among the Indians, Meunier relates, L'Archevêque and Grollet returned with two Indians to Fort St. Louis, hoping to bring the colonists back with them to the Tejas. They found the settlement uninhabited, "some having died of the pestilence and others shot through with Indian arrows." After setting off the 150 barrels of powder, they returned to give Meunier the news.[9]

On a trip with the Tejas to the Cadodacho nation, Meunier had been told of white people from beyond the river (the Red) who had been among neighboring tribes bestowing gifts of knives and beads. He did not know their nationality.

Meunier himself had seen the "buoys" at the mouth of the Río de San Marcos that had so upset the viceregal officials. He supported De León's testimony of the vague rumors of white settlers to the east, and the great distance to their purported settlement. Still the fears of the members of the junta were not allayed. They advised immediate steps to remove the buoys; the viceroy ordered a new maritime expedition.

The frigate *Nuestra Señora de la Encarnación*, commanded by Captain Francisco de Llanos, provisioned for a three-month voyage, set sail from Veracruz on October 12. Her mission was to remove the buoys, seek an inland water approach to the Tejas

reluctance by the survivors to name the actual murderer of La Salle, the elder Duhaut. Meunier's reference to "Río del Espíritu Santo" should not be taken as proof that La Salle was killed on the Brazos River, as Herbert Eugene Bolton ("The Location of La Salle's Colony on the Gulf of Mexico," *Southwestern Historical Quarterly* 27, no. 3 [January, 1924]:171-179) suggests that it should.

[9] Meunier, Declaration, pp. 196-198. Meunier here supports De León's conclusion (refuted by L'Archevêque and not mentioned by other survivors) that an epidemic had decimated the colony's ranks.

country, map Espíritu Santo Bay, and determine the suitability of the Fort St. Louis site for a future Spanish presidio. Sailing with Llanos was Juan de Triana as pilot, Captain Gregorio de Salinas Varona in charge of land operations, and Manuel Joseph de Cárdenas y Magaña as mapmaker.[10]

The Spaniards had special reason for their seemingly inordinate concern over the report of the buoys. With a Spanish mission now established in East Texas, it was feared the objects might mark the entrance to a river affording access to the new settlement. Nevertheless, the whole affair attests to official ineptness and a bad sense of timing. The wreckage of two French ships had failed to inspire any such diligence in exploring Espíritu Santo, or San Bernardo, Bay. While the Llanos expedition was outstanding in its accomplishment, the effort should have been made at least three years earlier.

The voyage proceeded up the coast from Veracruz with no more serious mishap than a sudden gust of wind that ripped away the main topsail and split the fore-topgallant mast. A jury rig sufficed until a log was found on the beach near the mouth of San Bernardo Bay. After sounding the mouth of the Río Grande, *La Encarnación* stood off Pass Cavallo, at San Bernardo's entrance, on the twenty-fourth. Anchored in two fathoms, with mud bottom, she put the launch over to sound the passage. Thus began the remarkably accurate and detailed Cárdenas mapping, color coded in the original, that solved many of the bay's riddles (see Plate 11 in the picture section). The dotted lines indicate the exploration by water, with crosses designating the ship's anchorages from which the launch departed. Letters and numbers correspond to points mentioned in the diary.[11]

[10] Viceroy Conde de Galve, "Decreto," in "Testimonio de las Diligencias ejecutadas para quitar las Boyas ó Valisas en el Lago de San Bernardo que llaman Bahía del Espíritu Santo," A.G.I., México, 1688-1690 (61-6-21), pp. 256-260.

[11] Francisco de Llanos, "Diario y derrota del Viaje que se hecho y Ejecutado a la Bahía de San Bernardo," ibid., pp. 260-287. Manuel de Cárdenas y Magaña presents his own version ("Diario," ibid., pp. 306-321). Cárdenas's map proves beyond a doubt that the French colony was located on Garcitas Creek, on or near the site later occupied by the Spanish Presidio de Nuestra Señora de Loreto de la Bahía (see Kathryn Stoner O'Connor, *The Presidio La Bahia del Espiritu Santo de Zuniga, 1721 to 1846*, p. 10, and Bolton, "The Location of La Salle's Colony," pp. 171-179). Cárdenas's map stands out for its thoroughness and accuracy. It won him a note of special thanks from the viceroy, but nothing more.

By the end of the fourth day the explorers had sounded the entrance as far as the site of the *Aimable* disaster (Point H) and brought the frigate in that far. On October 30 they reached Sand Point. Llanos believed that the sand reef extending across the entrance of Lavaca Bay had been responsible for the failure of other maritime searchers to find the passage to La Salle's colony. Llanos, Cárdenas, and Salinas entered the bay by launch on November 1, naming it Lago de Todos Santos, for All Saints' Day. They proceeded in turn to the site of the "buoys," which they found to be upended logs, to Garcitas Creek (named Río de los Franceses), and to an Indian village, with whose inhabitants they were unable to communicate.

From the *ranchería* they continued up the Garcitas until they saw the remains of the French settlement, on the highest elevation (Pueblo de los Franceses). The buildings of Fort St. Louis had been burned by Alonso de León's party several months previously. The remains consisted of gun-carriage wheels, musket breeches, and charred planks and beams.

On another day the Llanos party explored Chocolate Bay (near present-day Port Lavaca), which Cárdenas thought might be the mouth of the Medina River mentioned in De León's diary. Exploring a creek farther up Lavaca Bay, he thought it might be the Guadalupe River.

Passing a second time by the ravaged Fort St. Louis, the explorers uncovered the French artillery pieces that De León had buried, examined them, and left them where they lay. They then rowed on to Point P, where they camped for the night before proceeding upstream until the water became too shallow for the launches.

Coming again to the drift logs at the mouth of the Lavaca River, they raised them and cut off some pieces to take to Veracruz as evidence. They ascended the Lavaca (Río de San Marcos) to the Navidad fork, just east of Vanderbilt, and followed the Navidad until a pile of drift barred the way. Cárdenas called this stream Río del Espíritu Santo, in confusion typical of this period of nascent Spanish exploration of the region.

After reconnoitering Cox and Keller bays (Points 6 and 7), the mariners crossed Lavaca Bay to camp opposite Sand Point (8). There they found a temporary camp used by the French while the colony was being moved from its first site to the second. This, they inferred, was as far as La Salle's smallest ship was able to go toward the settlement.

On November 12 the frigate weighed anchor and sailed across the main bay to Point 11, thus beginning the reconnaissance of San Bernardo Bay proper. In the days following, the launch coasted Tres Palacios Bay, then rounded the point and proceeded northeastward to the mouth of the Colorado. Cárdenas's map calls the latter stream Río de la Santísima Trinidad, borrowing again from names used by De León. The explorers ascended the river several miles.

Coasting Matagorda Peninsula, they returned to a point near Port O'Connor. There a soldier died, and his body was interred in the bay. The crew took on water and brought a log from the beach to repair the broken mast, while the officers in the launch spent several days sounding around the entrance. On November 29 the frigate *La Encarnación* crossed the bar and steered for Veracruz, to arrive December 9, 1690.[12]

The buoys on the San Marcos River had proved false, and no navigable stream to Tejas country had been found. Llanos, in his report, praised the Fort St. Louis site, which dominates the landscape, but noted the lack of building materials. The French cannon would remain buried until the Spaniards got around to building a fort of their own on the site. Thirty-one years later, in 1721, the second Marqués de San Miguel de Aguayo was responsible for building the Presidio de Nuestra Señora de Loreto on the same eminence overlooking the Garcitas. It protected the Mission Nuestra Señora del Espíritu Santo de Zúñiga, upstream and on the creek's opposite bank (see Plate 12 in the picture section).

In the meantime a junta on October 16 had ruled favorably on Massanet's proposal for intensifying the missionary effort in East Texas. De León's military plan again was shoved into the background. The stalwart Indian fighter remained in disfavor, perhaps in part because of Massanet's headstrong opposition, but also because of the unreasoned attitude toward De León's failure to investigate the spurious buoys and the rumored French settlement

[12] Llanos, "Diario," in "Testimonio de las Diligencias," pp. 264-280; Bolton, "The Location of La Salle's Colony," pp. 179-184.

to the east. One of his own officers, Captain Francisco Martínez, now was pressing charges of fraud against him in connection with purchase of supplies for the previous expedition. Using an old ruse, the junta ruled that De León's presence in Coahuila was indispensable because of the continued hostilities of the Indians. A higher court was to rule on the question of the general's indispensability; in March, 1691, before the new *entrada* was yet underway, he was removed from the Coahuila scene by death.[13]

Chosen to head the military phase of the new expedition into Texas was a comparative stranger. Domingo Terán de los Ríos never before had crossed the Río Grande. Yet he became the first man to hold the title of governor of Texas. Primarily, the new venture was designed as a missionary enterprise, charged with expanding the missions already established and founding seven others among the Tejas and the Cadodachos. It also was to search out the country for Frenchmen or intruders from any other European nation, and to explore the lands north of the Mission San Francisco de los Tejas. Terán's force of fifty soldiers, ten priests, and three lay brothers took up the march from Coahuila in mid-May. Also on the expedition was the young Frenchman, Pierre Meunier, "whom the King our Lord and the Most Excellent Lord Viceroy had sent us in his royal name to convoy and conduct the fathers of the Santo Evangelio."[14] Pierre Talon, though not specifically mentioned, probably went along as well.

Reaching the Río Grande at Paso de Francia on May 28, they remained on the right bank four days, rounding up horses scattered in a stampede. Arriving June 19 at the Guadalupe, they met a large band of Indians of the Jumano and Cíbolo nations, together with various allied tribes from Nueva Vizcaya and New Mexico, estimated to number more than two thousand. The chief who came forward to greet them was none other than Juan Xaviata, who early in 1689 had carried to Governor Pardiñas in Parral firsthand news of the demise of La Salle's settlement. With him was the Christian Indian Nicolás of the Catqueza nation. Nicolás had served Pardiñas as interpreter in the taking of depositions

---

[13] Vito Alessio Robles, *Coahuila y Texas en la época colonial*, p. 364.
[14] Domingo Terán de los Ríos, "Diario del general Domingo Terán de los Ríos, en su expedición a Texas," in Lino Gómez Canedo (ed.), *Primeras exploraciones y poblamiento de Texas (1686-1694)*, p. 183.

from the natives who had visited the Tejas and Fort St. Louis. Father Massanet found him to be "very knowledgeable of the Mexican and Spanish languages."[1][5]

It was from these peripatetic Indians, who each year journeyed eastward from La Junta de los Ríos to hunt buffalo and trade, that the Terán expedition got its first news from Mission San Francisco. From two letters the natives carried, the Spaniards learned that a severe epidemic had fallen upon the nascent mission settlement and that Father Fontcuberta had died of a fever the previous February.

Xaviata carried a commission from Pardiñas as governor of the Jumanos, another Indian as lieutenant governor. Nicolás and some of the others carried saints' images or crucifixes attesting to their conversion. These religious tokens did not place them above suspicion, however, when on the night of the twentieth the horses stampeded, with a net loss of fifty. Another twenty-five mounts were lost the same way a week later.

While Terán's force advanced slowly across Texas, the ship *Santo Cristo de San Román*, already known for having made the third and fourth maritime expeditions in search of La Salle, set sail from Veracruz for Espíritu Santo Bay on June 25. The vessel carried fifty soldiers under command of Captain Salinas Varona and a cargo of provisions. She was commanded by Captain Juan Enríquez Barroto, who had formed a part of the first expedition in search of La Salle and had been involved in the quest until it was over. With the *Santo Cristo* went a smaller vessel commanded by Joseph de Aramburu.[16]

When the Terán expedition reached the Colorado River several miles below present-day Austin, Captain Francisco Martínez took 20 men, 150 horses, and 50 pack mules and set out to rendezvous with the two ships. The extra horses and mules were for mounting Salinas's soldiers and transporting the provisions from the ships to the Mission San Francisco. With Martínez went Pierre Meunier, for ancillary to meeting the ships was seeking the other two French children still among the Karankawas of the coastal country.

---

[15] Damián Massanet, "Diario Derrotero," 1691, ibid., p. 241. Massanet identifies the nations in this band as Choma, Cantona, Chomanes, Síbola, Cholome, Catqueza, and Caynaaya.

[16] Carlos Eduardo Castañeda, *Our Catholic Heritage in Texas*, I, 365-366.

Approaching the bay on July 7, Martínez began sending up smoke signals in hope of receiving an answer from the ships. He crossed the "Arroyo de los Franceses"—Garcitas Creek—and, traveling down the right bank, soon came upon an Indian from the tribe that had yielded up the three Talon children the year before. The savage could give no news concerning ships in the bay. Two leagues farther downstream the Spaniards came to the ashes of Fort St. Louis, where they found no signs whatsoever of anyone's having visited the tragic site. Martínez, with four companions, traveled down the Garcitas until he reached the bay, and, seeing no evidence of a ship, he returned to camp.

Continuing to reconnoiter the upper end of Lavaca Bay, Martínez on July 9 reached a *ranchería* of Indians on the bay shore. "Seeing us, they got into their canoes, and likewise made some smoke signals. As soon as I reached the place where, on the previous journey, Governor Alonso de León took the three French children and the woman [*sic*] from them, I sent Pedro, the Frenchman [Pierre Meunier], our interpreter, on ahead. He called to them, and, seeing him alone, one of the said Indians approached him and told him that they were our friends."[17]

Overcoming their fear, others joined him, and Martínez instructed the young Frenchman to assure them of the Spaniards' friendship and to inquire if they had seen a ship. They replied that since a vessel carrying corn or flour had been lost five moons previously, half a league off the bar at the bay's mouth, they had seen none. Martínez began to bargain through the interpreter for the two French children whom he had been informed were in their village. He promised horses in exchange for the children, enmity of his troops if the Indians refused. But the Indians vowed they did not have the white children. For the moment Martínez accepted this answer and left with the natives a written message for Captain Salinas, asking them to take it to the mouth of the bay.

On the tenth, pursuing a lead tendered one of his soldiers by an Indian, Martínez overtook some of the same natives and obtained the release of a little French boy. The lad was not the Talon boy he had expected but Eustache Bréman. Since Martínez had under-

---

[17] José Antonio Pichardo, *Pichardo's Treatise on the Limits of Louisiana and Texas*, I, 467.

stood that there were two Talon children, this seemed to indicate there were three children instead of two. He gave the Indians a horse and some presents in exchange for the boy but held one of the natives as hostage. He released the other two with instructions to bring the remaining two children in order to secure the release of their companion. One of the two natives replied that some Indians from farther inland had taken the girl[18] but promised to bring the other boy. Martínez remained in camp and waited, continuing to send up smoke signals for the two ships.

About noon on July 12 one of the Karankawas returned with Jean Baptiste Talon and news that no ships were to be found in the bay. Martínez rewarded him with two horses and some tobacco, then wrote another message for Captain Salinas informing him that he was departing for the Tejas mission and would return later to see if the ships had come. Breaking camp the same day, the captain and his soldiers began the march northward, leaving the little French girl, if indeed she existed, to her unknown fate among the untamed Indians of the wilderness coast. The gathering of the survivors of the ill-conceived, ill-planned, ill-timed, and ill-placed French settlement on the Texas coast now was as complete as it ever would be.

As Martínez and his soldiers rode over the northern horizon, sails appeared out of the blue haze beyond Pass Cavallo at the mouth of Espíritu Santo Bay. The two ships from Veracruz arrived just a few hours too late to make contact with the troops that had awaited them. Martínez returned to the Terán camp on the Colorado on July 17.

During his absence Indians had come from the Tejas mission. Through Bernardino, the Tejas chief who had gone to Mexico with De León the year before and now was returning, they related that the priests at Mission San Francisco were well and tending a large corn crop planted the previous spring. Massanet then dispatched two natives of the Cantona nation with a letter for the two priests at San Francisco. The message informed them that the caravan

---

[18] Martínez evidently was mistaken about the girl, for the Talons (Pierre Margry [ed.], *Découvertes et établissements des Français dans l'Ouest et dans le Sud de l'Amérique septentrionale*, III, 614-615) list their sister, Marie Madelaine, as the only girl captive, and she had been rescued the year before.

would proceed to the mission as soon as the soldiers returned from the coast.

But from the Tejas village, there was other news. Four Indians from the Cadodacho nation had brought word that ten white men, companions of those who had lived at the settlement on the bay, had come bringing many gifts from the direction of the sunrise, where they lived on the bank of a river.[19]

Martínez's return without having made contact with the ships at the bay touched off a controversy between Governor Terán and Father Massanet. The governor favored sending a new detachment to await the vessels while the main force remained in camp on the Colorado. Massanet, supported by the other priests, strenuously objected. Terán yielded, but as the expedition advanced, the pace was so slow that the religious, on reaching the Trinity, pressed on in advance of the main body without bothering to inform the governor.

On reaching Mission San Francisco, Terán learned that a second mission, Santísimo Nombre de María, had been founded on the banks of the Neches River, about five miles east of the first. The Indians, however, were responding to the missionary effort with growing impudence. They were more interested in stealing the Spaniards' horses than in hearing the gospel. Terán, having suffered disillusionment almost from the start of the expedition, now was possessed by a feeling of utter uselessness concerning the whole affair. Fearful that the supplies would become exhausted, he waited twenty days, then marched with most of his soldiers for the coast. Hoping to find the supplies and reinforcements that had been sent by sea, he was determined to return immediately to Mexico if they had not arrived.

Reaching Fort St. Louis, however, he found Captain Salinas Varona waiting, the two vessels moored in the bay. Salinas, much to Terán's disappointment, had brought new instructions from the viceroy that left him no safe recourse but to continue the exploration.

By the time the supplies were transported from the bay to the two missions and Terán was ready to reconnoiter the country

[19]Massanet, "Diario Derrotero," in Canedo, *Primeras exploraciones*, p. 249.

toward the land of the Cadodachos, it was November. Accompanied by Father Massanet, two other missionaries, and a number of soldiers, he began the march to the northeast on November 6. Severe winter weather closed in to turn the journey into a nightmare. Trudging through snow and sleet, the expedition on November 28 reached the native villages on the "Río de los Cadodachos."[20] The Indians were friendly, and no evidence was found that Frenchmen were living in the region. But even the religious, recognizing the lack of supplies, admitted the futility of attempting to found the four projected missions.

On the return march, begun December 5, the weather worsened, and nearly all the horses died in the persistent blizzard. The travelers were forced to walk most of the distance back to the settlement on the Neches. Terán, over Massanet's vociferous objections, commandeered the mission's horses for the return to Mexico. When the governor departed on January 9, six of Massanet's disheartened friars went with him.[21]

Swollen streams and inclement weather continued to impede the March, as Terán's troops made their way toward the bay. Not until March 5 did they rendezvous with Captain Barroto, who in the intervening months had made a trip to Veracruz for additional supplies.

Terán remained in camp on the bay more than two weeks, writing his reports and collecting testimony from participants in the *entrada* to prove that he had not been remiss in his efforts. But there was no concealing the fact that the expedition was a miserable failure. It had been plagued by bad management from the beginning. Yet in one respect Terán claimed success: he had proved the nonexistence of the French among the Cadodachos. There was, he insisted, nothing further to fear from this foreign enemy whose hapless minions on the Texas shore had caused such grave concern.

The governor, leaving his troops to return to Coahuila in the charge of Captain Martínez, boarded one of the vessels for the return to Mexico. Captain Barroto set an easterly course, bent on carrying out his instructions to explore the mouth of the Río de la

[20] Presently known as the Red River, probably in present-day Miller County, Arkansas.
[21] Terán, "Diario," in Canedo, *Primeras exploraciones*, p. 213.

Palizada—the Mississippi—but foul weather thwarted even this achievement. The ships finally turned toward Veracruz, where they arrived April 15.

In the face of Terán's failure, interest in the conquest of Texas waned. The missions were failing, and despite a relief expedition in 1693, led by Captain Salinas Varona, the new governor of Coahuila, they soon were abandoned. Father Massanet and the rest of his friars, defeated and heartsick, recrossed the Río Grande on February 17, 1694. They left behind only four soldiers who had deserted Spanish service to live among the natives.

The Sieur de la Salle had caused the Spaniards to make an inordinate expenditure of resources to penetrate Texas at a time and under circumstances not of their own choosing.[22] They must now withdraw and begin anew. The road back was more than twenty years long.

[22] Robert S. Weddle, *San Juan Bautista: Gateway to Spanish Texas*, p. 17.

20. THE FRENCH WEDGE

We left France on the 15th of October, 1698 . . . and arrived on the coast of Florida on the 24th of [January, 1699]. We followed the coast . . . making continual soundings in the long-boats for the purpose of discovering a port. . . . We would not have been obliged to go further than Pensacola-de-Galvez, had we not found the port occupied by the Spaniards, who have been established there since September, 1698."

—An officer of the frigate *François*
French, *Historical Collections*, n.s., p. 21

As the Terán expedition withdrew from Texas, it did so with the knowledge that the last remnants of La Salle's colony had been removed. La Salle himself was dead as the result of the mutinous bloodletting that claimed seven others before it finally ran its savage course. There remained, of the 180 persons in the colony when La Salle had set out on his first exploration from the bay, only the nine captured by the Spaniards and the six who had returned to France by way of Canada. Of the nine, several would yet participate in the making of history in the South and the Southwest, in a way their leader scarcely had envisioned when he brought them to the wilderness shore.

The four-year manhunt by the Spaniards likewise had brought to the forefront the names of some whose role in the history of the southern United States was not yet done. The most valiant of the searchers, Alonso de León, had followed La Salle to a premature grave. His energies spent from having led five expeditions, and from the rigors of founding a new colony in a province constantly harassed by savage Indians, the general had passed from the scene in March, 1691.

Of Fray Damián Massanet, who returned from the land of the Tejas so discouraged and soulsick that even the name of that Indian tribe was odious to his ears,[1] it has been said that he disappeared from history.[2] Though he never reappeared on the northern frontier, this assessment is hyperbolic. Massanet returned briefly to the missionary college at Querétaro, then served in the province of Michoacán. In 1715 he appears as the *visitador* of the Franciscan province of Guatemala. As late as October, 1716, he was serving as secretary to the provincial, Fray José González, on his official visit to the Colegio del Cristo Crucificado.[3]

But Fray Damián's career had passed its zenith when he withdrew from the Tejas. He felt his failure so deeply that he spurned official requests to suggest other mission sites on the northern frontier, yet blamed his inefficacy on others. Father Massanet had a strong personality, and his writings must be counted among the most important sources of knowledge of the beginnings of Texas.[4] Yet he suffered from human weakness and fell far short—as have many clerics and laymen before and since—of the Example he sought to follow. Unfortunately, his pettiness had its effect on history, the same as his more admirable qualities.

There was one in Massanet's company of friars who was made of sterner stuff: Fray Francisco Hidalgo. It was he who lamented the unfinished work at Mission San Francisco de los Tejas, and he who contrived, after more than twenty years of effort, to bring about renewal of the abandoned task.[5]

The abortive attempt to win the Tejas, however, was by no means the only effort to which the Spaniards would devote them-

---

[1] Robert S. Weddle, *San Juan Bautista: Gateway to Spanish Texas*, p. 18; Juan Domingo Arricivita, *Crónica seráfica y apostólica del Colegio de propaganda fide de la Santa Cruz de Querétaro en la Nueva España, segunda parte*, p. 221.

[2] Herbert Eugene Bolton (ed.), *Spanish Exploration in the Southwest, 1542-1706*, p. 350.

[3] Lino G. Canedo in Isidro Félix de Espinosa, *Crónica de los colegios de propaganda fide de la Nueva España*, pp. 681-682 n.

[4] Bolton, *Spanish Exploration*, p. 350. Canedo in Espinosa, *Crónica*, p. 682 n.

[5] Weddle, *San Juan Bautista*, pp. 94-95, 97-99. For a biographical sketch of Hidalgo see Arricivita, *Crónica seráfica*, pp. 206-226.

selves as a result of the La Salle episode. One important fruit of the search was the rediscovery of Pensacola Bay, a site that had figured prominently in early Spanish activities in Florida. New interest in this region sprang from fear that the French might attempt to follow up their failure on the Texas coast by planting a colony elsewhere on the Gulf of Mexico. There appeared to be no bay more suitable than that of Pensacola. This was the bay to which Tristán de Luna y Arrellano had brought fifteen hundred colonists near the middle of thy sixteenth century, only to have the remnants removed the following year by his successor, Angel de Villafañe. It also was the one that Juan Jordán de Reina, diarist of the Romero-Barroto expedition, had termed "the best bay I had ever seen in my life."[6]

But the chief advocate of fortifying the site was not Jordán—or Romero or Barroto—but Captain Andrés de Pez, whose ascending star would shine more brightly than that of any other searcher. Although Pez had commanded three of the maritime expeditions in search of La Salle, one of which had coasted Florida, he had never been inside Pensacola Bay. Nevertheless, he drew up a memorial detailing the many advantages of the region and set about his effort to win approval for his plan. Shortly after the news reached Mexico City that Alonso de León had found Fort St. Louis and captured some of its survivors, Pez presented his memorial to the viceroy, Conde de Galve. The bay region possessed such advantages, he said—abundant fruit, timber, and buffalo, as well as an easily defensible entrance to the bay itself—that it was incumbent upon Spain to fortify and settle it before the French did. Since the French had gone to great lengths to plant a colony at such a worthless site as San Bernardo (Espíritu Santo) Bay, he reasoned, they may well cast a covetous eye upon a more suitable port like Pensacola. Should these colonial rivals of Spain occupy this bay, he averred, they would be able to attack at will the galleons that sailed the coastal waters of Florida; they even might form a communication link with their settlements in Canada and would be in position to invade the frontier provinces of New Spain.[7]

The viceroy quickly grasped the validity of Pez's reasoning.

[6] Juan Jordán de Reina, "Diario y derrotero del viaxe," A.G.I., México, 1685-1688 (61-6-20), p. 29.

[7] Andrés de Pez, "Memorial," in Irving A. Leonard (trans.), *Spanish Approach to Pensacola, 1689-1693*, pp. 77-92.

Since Pez proposed suppressing the post at St. Augustine in order to divert its resources to this new enterprise, however, the Conde de Galve resolved to send the naval officer to Spain to plead his own case. In the summer of 1689, Pez sailed for Spain. As visible evidence of French designs on Spanish territory he took with him the two French captives whom De León had just brought back from Texas: L'Archevêque and Grollet.[8]

While General De León and Father Massanet were making preparations for the mission-founding expedition of 1690, Captain Pez was in Madrid sounding out the channels of official procedure. He found them tortuous. Not until October of that year did his plan come up for formal discussion by the *junta de guerra*. At the council's hands the naval officer did not fare well. In a majority report dripping with innuendo and sarcasm, the Marqués de la Granja carefully dissected the plan. He dealt the Pez proposal a blow that under ordinary circumstances would have been lethal.[9] King Charles II, however, rejected the council's recommendations and resolved that the plan of Captain Pez, with the exception of that part which called for abandonment of St. Augustine, should be carried out.

The dissatisfaction of the junta was to surface in an effort to put as many obstacles as possible in Pez's path. In September, 1691, the body of advisers warned the king against acting upon the Pez memorial without first verifying its claims. It was evident from the diary of the Pez-Gamarra expedition, it was noted, that he had not examined the bay personally, or even landed on its shores. The viceroy should be instructed to send capable pilots and engineers to examine Pensacola Bay, while making thorough land and sea explorations of the region between Pensacola and Espíritu Santo Bay.[10]

But the old confusion concerning the appellation "Espíritu Santo Bay" persisted. The junta surely had in mind the bay on which La Salle's colony had been situated. Colonial officials, however, seem to have preferred to call this bay San Bernardo, and when the name Espíritu Santo was used, they took it to mean

---

[8] Viceroy Conde de Galve to Marqués de los Vélez, June 29, 1689, ibid., pp. 99-102.
[9] Marqués de la Granja, "Opinion," ibid., pp. 103-110.
[10] "Report of War Committee," September 27, 1691, ibid., pp. 132-136.

Mobile Bay. The proposed land expedition, as it developed, was of little consequence anyway.

The king accepted the junta's recommendations this time and issued his formal decree implementing them June 26, 1692.[11] Captain Pez, disgruntled at the lost motion engendered by the official bickering, already was in Cádiz preparing to sail for America.

While Pez battled official red tape, the two French prisoners he had brought to court languished in the royal jail. Evidently having arrived in Madrid by early January, 1690, they petitioned the court five months later for two reales per day for sustenance for the "poor, dying foreigners who have no recourse." The request finally was granted after another five months. Then, except for paying the stipend, Spanish officials evidently gave them little thought for almost another two years.[12]

Early in May, 1692, with Pez already in Cádiz, the two Frenchmen submitted another petition. They had, it was pointed out, been in jail two and one-half years without having committed a crime. In addition, they had been forced to live for five years—a slight exaggeration—a life of severe deprivation among barbarous Indians. They asked either to be returned to the Indies with Captain Pez to serve the king of Spain or to be given their freedom outright.[13]

In considering the matter, the Junta de Guerra de Indias reviewed the prisoners' connection with La Salle's intrusion, their life among the Indians, and their capture by Alonso de León. Not without sympathy for the hardships they had suffered, the junta nevertheless could not recommend that they be set free. On the other hand, the council reasoned, the two men did not deserve to be placed in stocks; to allow them to associate with other prisoners would be to risk spreading in France the knowledge they had acquired of the region from which they had been taken. Such an outcome could prejudice seriously the interests of Spain. To

[11] Charles II, "Royal Decree," ibid., pp. 138-141.

[12] Jean L'Archevêque and Jacques Grollet, Petition, May 27, 1690, A.G.I., México, 1688-1690 (61-6-21), p. 242; Council to the treasurer, November 8, 1690, ibid., p. 243. It may be assumed that L'Archevêque was the author of the petition, since Grollet was illiterate.

[13] L'Archevêque and Grollet, Petition, undated, ibid., p. 245.

keep them as they were, in an isolated cell of the royal jail, in peacetime, would mean that the French king might insist on their repatriation. For the same reason they could not be sent to work in the mines of Almadén. The best solution, therefore, seemed to be to send them back to America, where the viceroy might order them as he saw fit, and where they would be beyond reach of any claim by Louis XIV.[14]

L'Archevêque and Grollet were given a stipend with which to clothe themselves and were to be delivered to Captain Pez at Cádiz. Pez was to allow them each a soldier's ration for the voyage. The prisoners, reconciled to turning their backs on their native land forever, were jubilant at the decision. Reported one official, "They go very gladly in the service of His Majesty."[15] Their back allowance was paid up, and they departed for Cádiz, probably early in July, 1692. Their names appear again in connection with the resettlement of New Mexico, from which the natives had driven the Spaniards in 1680.

Pez, who shortly after his return to Mexico became admiral of the windward fleet, was chosen to command the Pensacola exploration from the sea. The viceroy chose Dr. Carlos de Sigüenza y Góngora, eminent scholar and scientist, professor of mathematics at the Royal University of Mexico, and chief cosmographer of New Spain, to assist him. Picked to lead the land expedition was Laureano de Torres y Ayala, governor-elect of Florida.

The Pez-Sigüenza expedition sailed from Veracruz on March 25, 1693, setting a course directly for Pensacola, with orders to sound the bay and locate sites for presidio and settlement. The reconnaissance then was to extend to Mobile Bay and the Río de la Palizada, with Sigüenza to prepare maps and scientific description of the places visited.

On taking possession of Pensacola Bay in the name of the king, they rechristened it "La Bahía de Santa María de Galve." Sigüenza, recalling that the expedition of Luna y Arrellano had entered the bay on St. Mary's Day (August 14), suggested the name, linking the names of the viceroy and the Virgin. The two leaders then proceeded to explore the bay in company of their pilot, Pedro

---

[14] Enrique Enríquez and others, Report of Junta de Guerra de Indias, Madrid, May 6, 1692, ibid., pp. 237-240.
[15] Antonio Ortiz de Otálora, Report of Council of June 21, 1692, ibid., pp. 249-250.

Fernández Cenrra, and Captain Juan Jordán de Reina. It was this latter officer who, as diarist of the first maritime expedition sent in search of La Salle, had written such a glowing report. He was to be closely associated with its later occupation.

As they explored, they christened the prominent landmarks: the point on the east side of the entrance was named Punta de Sigüenza, the one on the left Punta de San Carlos; a ravine that enters the bay in the southern part of the present city of Pensacola was named Barranca de Santo Tomé; the Yellow River, Río Jordán; the Escambia River, Río de Jovenazo, and the one to the east of it, Río del Almirante, in honor of Admiral Pez. Twice during the exploration the group frightened away bands of Indians but never succeeded in making contact with the natives.

The reconnaissance completed, the ships took on wood and water, and one installed a new mainmast. Leaving a large cross standing on Sigüenza Point, the explorers sailed out of the bay and proceeded westward along the coast. Soundings at Mobile Bay revealed a channel depth of only twenty palmos—considered too shallow to warrant further exploration. On May 2, at 29° 27', sixteen men left the main vessel in a shallop to explore the ragged coastline in search of the mouth of the Mississippi. On May 5 the small vessel sailed along the swampy coast, impeded by mudbanks and floating logs. Surrounded by flocks of pelicans and screeching gulls, the men dropped anchor in Breton Sound. The following day they reached the cape that the Gamarra-Pez expedition, on August 7, 1687, had named San Luis (North Pass), and viewed one of the mouths of the great river. Attempting to enter, they found the mouth obstructed by sand bars and a mass of driftwood, with current so swift that entry in the shallop was impossible. But Pez, who had examined the many mouths of the mighty river in 1687, added to his knowledge of the nature of the stream, which had been passed up repeatedly as affording no likely place for ships to enter or a settlement to be formed. Still it appears doubtful that he fully realized its significance. The boatmen back on board the ship, they set sail for Veracruz, which they reached in five days, on May 13, 1693.[16]

[16] Andrés de Pez, "Report," Mexico City, June 1, 1693, in Leonard, *Spanish Approach*, pp. 149-150; Carlos de Sigüenza y Góngora, "Description of the Bay of Santa Maria de Galve . . . ," ibid., pp. 154-180.

Both Pez and Sigüenza, in their official reports, stressed the strategic position of Pensacola Bay and the urgency of fortifying it. The French king already had made one attempt to plant a colony at the mouth of the Río de la Palizada to facilitate communication with the settlements of New France. The plan had failed only because of La Salle's misfortune. When France was free of the war in which she presently was engaged, she almost certainly would renew the effort to secure a port on the gulf shore.

Sigüenza then issued a second report in which he praised the Bay of Santa María de Galve as "the finest jewel possessed by His Majesty . . . not only here in America, but in all his kingdom."[17] Deep-draft vessels could anchor at the beach itself without danger of running aground, and, in his hyperbolic description, the bay was capacious enough to harbor all the fleets of the world. With lumber and masts for vessels of all sizes available on its shores, it was large enough for a hundred shipyards. If Spain did not occupy it, some foreign nation almost certainly would.

Although Torres y Ayala had not yet made his land expedition, a junta met early in June and decided that the blanket permission accorded the viceroy by the king to put the bay in a state of defense should be exercised at once. It named Pez, Sigüenza, and the *factor*, Sebastián de Guzmán, to a committee charged with drawing the procedure for doing so. The panel soon bogged down in disagreement. Sigüenza and Guzmán favored sending a small force immediately to assert the king's claim, but Pez opposed such a plan. A weak garrison, he maintained, would merely invite attack, either by Spain's colonial rivals or by the voracious pirates who still prowled the gulf. The outgrowth of the dispute was that the viceroy once again sent Pez to Spain to seek necessities of men and supplies for founding the settlement.[18]

Meanwhile, the expedition of Governor Laureano de Torres y Ayala was carried out, accomplishing little that had not already been done better by the Pez-Sigüenza exploration. Torres, accompanied by Fray Rodrigo de la Barreda and twenty-five soldiers, reached Apalache on May 15 from Havana to begin the reconnaissance. With reinforcements and Indian guides obtained there, they

[17] Carlos de Sigüenza y Góngora, "Report," June 1, 1693, ibid., p. 193.
[18] William Edward Dunn, *Spanish and French Rivalry in the Gulf Region of the United States, 1678-1702*, pp. 168-169.

proceeded in June to Pensacola, arriving on July 2. A vessel sent to follow the coast from Apalache to Pensacola was found waiting in the bay. Torres's men found the Panzacola village deserted. The native guides told them that this tribe at last had been exterminated in their war with the Mobilas. Torres then proceeded to duplicate the efforts of Sigüenza and Pez, examining the area in the same careful manner. Plans for continuing to Mobile Bay by land were abandoned on advice of the guides, who warned that intervening swamps and creeks would make travel difficult. The vessel made a ten-day voyage to Mobile Bay, however, during which this site was examined thoroughly. After writing a report to the viceroy and the king, describing Pensacola as a good port that easily could be fortified, Torres departed August 5 for St. Augustine.[19] His expedition had been delayed until it had little bearing on plans for occupying Pensacola Bay.

By December, Pez was in Spain, armed with all kinds of documents, as well as arguments, for pushing his advocacy of the occupation of Pensacola. But he found that resistance among the members of the War Council had melted. As a result of their recommendations, a royal decree issued June 13, 1694, instructed the viceroy to proceed with the occupation and fortification of Santa María de Galve.

While opposition in Spain had waned, however, so in New Spain had interest. The Conde de Galve, still a strong proponent of the settlement, pleaded a lack of resources, which somehow failed to come from Spain as expected, and when he died early in 1696 no action had been taken. Not until after the Treaty of Ryswick was signed September 20, 1697, restoring peace to the nations of Europe, were the old fears of French aggression revived sufficiently to end the period of inaction.

The year 1698 brought fresh reports that Louis XIV was having four vessels fitted out preparatory to sending families from the Caribbean islands to settle on the gulf coast. Spanish officialdom roused to action. On April 19 a royal decree called for making the founding of a presidio at Pensacola the empire's most urgent business. With this new cedula went orders for raising the men and supplies that the Conde de Galve had so long sought. The new

[19] Laureano de Torres y Ayala, "Journal," Leonard, *Spanish Approach*, pp. 228-254.

viceroy, José Sarmiento de Valladares, Count of Moctezuma, was commanded to begin occupying La Bahía de Santa María de Galve. But reliance was not to be placed on this measure alone. Secret orders were issued to two other officers giving them a responsibility for ensuring that the fortification of Santa María de Galve was carried out.

Admiral Pez had fallen under a cloud the year before, and his association with the enterprise, for all practical purposes, was ended. In 1697 he had been accused of cowardice and neglect of duty in connection with a battle with pirates off the coast of Cuba. Although he continued to command the windward fleet, he was not cleared of charges until 1701. In the interim his prestige suffered. Even Don Carlos de Sigüenza y Góngora, who had been unstinting in praise of Pez during their 1693 exploration, now stepped forward to criticize him. Sigüenza, asked again to recommend procedure for occupying Pensacola, used the occasion to berate his former associate. The original Pez memorial, he intimated, had been a plagiarism. The document had been the work of Juan Enríquez Barroto—who incidentally was one of Sigüenza's former students—but Barroto, being of retiring nature, had not pressed the matter. Pez, then, had appropriated the report and claimed it as his own. The admiral, according to his critic, had gone to Spain unnecessarily to promote the project in order to increase the benefit he himself might derive from it. His selfish motives had occasioned the long delay in carrying out the enterprise and had burdened the royal treasury unduly.[20] Sigüenza's remarks were reminiscent of the vilification of Alonso de León by Father Massanet.

Pez being out of the picture, the viceroy chose another prominent naval officer to head the enterprise: Andrés de Arriola, famed for having set a new record for navigation to and from the Philippines in 1694. Arriola, while leading a maritime expedition against a pirate fleet that was preying on gulf shipping, had entered Pensacola Bay in 1695 and also had approached the mouth of the Mississippi. Arriola was forthright in stating his belief that the wrong location for settlement had been chosen. The real objective of the French, he maintained, was the Río de la Palizada, ob-

[20] Dunn, *Spanish and French Rivalry*, pp. 175-178.

viously the river for which La Salle had been searching when his misfortunes carried him beyond it to San Bernardo Bay. Nevertheless, the king's orders had to be carried out, and Arriola stood ready to do what he could to that end. As his second in command he was given a soldier who had played an important part in the search for La Salle—De León's old lieutenant, Francisco Martínez. A military engineer named Jaime Franck was chosen to supervise the building of fortifications. On October 15 they sailed from Veracruz with three vessels and a crew composed largely of conscripts, beggars, and convicts. After a stormy voyage they reached Pensacola on November 21 to find it already occupied by Captain Juan Jordán de Reina and a force of fifty soldiers from Havana.

The previous April, when the Council of the Indies had placed top priority on fortification of Pensacola, Jordán and Captain Martín de Aranguren Zavala each had been given secret and separate orders. Zavala at that time commanded two vessels being made ready at Cádiz to go in search of overdue treasure galleons from South America, which it was feared had been victimized by pirates. Zavala, should he find on reaching Havana that the galleons were safe, was to proceed to Veracruz and add his force to the expedition being sent to Pensacola by the viceroy. Jordán's orders were to embark on one of Zavala's vessels as far as Havana. There he was to requisition a frigate, men, arms, and supplies from the port governor and proceed to Pensacola Bay to hold it until the expedition from Mexico arrived. Two of the three plans formulated by the home government for occupation of Pensacola succeeded in reaching the site more or less on schedule, with Jordán and his force from Havana being the first to arrive.[21]

Under Franck's direction the Presidio of San Carlos de Austria, made of pine logs, rose near the Barranca de Santo Tomé (see Plate 13 in the picture section). Its redoubts overlooking the mouth of the bay bristled with sixteen guns. The plan to build a second fort on the eastern point, Punta de Sigüenza, was abandoned as impractical because the site was deemed too swampy. In fact, the enthusiasm of the builders for the entire project waned rapidly. Neither Arriola nor Franck was able to see the merits

[21] Ibid., pp. 178-181.

extolled a few years previously by Pez and Sigüenza. The naval officer, viewing the inhospitality of the site, remained convinced that the French could have no designs on it, that their real objective would be the Mississippi instead. The military engineer apparently shared these views.

Meanwhile, the convicts brought from Veracruz proved worse than useless. Forty of them deserted in a body. Though most soon were captured, they still created more problems than they solved. Food was scarce, thievery rampant. The camp splintered into vindictive factions, with quarreling and fighting a constant bane to those in charge. Then, on January 3, 1699, fire leveled eight of the settlement's buildings, including the chapel, Captain Jordán's quarters, and the main storehouse. Beset by such difficulties, Arriola dispatched a vessel to Mexico with an appeal for aid. With it went the melancholy reports of Arriola and Franck.

A few weeks later a series of resounding cannon shots split the misty morn, heralding the arrival of the very threat these miserable minions of King Charles II had come to forestall. Like ghosts out of a sepulcher the outline of five ships took shape through the fog at the harbor's mouth. The morning sun quickly burned away the shroud and a gentle breeze unfurled the limp cloth that draped from the command vessel's mizzen. Her colors were those of France.

The Spanish flag promptly rose above the unfinished log structure on shore, as Arriola deployed his small fleet of two vessels in defense of the port entrance. Martínez, the sergeant major, took charge of the presidio, granting the deserters hasty pardon to station them along the parapets. But the French had not come for confrontation. The following day Arriola permitted a launch bearing the emissary of the French naval commander, the Marquis de Chasteaumorant, to enter the bay, the envoy and one companion to come ashore. From this representative the Spanish officers received a spurious report of the expedition's purpose: to reconnoiter the Gulf of Mexico and to seek out some Canadian renegades believed to be harboring in the region.

In reality, the French had come to plant a settlement. The name of Chasteaumorant, though it actually was he who commanded the vessels, was but a front for Pierre Le Moyne d'Iberville. The mission was "to found, on the Mexican Gulf, a colony to be named Louisiana."[22] The report of preparations for such an expedition received the previous year had been no idle rumor.

Chasteaumorant, through his envoy, asked permission for his ships to enter the bay to take on wood and water. In return he would gladly furnish the Spaniards provisions from the ships, should they be in need. The envoy freely answered questions concerning the strength of the squadron, whose flagship, the *François*, carried fifty-eight guns. The *Marin* had thirty-eight, the *Badine* thirty-two, the two ketches six guns each.

Arriola, however, steadfastly refused to permit the vessels to enter the harbor, saying that his orders from the king strictly forbade it. Instead he sent Francisco Martínez, along with a pilot and a number of other men, back with the envoy to guide the French ships to a safer place on the coast where they might obtain the needed wood and water. Once again Martínez's fluency in the French language served in good stead, as it had in dealings with La Salle's survivors in the Texas wilderness.

The Spaniards from the destitute colony gratefully accepted the food and drink tendered by their hosts on the *François*, while gleaning all the information they could. They learned that the expedition carried one thousand men, together with cattle, horses, and supplies far more abundant than would seem necessary for the kind of mission the envoy had described. Martínez observed that the two vessels—said to be captured corsairs—were kept some distance away. He surmised that they contained women and children destined for the founding of a colony.

The *sargento mayor* found most interesting the Frenchmen's choice of a pilot and interpreter: he was the notorious pirate, Laurens de Graff[23]—"Lorencillo," as the Spaniards called him—

[22] José Antonio Pichardo, *Pichardo's Treatise on the Limits of Louisiana and Texas*, I, 232. See letter of anonymous officer of the *François* in B. F. French, *Historical Collections of Louisiana and Florida*, new series, pp. 21-22.

[23] French, *Historical Collections*, p. 34; Pierre Margry (ed.), *Découvertes et établissements des Français dans l'Ouest et dans le Sud de l'Amérique septentrionale*, IV, xxiv. Margry (p. 88) reproduces a letter from Iberville to the minister of marine, dated December 19, 1698, stating that De Graff had told him he had engaged "a Flemish-Spanish pilot" who had taken part in the search for La Salle. This unidentified pilot had been sent to discover "all the south coast of Florida," De Graff claimed, and had told him of a good harbor or river fifty or sixty leagues west of Apalache, where the Spaniards planned to settle to keep other nations out. It was this harbor that Iberville was seeking.

who had been one of the two leaders in the rape of Campeche in 1685, and of Veracruz two years before that. Eagerly, the French pressed for information on the gulf region and its ports: the Río de la Palizada, San Bernardo Bay, the Río Bravo, and the Pánuco. But Martínez was wary. All these places, he said, were shallow and uninviting.

Instead of accepting the assistance of his Spanish guests, however, Chasteaumorant wrote a letter to Arriola again requesting permission to enter the bay. Again Arriola refused. The following day French boats were observed in the channel taking soundings, in the charge of "Lorencillo." When Arriola sent an officer to order them to cease, they obligingly complied. On January 30, after sending a farewell message to Arriola protesting his lack of hospitality but thanking him for his courtesy, Chasteaumorant sailed westward.[24]

For Spain the events that followed this first encounter between Spanish forces and the well-known Iberville expedition were tragically inept and indecisive. While Arriola could do no more than speculate upon the real intentions of the French aboard the vessels, his gravest suspicions later were justified. Iberville's forces, having landed at Santo Domingo, where they were reinforced by De Graff and his buccaneers, had failed to obtain accurate information on the location of the Mississippi. Not suspecting that Pensacola was occupied, they had decided to sail for the Florida coast and follow the shoreline to the river's mouth, thus avoiding La Salle's error. From Pensacola they passed Mobile Bay and proceeded westward until March 2, when they entered the mouth of the Mississippi. Then, before Iberville returned to France to report his success and make plans for fostering the new colony, a fort was built at temporary Biloxi. A full year was to elapse before the Spaniards had definite knowledge of the colony's existence.

Hardly had the French sails disappeared on the western horizon when Arriola called his officers into council. In accord with their decision, he took one of his vessels and sailed on February 2 for Veracruz. Six days later Martínez sent a pilot and four men to Mobile Bay, where they found signs of the French, but no ships were to be seen.

[24] This account summarizes that given in Dunn, *Spanish and French Rivalry*, pp. 185-190.

Arriola's diligence at Santa María de Galve might have saved the gulf coast for Spain had it not been for the indecision that followed. On reaching Mexico he found all-out preparations underway to repel a Scotch settlement on the Isthmus of Darién. In response to Arriola's appeal, viceregal officials decided the French posed the more serious threat and should be dealt with first. But developments caused them to vascilate. In April the decision was reversed; better to be invaded by French Catholics than Scotch Calvinists. Captain Zavala, still in Veracruz with his small fleet, was directed to sail for Havana and thence to Cartagena to assume command of forces being organized for the expulsion of the Scots. When the mission was completed, he was to return to Veracruz for further orders.

The deliberation with which Zavala proceeded to carry out his instructions fell short of the urgency demanded by the dual threat to Spain's possessions. It was August before he reached Havana to receive the welcome news that the Scots had retired from Darién of their own accord. Instead of returning to Veracruz he set sail for Spain, taking with him all the forces that might have been available for expulsion of the French from the mouth of the Mississippi. For the beleaguered government of New Spain, there was little comfort in the fact that Zavala was placed under arrest and severely censured after he reached the homeland.

By this time the French scare had given way to alarm over the threatening posture of the English. The garrison at Pensacola was reduced to starvation. Many died from malnutrition, others went mad. Jordán and his men mutinied and won the right of a separate command from that of Martínez.[25]

In view of continued rumors of an English settlement west of Mobile Bay, Martínez twice sent reports to Veracruz. As a result an order was dispatched to Havana for Captain Zavala to reconnoiter the gulf coast and exterminate any foreigners who had settled there. But Zavala, of course, had removed himself from the scene, having already sailed homeward.

Finally, in late October, provision was made by a *junta general* to send Arriola to drive out the English. He was provided with a twenty-six-gun frigate in addition to the vessel that recently had

[25] Ibid., pp. 191-197.

brought Martínez's reports and a cargo of ailing men from Pensacola. Added to his force were another hundred men from the slums and prisons of Mexico. Still protesting the conditions at Pensacola and advocating its abandonment, Arriola at last set sail to return to his post in December. In March he sailed westward with four vessels to seek the rumored English settlement.

Some distance west of Mobile Bay the Spaniards overtook a small boat flying the English flag. The occupants of the craft, however, were not English but French from the fort at Biloxi, and the grand hoax of Iberville's settlers at last was revealed. Proceeding on to Biloxi, Arriola protested the settlement to the French commandant while enjoying good food and drink, the likes of which the Spanish settlement at Pensacola had not known in months. In reply to his protest, Arriola was informed that the French had occupied the region to frustrate the designs of the English. There was little the Spaniards could do but go back to the miserable settlement whence they had come. Three days after the return voyage was begun a hurricane drove three of the four vessels upon the coast. After days of suffering, the survivors regained the French fort, where they again were treated hospitably until vessels came from Pensacola to return them to the Spanish settlement. So ended the only offensive move the Spaniards were able to muster against the French colony of Louisiana.[26] The French had driven a wedge between the Spanish-held regions of Florida and northern Mexico.

When the imbecile king, Charles II, died in November, 1700, the young grandson of Louis XIV, Philip V, came to the Spanish throne. In the diplomatic maneuvering over the Louisiana question, Spain was forced to admit to her diminishing resources. The fact was justified by the rationalization that Spain should not attempt to prevent France from developing a region that she herself would never be able to utilize. Furthermore, the French, in forming the Louisiana settlement, had erected a barrier to the ever-advancing English. In Spanish eyes, it was better to yield ground to French Catholics than to English heretics.

In December, 1701, Iberville came to Pensacola, and Martínez permitted his four ships to enter the harbor. Then the French

[26] Ibid., pp. 200-205.

colonizer announced that he had orders from his king to occupy Mobile Bay ahead of the English. Martínez's report of the incident alarmed the Spanish War Council, but Philip V refused to be concerned. His disapproving response suppressed the zeal of the junta. To the French occupation of Louisiana, Spain tacitly acquiesced.

In straining at a gnat—La Salle's colony—Spain had swallowed a camel—Iberville's. The impotent threat posed by La Salle had spurred the Spaniards to new exploration and discovery from the Florida keys to Tampico, from La Junta de los Ríos to the Tejas country, from Apalache to the land of Tiqui Pache. But surprisingly little came of the effort. Pensacola was the only lasting settlement to result. The whole region of Texas now stood abandoned, as it had since the withdrawal of Father Massanet's disheartened friars in 1693. Near Paso de Francia on the Río Grande, where De León had blazed the trail on his way to find the devastated Fort St. Louis, a struggling mission settlement recently had come into being. Even this distant outpost, San Juan Bautista, eventually would be visited by French intruders, among them two of La Salle's survivors. Until it was, the area beyond would lie dormant, while the overspent viceregal government of New Spain waited in lethargy to feel the spur that would send her once again to new conquests.

21. LA SALLE'S REMNANTS

...I have reported that there is one Juan Larchevêque. In accordance with the order, condition and arrangement under which he came here, he is at present married, with sufficient means to live respectably, and is very loyal to his Majesty. He has accompanied me on this journey as a citizen, and as interpreter in his native tongue. He is ready to do whatever may be required in the royal service.

—Antonio de Valverde Cosío
Pichardo, *Treatise*, I, 194

Of the fifteen survivors of La Salle's ill-fated colony on the Texas coast, nine were captured by the Spaniards, the other six having returned to France. Of the six only Father Anastasius Douay, the Recollect friar remembered for the account he wrote of the 1684 La Salle expedition, appears again on the American scene. He returned to Louisiana with the Iberville expedition of 1699 and accompanied Iberville on explorations of the Louisiana coastal region.[1] The fate of the nine has been slow to emerge, and the full story is not found even today. Of those whose later life is known, that of Jean L'Archevêque is the most complete.

L'Archevêque was twenty-six years old at the time of La Salle's murder, in which he conspired. A servant of Duhaut, the actual murderer of the great explorer, L'Archevêque lured La Salle into the ambush from which he was shot.[2] Afterward he managed to warn Henri Joutel, La Salle's trusted lieutenant, of the danger to Joutel's own life, thereby forestalling further killing. Still later,

[1] B. F. French, *Historical Collections of Louisiana and Florida*, second series, 1527-1702, p. 45.
[2] Henri Joutel, *Joutel's Journal of La Salle's Last Voyage, 1684-7*, p. 134.

when the assassins had a falling-out among themselves, this coconspirator was saved from death by the intervention of Joutel and the two priests, Cavelier and Douay.

Having stated his intention of going with the group that was to return to France by way of Canada, L'Archevêque failed to show up at the appointed time, evidently preferring to remain among the Indians. But he and Jacques Grollet quickly tired of life among savages; when the opportunity arose, they sent messages to the Spaniards asking to be returned to civilization. This request eventually was granted in 1689 by De León, who took from the two captives the usual depositions and sent them on to Mexico City for further interrogation.

Shortly thereafter, the two Frenchmen were conducted to Spain on the ship of Captain Andrés de Pez. Though it seems natural to presume they were taken to the court of Charles II to give an account of the La Salle expedition, no such relation has come to light. They remained in the court jail until the summer of 1692, then returned with Pez to Mexico to enter the service of the king and accept their orders from the viceroy.

While they were in Spain, De León's 1690 expedition returned still more survivors to Mexico: Pierre Meunier, age twenty, and four of the Talon children. Meunier, and probably Pierre Talon, served the Terán expedition of 1691 as interpreters. This *entrada* brought back two more children, Jean Baptiste Talon and Eustache Bréman. All the children were sent to Mexico City and lived in the viceroy's household until the Conde de Galve died in 1696.[3]

The three men—Meunier, L'Archevêque, and Grollet—who would not have been permitted to return to their native France even if they had desired to, were allowed to become citizens of New Spain. While L'Archevêque and Grollet languished in the Spanish jail, preparations were made for the reconquest of New Mexico, which had been lost to the natives in the 1680 revolts.[4] Before they

---

[3] Pierre Margry (ed.), *Découvertes et établissements des Français dans l'Ouest et dans le Sud de l'Amérique septentrionale*, III, 610, 614.

[4] C. L. Sonnichsen, *Pass of the North: Four Centuries on the Rio Grande*, p. 64. Oakah L. Jones, Jr. (*Pueblo Warriors and Spanish Conquest*, p. 76) says L'Archevêque "had lived in New Mexico since 1691," an obvious error, since it has been shown in the preceding chapter that he and Grollet were still in Spain as late as July, 1692.

returned to New Spain, Diego de Vargas had taken over the government of New Mexico at El Paso del Norte.

The first Vargas expedition left El Paso on August 16, 1692. L'Archevêque and Grollet, too late for the first *entrada*, apparently hurried northward to join the second, which left the gateway settlement October 4, 1693. Despite some indication that Meunier was in Mexico at a later date, he must have joined them. In any event, all three were in Santa Fe by 1696. Meunier and L'Archevêque had come as soldiers, Grollet as a settler.

The following year L'Archevêque married Antonia Gutiérrez, a widow, and in 1701, while still serving as a soldier, he purchased a tract of land at Santa Fe. His wife died shortly afterward. In 1704 he was serving as a scout with Juan de Ulibarri. He was a member of a junta in 1714.[5]

L'Archevêque remained a widower until 1719, when he married the daughter of the alcalde mayor, Ignacio de Roybal, in the church of the pueblo of San Ildefonso. The governor of the province, Antonio Valverde Cosío, was a witness to the ceremony. "Captain Juan de Archibeque," as he now called himself, stood in high favor. Having served with honor in the military, he had retired to become a successful trader, his operations extending as far as Sonora, his business matters occasionally taking him even to Mexico City. Two sons, one by his first marriage, the other illegitimate, assisted him in the enterprise.[6] The conspirator in La Salle's murder had attained a position of high prominence and affluence. His views were influential with the government and the military; his new wife was the daughter of one of New Mexico's first families. But such a favored position would not endure long.

In the spring of 1720 the New Mexico governor, under orders from the viceroy, was making plans for a reconnaissance of the plains to the east, where it was said the French were thrusting westward with Pawnee Indian allies. Consulted by the governor, L'Archevêque advised that the expedition to block the intrusion by his countrymen be made at once. The campaign was organized with Don Pedro de Villasur placed in command of forty soldiers and seventy Indian auxiliaries. L'Archevêque was assigned to his

[5] Adolph F. Bandelier, *The Gilded Man*, p. 298; Jones, *Pueblo Warriors and Spanish Conquest*, pp. 76, 89.
[6] Bandelier, *The Gilded Man*, pp. 298-299.

staff as interpreter. The expedition marched from Santa Fe on June 16. In August it made camp "on the banks of a large river, which divided the nation of the Quartelejo Apaches, who are our allies, from that of the Pananas [Pawnees], who are allies of the French."[7]

Meeting envoys from the Pawnees, L'Archevêque had an unsatisfactory exchange of written messages with a French leader who the Indians said was among them, but whom he never saw; then the Spanish force withdrew for security to the south bank of the river.[8] On the morning of August 16, as the soldiers were saddling their horses, the Pawnees, perhaps guided and motivated by the French, as Valverde Cosío believed, fell upon the camp and wrought wholesale slaughter. Thirty-four Spaniards and eleven Indian auxiliaries died in the massacre, among them Villasur and L'Archevêque. The betrayer of La Salle thus died at the hands of his own countrymen or their allies on the first anniversary of his second wedding.[9]

Meunier filed written information on himself in the official records at Santa Fe in 1699, but nothing more is found concerning him. Grollet settled at Bernalillo, New Mexico, and married Elena Galuegos in 1699. He was still living six years later.[10]

While these three survivors figured in New Mexico history, two of the Talon brothers played a key role in that of Louisiana and Texas. Unfortunately, their activities can be viewed only in fragments, but enough information is available to alter some previous historical notions.

Parents of the Talon children who survived the French colony were Lucien and Isabelle Marchand Talon. Lucien, senior, a Canadian, probably was related in some way to the intendant of New France, Jean Baptiste Talon, whose name he gave to one of his sons. At least four of the family's six children were born in Canada.[11] The parents took them on La Salle's last voyage with grand

[7] Antonio de Valverde Cosío to the Viceroy, Marqués de Valero, October 8, 1720, in José Antonio Pichardo, *Pichardo's Treatise on the Limits of Louisiana and Texas,* I, 195.

[8] Probably the Arkansas, though considered by some to have been the North Platte.

[9] Valverde Cosío to the Viceroy, Pichardo, *Treatise,* I. 195-197; Jones, *Pueblo Warriors and Spanish Conquest,* p. 102 and n.

[10] Bandelier, *The Gilded Man,* pp. 294, 301. A recent Albuquerque, New Mexico, telephone directory listed 103 Gurules (Spanish version of Grollet) and 41 Archibecques.

[11] Cyprian Tanguay, *Dictionaire Généalogique des Familles Canadiennes depuis la Fondation de la Colonie Jusqu'à nos Jours,* I, 558.

visions of carving along the Mississippi River a new empire from which the children would reap the benefits. After the father's death, the mother sought for her youngest, also named Lucien, the special privileges granted by the king of France to the first born of the French colonists in America, as he had been born during the voyage from France.[12]

The oldest son, Pierre,[13] was not quite eleven when La Salle took him to the Tejas country to qualify him as an interpreter. When the survivors split and one group proceeded toward Canada, he remained among the Indians, with Pierre Meunier, who was ill at the time. By the time De León took them out three years later, in 1690, they had mastered the language beyond La Salle's expectations. While the knowledge failed to benefit the colonists of Fort St. Louis, it was to find utility otherwise.[14]

Pierre Talon, though he had sought to evade capture himself, asked De León to rescue his sister and three brothers living among the Clamcoëts (Karankawas).[15] De León did his best but had to leave one of the boys, Jean Baptiste, as well as Eustache Bréman, to be brought out a year later by General Terán.

When the Talon children reached Mexico, the viceroy's wife took them and Bréman into her household and made them her servants. Parkman relates superficially that Pierre and Jean Baptiste were enrolled in the Spanish navy, while their younger brothers and sister were taken by the viceroy to Spain.[16] Close examination of available French documents, however, reveals probable error in this statement.

The viceroy, Conde de Galve, died in office in 1696. Soon thereafter, it appears that all five of the children were embarked for Spain with a five-vessel fleet of the *armada de barlovento*. The three older boys sailed on one ship, while Marie Madelaine, and

[12] Joutel, *Journal*, p. 115.

[13] Pierre and Jean Talon, "Interrogations faites à Pierre et Jean Talon," in Margry, *Découvertes et établissements*, III, 611.

[14] That is, on the Spanish *entrada* of Domingo Terán de los Ríos in 1691 and the French expedition of Louis Juchereau de St. Denis in 1714, as will be seen. Joutel (*Journal*, p. 161) blames Meunier's fondness for "the course of Libertinism" for his remaining behind.

[15] Talon, "Interrogations," in Margry, *Découvertes et établissements*, III, 619.

[16] Francis Parkman, *La Salle and the Discovery of the Great West*, p. 333.

possibly the youngest boy, Lucien, accompanied the viceroy's widow on another.[17]

As the fleet coasted the Greater Antilles, it encountered the French squadron of M. Des Augers (or Desaugiers), and Captain Patoulet's ship, *Le Bon*, captured the Spanish vessel *Le Christ* on January 7, 1697. On board the captured ship were the three Talon brothers.[18]

The Sieur de Boissieux, who returned the repatriates to France "from the isles of America," interrogated Pierre and Jean Baptiste and wrote concerning them exactly one year later. The letter, dispatched from Morlaix, probably was addressed to the French minister of marine, Count Louis de Pontchartrain. Eustache Bréman, a paymaster's son, and Pierre Meunier, he related, still were in Mexico City, and the girl "presently is with the countess [the viceroy's widow]." One of the boys, Robert, who was younger than the two he had interrogated, was at Oleron.[19] He makes no mention of the youngest boy, Lucien, whose name has vanished from the record.

Boissieux, although he extracted considerable information from them, evidently found the Talon brothers shy, and cooperative only to a point. "They asked to be sent back to Spain, to be near the countess, by the Intendant [probably of Santo Domingo] did not wish it, nor did M. Desaugiers. They know nothing of the [Spanish] mines that they wish to tell."[20]

The minister of marine, on learning that the survivors of La Salle's colony had returned from New Spain, had immediate plans for them. Preparations were advancing rapidly for sending to America a new founding expedition under Pierre le Moyne, Sieur d'Iberville. Already Pontchartrain had learned of another survivor of the Texas colony "who has a precise account of the voyage made by the late Sieur de La Salle to the Gulf of Mexico in 1684." This man was Henri Joutel, who had taken employment as keeper

---

[17] "Lettre du sieur de Boissieux," in Margry, *Découvertes et établissements*, IV, 43, 44.

[18] Margry (*Découvertes et établissements*, IV, 44 n.) places the capture at "some distance from Santo Domingo." In ibid., III, 610, it is described as having occurred "before Havana." The ship *Le Christ* may well have been the *Santo Cristo de San Román*, which figured prominently in the Spanish search for La Salle's colony.

[19] "Lettre du sieur de Boissieux," in Margry, *Découvertes et établissements*, IV, 43.

[20] Ibid., p. 44.

of one of the city gates at Rouen. With this news the minister had written to the intendant at Rouen, asking him to obtain the journal and send it to him, adding, "You have my assurance that it will be returned in a month or six weeks."[21]

On receiving the journal, however, the minister sent it on to Iberville, who was to keep it with him during his voyage. Not until five years later was it returned, and then with part of it missing.[22] Pontchartrain wrote to Iberville of the journal, "I do not doubt that you will find it illuminating. I will try also to send you the man who wrote it." In this latter effort, however, Pontchartrain was to be frustrated, for "the historian of the 1684 enterprise did not wish to incur new risks."[23]

Pontchartrain also encountered frustration concerning his plans for the Talons. Having ordered the two brothers sent to Iberville at La Rochelle, he was provoked by the latter's dalliance, which resulted in miscarriage of the minister's intentions. Pierre and Jean, entering the roadstead at La Rochelle on June 7, aboard the *Ville d'Emden,* somehow were transferred to *La Gironde.* They sailed from the harbor on the second ship nine days later for an undetermined destination, without Iberville's having seen them. Pontchartrain expressed his disgust in a letter to Iberville: "It is your fault for not having removed them more promptly from the ship *Ville d'Emden.*"[24]

On order of Pontchartrain, the two Talons submitted on September 24 to a formal interrogation concerning the La Salle colony and their life among the Indians. The first question, directed at Pierre, concerned events surrounding the death of La Salle. Pierre told of the initial outburst of violence in the Texas wilds in much the same manner as had Joutel.[25] But he indicts "an Englishman named James [Hiens]" as the axe murderer of Nika, Moranget, and Saget, rather than the surgeon Liotot, and the younger Duhaut as the slayer of La Salle, instead of his

---

[21] Pontchartrain to M. de la Bourdonnaye, June 4, 1698, in Margry, *Découvertes et établissements,* IV, 50.

[22] Ibid., "Introduction," p. xxiii; Jean Cavelier, *The Journal of Jean Cavelier,* p. 12.

[23] Pontchartrain to Iberville, July 23, 1698, in Margry, *Découvertes et établissements,* IV, 72; ibid., "Introduction," p. xxiii.

[24] Pontchartrain to Iberville, June 25, 1698, ibid., p. 63.

[25] Joutel, *Journal,* p. 154.

older brother.[26] Hiens also is said to have lain in ambush for La Salle, in case he took a different route. Events following La Salle's death, as related by Pierre, differ considerably from Joutel's version.[27]

After the murders, Pierre relates, Duhaut established himself in command. Those who were to return to France then set out for Canada, preferring the wilderness to Duhaut's domination. They included La Salle's brother (the abbé); his young nephew, Cavelier, described as being only ten or twelve years old; Father Douay; "and two or three others."

Duhaut's rule was short-lived, however, for the assassins were divided among themselves. "Two or three days later" Hiens killed him with a pistol shot and replaced him in command. Hiens inspired the same kind of resentment among his followers as Duhaut had, and some days later he was slain by the sailor Ruter, who in turn was killed by the surgeon (Liotot).[28] "This surgeon, believing that someone else might do as much for him, removed himself to a nation of savages called Toho, close neighbors of the Cenis, who welcomed him, his gun, and ammunition."[29]

The surgeon, along with Pierre Talon, then joined the Tohos in their war with a nation called Paouïtes, or Lemerlauans. As the cowardly Tohos unexpectedly withdrew, the surgeon was left behind and killed. Talon escaped the same fate by fleeing on a horse the surgeon had given him before going into combat. The youth then returned to the Cenis village to remain with this nation until the Spaniards came, always in the company of Pierre Meunier. The others who remained in the wilderness became scattered among the natives.

Pierre Talon's version of the La Salle murders hardly casts doubt

[26] Talon, "Interrogations," in Margry, *Découvertes et établissements*, III, 610. The younger Duhaut, according to Joutel (*Journal*, p. 114), failed to return with the others from La Salle's expedition to the Cenis in September, 1686, and was presumed to have been killed by Indians. The Talon account cited here has been largely overlooked by historians. Robert Carlton Clark (*The Beginnings of Texas, 1684-1718*, pp. 20-31) draws from portions of it.

[27] Joutel, *Journal*, p. 154. Delanglez (Cavelier, *Journal*, p. 149 n.) says the few details given by the Talon children on La Salle's death agree with the corresponding ones related by Joutel. This is not entirely the case.

[28] Talon, "Interrogations," in Margry, *Découvertes et établissements*, III, 612.

[29] Ibid.

on Joutel's account, which charges Liotot with the three axe slay-
ings before La Salle was fatally shot by Duhaut. It does raise a
question concerning Talon's motives for the fabrication. It is rea-
sonable to speculate that the surgeon Liotot had served the Talon
family well, during the birth of one child and the fatal illness of
another, and Pierre could not bear—even after eleven years—to
speak of him as the villain he was.

Jean Baptiste Talon gives the only eye-witness account available
of the massacre at Fort St. Louis by the Clamcoëts, or Karankawas. These natives had harbored enmity for the French invaders
since La Salle, shortly after landing, had appropriated their canoes.
But they had assumed a guise of amity and, when they approached
the French settlement on the fatal day, they were received as
friends, in disregard of La Salle's explicit orders. It was the opportunity for vengeance that the Indians had long desired. They fell
upon the twenty to twenty-five persons in the settlement, ultimately killing all but the five children. These were rescued by the
Indian women who, moved to compassion by their youth, carried
them away on their backs.

The Talon children saw their mother slain before their eyes.
Their father having failed to return from an expedition, they never
knew the manner of his death. The older sister, Marie Elizabeth,
had succumbed to an illness in the settlement.

The Indian women also saved Madame Barbier, wife of the
officer whom La Salle had left in charge, who was nursing a three-
month-old baby. On returning to their village, however, the warriors killed her, then the infant by holding its feet and swinging its
head against a tree trunk. Yet the Talon children and Eustache
Bréman always were treated with the greatest kindness. Never
were they beaten or otherwise mistreated. "On the contrary, they
loved them tenderly and appeared to be extremely sorry when
someone caused them displeasure. They took their side on such
occasions, even against their own children."[30]

When the Spaniards came and took the first three children
away, Jean Baptiste relates, the Clamcoëts were moved to grief,
weeping bitter tears, even for a month afterward. When the Spaniards returned for the other two boys, the natives implored Talon

[30] Ibid., p. 617.

to escape his captors, steal their horses, and return to the Indians. He pledged his word, but without intention of keeping it, for he, too, longed to return to civilization.

In the conflict that grew out of the bartering of horses for the first three children, when several Indians were killed, the Clamcoëts showed themselves to be extremely afraid of firearms. Finally the Spaniards appeased them with tobacco, "which they like so much there is nothing they won't do to get it." They had been just as fearful, Jean Baptiste recalled, of the Frenchmen's drums that sounded the call to arms when the natives had resisted La Salle's confiscation of their canoes soon after landing. "By throwing themselves belly to ground, they believe they can avoid the blow of musket and cannonshot."[31]

Described in detail by the Talons is the method used by the Indians to tattoo them, a custom evidently followed by both the Tejas and the Karankawas. Charcoal, or black soot, was mixed with water, and the solution was injected into the skin and the flesh through many pricks of a sharp thorn. The process was excruciatingly painful to the victim, and the tattoos were impossible to remove. The marks were placed on the face, arms, hands, and "other parts of the body." When the Spaniards took the children from the natives, they tried "a hundred remedies" to remove the black streaks, but in vain.[32] The tattoos remained to serve as a passport for the two elder Talon brothers when, a quarter of a century later, they appeared once again among the Texas Indians.

The Talons learned the customs and language of the tribes with whom they hunted and went to war. They could shoot an arrow as true and run as fast as the Indians themselves, "which is to say, like a horse at a gallop," always keeping pace without tiring. They always went naked, and each morning at daybreak, regardless of season, they followed the native custom of bathing in the nearest river. They ate what the Indians ate, which often was meat from the hunt, either fresh or dried, but usually half raw. There was, however, one exception: human flesh. Jean Baptiste Talon found that the Karankawas liked to eat the flesh of their enemies. While

[31] Ibid., p. 620.
[32] Ibid., p. 615.

he never knew them to feed on the Frenchmen they had killed, he recalled going without food for three days rather than eat the flesh of the fallen "Ayennis," as the natives did.[33]

In some ways the Tejas, or Cenis, were scarcely less savage, as Pierre Talon found them. In making war upon their enemies, they observed no military discipline but relied solely on the element of surprise to carry their objective. They never attacked except at night or at daybreak and withdrew when it pleased them, without asking permission of their leader. They were prone to torture captives, and the warriors tore off the skin of their victim's head with the scalp, stuffing the skin with hay and hanging it at the ridgetop of their lodge as a trophy. Such human relics also were used in festivals, during which the victors carried them about exultantly as they danced and sang. Those who had the most scalps enjoyed the greatest esteem. In spite of this savagery, however, the Cenis accorded the most humane treatment to the French sojourners.

When the first Spanish expedition penetrated the Tejas country, L'Archevêque, whom Pierre Talon describes as being of good family and well educated, and Grollet gave themselves up. (The Talons saw them later in Mexico.) The others, including Talon and Meunier, chose to remain in the wilds. The Spaniards, relates Pierre Talon with a touch of hyperbole, came five hundred strong. They were armed with muskets, blunderbuses, and pistols, and all wore "coats of iron wire, made like nets, with small, strong stitches, to protect them from the savages' arrows." When the Spaniards returned the following year, this time with "no more than two hundred men," Talon and Meunier sought to flee but in so doing ran into De León's troop, were captured, and forced to lead their captors to the Cenis village.[34]

Finding these natives to their liking, the Spaniards left three Franciscan religious to establish missions, with some soldiers to guard them. The French youths observed the priests making a compilation of Indian words in an effort to learn the language. Since "the lieutenant"—Francisco Martínez—spoke fluent French, he was able to use the captives as interpreters of the Tejas idiom.

Impressed by the Spaniards' kindness, young Talon asked them

[33] Ibid., p. 616.
[34] Ibid., p. 618.

to rescue his sister and three brothers from the Clamcoëts and return them to civilization. De León, his business of assisting in the founding of Mission San Francisco de los Tejas finished, proceeded to the capture of Robert, Lucien, and Marie Madelaine Talon.[35]

According to the Talons, the Spaniards at this time also captured an Italian from among the Clamcoëts, but neither De León nor Massanet mentions him. Pierre Talon indicates he was of La Salle's company but endeavored to keep himself apart. The Abbé Prevost relates that the Spaniards "locked him up in prison from which place he probably did not leave" unless to work in the mines.[36]

Jean Baptiste Talon and Eustache Bréman remained with the Indians until 1691, when Martínez, making his third *entrada* with the Terán expedition, effected their rescue. At last all the Talon children and Bréman reached Mexico to serve in the viceroy's household until that official died in 1696.

Despite the initial desires of the minister Pontchartrain, Iberville departed from La Rochelle on his first voyage to Louisiana on September 5, 1698, without the Talon brothers. Of La Salle's survivors, only Father Anastasius Douay made the voyage. The Talons had been placed with two companies of Canadians, consisting of sixty-six men and three officers, one of whom was Louis Juchereau de St. Denis. In January, 1699, Pontchartrain ordered that the Canadian companies be kept in France, so they might be available as reinforcements for Iberville after he had made his discovery.[37]

On May 5, the Sieur de Bégon had a roll of the Canadians, then at Rochefort, drawn up. In addition to St. Denis, the list included "the celebrated Pierre and Jean Talon, survivors of the La Salle

---

[35] Ibid., pp. 619-620. The girl was given up by the Indians only after a fight. Fray Damián Massanet (to Don Carlos de Sigüenza, 1690, in Herbert Eugene Bolton, *Spanish Exploration in the Southwest, 1542-1706*, pp. 384-385) blames the conduct of De León's soldiers for provoking the affray, but Pierre Talon upholds the De León version (ibid., pp. 420-421): that the Indians, having agreed to exchange the prisoners for a horse, then threateningly demanded additional remuneration.

[36] Talon, "Interrogations," in Margry, *Découvertes et établissements*, III, 621; Pichardo, *Treatise*, I, 160.

[37] Marcel Giraud, *Histoire de la Louisiane Française*, I, 33.

expedition who once again were taking the road to Louisiana."[38] The Canadians were placed aboard *La Gironde* which, along with *La Renommée*, sailed from La Rochelle on Iberville's second expedition October 17, 1699, and arrived at Biloxi on February 9, 1700.[39]

"The celebrated Pierre and Jean Talon" were privates in the company of Canadians, and their destiny was Fort Maurepas, near present Ocean Springs, Mississippi. Their activities at this primitive outpost and their role in exploring the new land are not found. They next appear in a letter written by Iberville, at La Rochelle, to the Abbé Cavelier, more than four years later. The letter was in reply to an inquiry by La Salle's brother concerning the possibility that additional survivors of Fort St. Louis might remain alive among the Texas Indians. Iberville attached to his reply a summary of the testimony taken from the brothers in 1698.

Enclosed, Monsieur, is the extract from the report of Pierre and Jean Talon, two natives of Canada from a village near Québec, who were returned here from Mexico, and whom I had two years in Misisipy, in the King's pay. They were returned two years ago and presently are in the prisons of Portugal. I render testimony that they have assured me repeatedly that M. de Chedeville, the Recollect Fathers, and the others have been killed by the Savages. Thereafter, Fransisquo Martine, sergeant major of the fort of Pansacola, twenty leagues from Misisipy, where I have been for three months, commanded the last two expeditions which the viceroy of Mexico sent to aid the settlement they have made among the Cenis and on the seacoast. He has taken practically all the French from the hands of the Savages. I asked him for news of M. Chefdeville [*sic*], the Recollects, and Gabriel Minime, or Barbier, with whom I was

[38] Ibid.; Sieur de Bégon, "Rolle des canadiens passez de Plaisance en France pour servir sur les vaisseux que doivent aller à Mississipy pendent la putz, Anée 1699 avec leur solde par mois," Rochefort, May 5, 1699, French National Archives of Paris: Colonies, Documents Relating to France in the Mississippi Valley, 1699-1803 (A.C., C 13C, 2:15), pp. 64-67.

[39] Margry, *Découvertes et établissements*, IV, xliii. Estelle M. Fortier Cochran (*The Fortier Family and Allied Families*, p. 236) says, "In the Archives of Paris, we find Jean and Pierre Talon listed as first soldiers at Fort Maurepas, in a census list of August 2, 1699." I have not found the document referred to, but it appears to be in conflict with Bégon's list. The document file of the Louisiana State Museum Library in New Orleans lists Pierre Talon as "private of the Canadian army stationed at Fort Rochefort and transferred to Fort Maurepas on the Mississippi River in Louisiana, who embarked on the frigate *La Renommée*, commanded by M. d'Iberville."

acquainted. He assured me that these persons have been killed, and that by order of the King, he took from the Savages their breviaries and their chalices. From Misisipy I sent [a party] along the coast to the west without getting news that any Frenchmen remained. This I certify as the truth. La Rochelle, 3 May 1704.

D'Iberville

Captain of the King's vessels, knight of the military order of Saint-Louis, commandant for the King of Louisiana.[40]

Nothing more is heard of the Talons until ten years later, when two of them returned to Texas as members of the expedition of Louis Juchereau de St. Denis.[41] Their part in this important episode generally has been obscured, thanks to the mixing of fact and fiction by one André Pénicaut, with the emphasis on the latter.[42] Pénicaut wrote in the first person, claiming that he himself was on

[40]Pierre Le Moyne d'Iberville, "Lettre autographe à l'abbé Cavelier," May 3, 1704, in Margry, *Découvertes et établissements*, III, 622. The reconnaissance must have been made in 1702, when Francisco Martínez asked the Sieur de Bienville for "two or three Frenchmen" to accompany three Spaniards he was sending to examine the Texas coastal region (M. Duclos to Spanish officials at Veracruz, August 13, 1714, French National Archives of Paris: Colonies, Documents Relating to St. Denis and Florida, 1714-1718 [A.C., C 13, 3:675], p. 38). One of the Spaniards, Felipe Mendoza, reached San Juan Bautista in 1703, claiming to have fled from the three Frenchmen after they had killed his Spanish companion near the Texas coast (Robert S. Weddle, *San Juan Bautista: Gateway to Spanish Texas*, pp. 67-70).

[41]Giraud (*Histoire de la Louisiane Française*, I, 337) makes fleeting mention of a reconnaissance attempted by Jean and Pierre Talon toward the Madelaine River (Río Grande) prior to the St. Denis expedition of 1714. The inference is drawn that Antoine Crozat, holder of the Louisiana trade concession, had hopes of occupying the mouth of the Río Grande, and that the reported exploration was made in furtherance of such a plan.

[42]André Pénicaut, "Relation de Pénicaut," in Margry, *Découvertes et établissements*, V, 500-534. Several writers have perceived Pénicaut's unreliability. Perhaps the best assessment is made by Elizabeth McCann ("Pénicaut and His Chronicle of Early Louisiana," *Mid-America* 23, no. 4 [October, 1941]: 293), who says that Pénicaut's account of the Iberville expedition after it reached the gulf coast contains "so many omissions, distortions, and abbreviations as to render his account practically worthless." Unfortunately, this article covers only the years 1698-1704. Lester G. Bugbee ("The Real Saint-Denis," Texas State Historical Association, *The Quarterly* 1, no. 4 [April, 1898]: 267) detects Pénicaut's distortion of the St. Denis episode but still incorrectly credits him with being a member of the expedition. Writers who have been led astray by falsehoods in the narration are too numerous to mention. Ross Phares (*Cavalier in the Wilderness*) drew heavily, either directly or indirectly, from Pénicaut for his narration of the St. Denis expedition and St. Denis's biography. Richebourg Gaillard McWilliams translated the relation into English (*Fleur de Lys and Calumet*), giving no indication that he detected Pénicaut's falsity. I (*San Juan Bautista*, p. 100) succumbed to the oft-repeated error in names of the members of the St. Denis expedition, which stems from Pénicaut.

the expedition—which he was not—and fictionalizing names throughout. But the truth, as near as it can be determined, is found in a letter written by a Spanish officer on the Río Grande, reporting the arrival at his post of four Frenchmen: St. Denis, Medar Jalot, and Pierre and Robert Talon.[43]

At the time of the St. Denis expedition the East Texas mission field had been abandoned for twenty years. The most advanced Spanish outpost on the northeastern frontier was San Juan Bautista, the mission settlement on the Río Grande not far from Paso de Francia, where De León had crossed when seeking La Salle's colony. St. Denis's journey was made in response to a letter written from that post, inviting French participation in renewing religious activity among the Tejas. The writer of the letter was Father Francisco Hildago, who reluctantly had withdrawn in 1693 from the first East Texas missionary undertaking, and who had pledged himself to return to the unfinished task.[44]

The letter, written January 27, 1711, finally found its way to the French governor at Mobile, Antoine de la Mothe, Sieur Cadillac, two and a half years later. Cadillac, as commercial agent for the holder of the government trade concession, Antoine Crozat, saw in Hidalgo's proposal the possibility for opening an overland trade route with the provinces of northern Mexico. To accomplish this mission he sent St. Denis, commandant of the French post at Biloxi, with twenty-four men.

On reaching the Tejas, all but three of the twenty-four took leave to return to Mobile. Remaining with St. Denis were Medar Jalot and the two Talon brothers, Pierre and Jean. It was here that the Talons began to fulfill their important purpose on the expedi-

---

[43] Diego Ramón to Francisco Hidalgo, July 22, 1714, in Archivo Santa Cruz de Querétaro, K. Legajo 1, No. 7. Herbert Eugene Bolton ("The Location of La Salle's Colony on the Gulf of Mexico," *Southwestern Historical Quarterly* 27, no. 3 [January, 1924]: 175) says in reporting the capture of the Talons, "Just a quarter of a century later two of the boys, Jean and Robert Talon [*sic*], reappeared in Texas as guides of the famous St. Denis, when in 1714 he made his historic journey from Natchitoches to the Rio Grande." Bolton's vague citation is to "MS correspondence of St. Denis with the mission authorities of San Juan Bautista, 1714, and of Santa Cruz de Querétaro." I have found no other reference published in English to the Talons, in any combination, having accompanied St. Denis to the Río Grande. The two Talons with St. Denis probably were Pierre and Jean, instead of Pierre and Robert or Jean and Robert.

[44] For an account of Father Hidalgo's role in the episode see Weddle, *San Juan Bautista*, pp. 97-100.

tion. By the tattoo marks still on their faces, the Indians recognized them and accorded welcome.[45] Pierre, having first come to the Tejas to learn their language and having spent three years among them, undoubtedly retained some knowledge of their idiom.

St. Denis, failing to find Father Hidalgo among the Tejas as he had hoped, decided to push on to the Río Grande with his three companions. The Tejas chief, Bernardino, and twenty-five braves accompanied him, though all but four of the Indians turned back after repelling an attack by Karankawas on the Colorado River. The party of eight then proceeded to the Río Grande and the frontier mission settlement of San Juan Bautista.

In command of the Presidio de San Juan Bautista del Río Grande was Captain Diego Ramón, the old lieutenant of General Alonso de León, who undoubtedly had seen the Talon children when they were brought from East Texas. Father Hidalgo having retired to the missionary college at Querétaro two years previously, Ramón wrote to him on July 22, 1714, to apprise him of the arrival of the Frenchmen:

> You will be very glad to receive these lines, for in them I communicate to Your Reverance that in this Presidio are four Frenchmen: a Captain called Luis de Sn. Dionisio, another Pedro Talon and the other Roberto, who were among those recued by General Alonso de León. The Captain does not speak Spanish, nor does his other companion [Medar Jalot]. God has been served that my *cajero* should speak the French language. He has examined them in every way, and I say that if His Majesty (God keep him) does not intervene and the villages of the Naquitoies are not settled, the French will be masters of all this land.[46]

This letter, so many times overlooked by writers on the St. Denis expedition, shatters the illusion that the glib Pénicaut had any part in it, placing in his stead the Talon brothers. It also casts St. Denis in a different light; instead of the bold, confident cavalier who spoke fluent Spanish, he had to resort to an interpreter in

[45] Antoine de la Mothe, Sieur Cadillac to M. Raudot, April 10, 1714, in French National Archives of Paris: Colonies; Documents Relating to St. Denis and Florida, 1714-1718 (A.C., C 13, 3:469), p. 31; Charmion Clair Shelby, "International Rivalry in Northeastern New Spain, 1700-1725," p. 118.

[46] Ramón to Hidalgo, July 22, 1714.

order to address himself to Ramón. He undoubtedly found the Talon brothers, who had lived among the Spaniards six years, quite useful in this regard.

Once again the alarm capable of stirring officials of New Spain to action had sounded: the French threatened to lay claim to the vast, fertile region of Texas. The time had come to move. Out of the threat at last came the 1716 *entrada* to establish five missions in East Texas and one in present-day Louisiana (see Plate 14 in the picture section). Led by Captain Diego Ramón's son Domingo, it was accompanied by St. Denis himself, newly married to Don Diego's granddaughter, as guide and conductor of supplies. The Spaniards, as officials in faraway Mexico City saw it, were responding to a threat. But St. Denis cared only that he was bringing the Spaniards closer to his own base, in order to utilize them in his trade schemes.

"Like a good vassal in old feudal days, he served his immediate lords, Cadillac and Crozat, better than he served his king; and it is probable that if the government of either France or Spain had really understood what he was about, he would have been rewarded with a halter. But Spain owed him much; for he had given it possession of a goodly land. Thenceforth, until the Anglo Americans came, Texas followed the fortunes of Mexico."[47]

The Talon brothers, from all accounts, had long since returned to Mobile carrying letters to Cadillac.[48] When Domingo Ramón listed the members of his expedition, he included three Frenchmen: "Don Luis de San Dionisio, *cavo convoyador*, Don Juan de Medar and Don Pedro Largen."[49] But the Talons already had fulfilled their role in the grand plot, which was nothing more or less than the bartering of Texas to the Spaniards to establish illicit trade—surely one of the biggest real estate giveaways in history.[50]

---

[47] George P. Garrison, *Texas: A Contest of Civilizations*, p. 52.

[48] Louis Juchereau de St. Denis to Antoine de la Mothe, Sieur Cadillac, San Juan Bautista, February 21, 1715, in Margry, *Découvertes et établissements*, IV, 195. Cadillac ("Extrait des lettres de Lamothe-Cadillac," ibid., p. 198) reports the return of "the two men named Talon."

[49] Domingo Ramón, "Derrotero para las Misiones de los Presidios Internos," Archivo San Francisco el Grande, VIII, 70-71. Pedro (or Pierre) Largen was not among those whose arrival had been reported by Captain Diego Ramón; whence he had come is not explained.

[50] The ultimate destiny of the Talon children has been elusive. One source records that

France's claim to the land for which La Salle's hapless colonists had paid such a dear price was, for all practical purposes, ended forever.

Out of Spain's persistent search for the miserable little fort on a nebulous bay mistakenly called Espíritu Santo at last had come her right to vie with the natives for control of the region for a century. At the end of that period, citizens of the new American nation, brimming with ideals of Manifest Destiny—less euphemistically called greed—inherited the land and the problems that had defeated the minions of France, then of Spain, For the peoples who had gone before, and the tribulations they had suffered in blazing the trail, these newcomers could scarcely spare a backward glance.

Pierre died in France (*Who Was Who in America*, Historical Volume, 1607-1896, Revised Edition, p. 591). Of Lucien nothing is found after he was taken from the Indians by Alonso De León. Robert—probably the one who was at Oléron when Boissieux wrote of returning the three brothers from "the isles of America"—is mentioned by name only by Diego Ramón at San Juan Bautista, and that in error. Professor Marcel Giraud of the Collège de France in Paris, however, writes that Robert was settled in Mobile, 1719-1721: "He is listed as a *menuisier* (carpenter or joiner) on the Mobile parish register. He has married Jeanne Prot or Praux, from whom he had two children, born 5 January 1719, 4 October 1721. He is quoted on the same register as being godfather at a baptism at Mobile on April 6, 1722. The census of Mobile, June 28, 1721, shows him as an inhabitant of Mobile, owning 5 black slaves, 1 Indian slave, 2 horned cattle" (Marcel Giraud to author, letter, February 9, 1972).

Marie Madelaine, reported to have been still with the Spanish viceroy's widow in January, 1698, was married shortly thereafter to a Frenchman, Pierre Simon, of the St. Paul section of Paris. She gave birth to a son, also named Pierre, in 1699. The family probably took up residence in Canada, for the son married Marie Charlotte Bouvier at Charlesbourg on February 10, 1719. They later lived in Quebec (Tanguay, *Dictionaire Généalogique*, VII, 187-188).

BIBLIOGRAPHY

Unpublished Material

NOTE: The Archivo General de Indias, Dunn Transcripts, in The University of Texas Archives, Austin, are typescripts of original documents preserved in the Archivo General de Indias at Seville, Spain. Dates included in the citations are those under which the typescripts are filed, with the file numbers of the originals (old system) following in parenthesis. Typescripts from the French National Archives of Paris, Library of Congress Transcripts, are treated in the same manner.

Aguayo, Marqués de San Miguel de. Letter. Archivo General de Indias, Audiencia de México, 1685-1688 (61-6-20), Dunn Transcripts. The University of Texas Archives, Austin.
———. "Testimonio." Archivo General de Indias, Audiencia de México, 1685-1688 (61-6-20), Dunn Transcripts. The University of Texas Archives, Austin.
Alcano, Fray Martín de. "Certificación." Archivo General de Indias, Audiencia de México, 1678-1686 (61-6-20), Dunn Transcripts. The University of Texas Archives, Austin.
Amolar, Francisco de. Letter. Archivo General de Indias, Audiencia de México, 1685-1688 (61-6-20), Dunn Transcripts. The University of Texas Archives, Austin.
Arechaga, Juan de. Report of Junta. Archivo General de Indias, Audiencia de México, 1685-1688 (61-6-20), Dunn Transcripts. The University of Texas Archives, Austin.
Arroyo, Francisco Garcí de. Letters. Archivo General de Indias, Audiencia de México, 1678-1686, (61-6-20), Dunn Transcripts. The University of Texas Archives, Austin.
Astina, Antonio de. "Acuerdo." Archivo General de Indias, Audiencia de México, 1678-1686, (61-6-20), Dunn Transcripts. The University of Texas Archives, Austin.
———. Letter. Archivo General de Indias, Audiencia de México, 1685-1688 (61-6-20), Dunn Transcripts. The University of Texas Archives, Austin.
Astorga, Francisco Osorio de. "Auto de Acuerdo." Archivo General de Indias,

Audiencia de México, 1678-1686 (61-6-20), Dunn Transcripts. The University of Texas Archives, Austin.

——. Letter. Archivo General de Indias, Audiencia de México, 1678-1686 (61-6-20), Dunn Transcripts. The University of Texas Archives, Austin.

Ayala, Juan de. Report. Archivo General de Indias, Audiencia de México, 1685-1688 (61-6-20), Dunn Transcripts. The University of Texas Archives, Austin.

Barroto, Juan Enríquez, and Andrés de Pez. "Paracer de Pez y Barroto." Archivo General de Indias, Audiencia de México, 1685-1688, Dunn Transcripts. The University of Texas Archives, Austin.

Bastida, Pedro de la. "Repuesta." Archivo General de Indias, Audiencia de México, 1678-1686 (61-6-20), Dunn Transcripts. The University of Texas Archives, Austin.

——. "Repuesta del Fiscal." Archivo General de Indias, Audiencia de México, 1671-1685 (61-6-20), Dunn Transcripts. The University of Texas Archives, Austin.

——. "Repuesta del Señor Fiscal." Archivo General de Indias, Audiencia de México, 1678-1686 (61-6-20), Dunn Transcripts. The University of Texas Archives, Austin.

Bégon, Sieur de. "Rolle des canadiens passez de Plaisance en France pour servir sur les vaisseux que doivent aller à Mississipy pendent la putz, Anée 1699 avec leur solde par mois," French National Archives of Paris: Colonies. Documents Relating to France in the Mississippi Valley, 1699-1803 (A.C., C 13c, 2:15), Library of Congress Transcripts. The University of Texas Archives, Austin.

Brigaut, Nicolás. Confession ("Confesión del Capitán de la galeota de nación francés Corsario pirata" and "Otra ratificación"). Archivo General de Indias, Audiencia de México, 1671-1685 (61-6-20), Dunn Transcripts. The University of Texas Archives, Austin.

Cabrera, Juan Márquez. Letters. Archivo General de Indias, Audiencia de México, 1671-1685 (61-6-20), Dunn Transcripts. The University of Texas Archives, Austin.

——. Order ("Derrotero y Orden que ha de guardar Marcos Delgado que va al descubrimiento de la Bahía del Espíritu Santo"). Archivo General de Indias, Audiencia de México, 1671-1685 (61-6-20), Dunn Transcripts. The University of Texas Archives, Austin.

——. Reports. ("Autos" and "Ynforme"). Archivo General de Indias, Audiencia de México, 1671-1685 (61-6-20), Dunn Transcripts. The University of Texas Archives, Austin.

Cadillac, Antoine La Mothe, Sieur. Letter. French National Archives of Paris: Colonies. Documents Relating to St. Denis and Florida, 1714-1718 (A.C., C 13, 3:675), Library of Congress Transcripts. The University of Texas Archives, Austin.

Cárdenas y Magaña, Manuel de. "Diario." Archivo General de Indias, Audiencia de México, 1688-1690 (61-6-21), Dunn Transcripts. The University of Texas Archives, Austin.

Carrasco, Pedro Fernández. Diary ("Diario del Viaje"). Archivo General de Indias, Audiencia de México, 1688-1690 (61-6-20), Dunn Transcripts. The University of Texas Archives, Austin.

Castro, Diego de. "Testimonio." Archivo General de Indias, Audiencia de México, 1678-1686 (61-6-20), Dunn Transcripts. The University of Texas Archives, Austin.

Charles II of Spain. Decree ("Real Cédula"). Archivo General de Indias, Audiencia de México, 1678-1686 (61-6-20), Dunn Transcripts. The University of Texas Archives, Austin.

———. Letter. Archivo General de Indias, Audiencia de México, 1678-1686 (61-6-20), Dunn Transcripts. The University of Texas Archives, Austin.

De León, Alonso. "Declaración." Archivo General de Indias, Audiencia de México, 1685-1688 (61-6-20), Dunn Transcripts. The University of Texas Archives, Austin.

———. Letters. Archivo General de Indias, Audiencia de México, 1685-1688 and 1688-1690 (61-6-20), Dunn Transcripts. The University of Texas Archives, Austin.

———. Petition. Archivo General de Indias, Audiencia de México, 1678-1686 (61-6-20), Dunn Transcripts. The University of Texas Archives, Austin.

Delgado, Fructos. Reports of Junta. Archivo General de Indias, Audiencia de México, 1678-1686 (61-6-20), Dunn Transcripts. The University of Texas Archives, Austin.

Delgado, Marcos. Diary ("Derrotero"). Archivo General de Indias, Audiencia de México, 1671-1685 (61-6-20), Dunn Transcripts. The University of Texas Archives, Austin.

———. Letters. Archivo General de Indias, Audiencia de México, 1671-1685 (61-6-20), Dunn Transcripts. The University of Texas Archives, Austin.

Duclos, M. Letter. French National Archives of Paris: Colonies. Documents Relating to St. Denis and Florida, 1714-1718 (A.C., C 13, 3:675), Library of Congress Transcripts. The University of Texas Archives, Austin.

Durango, Juan de la Cruz. Letter. Archivo General de Indias, Audiencia de México, 1685-1688 (61-6-20), Dunn Transcripts. The University of Texas Archives, Austin.

Enríquez, Enrique. Report of Junta. Archivo General de Indias, Audiencia de México, 1688-1690 (61-6-21), Dunn Transcripts. The University of Texas Archives, Austin.

Evans, Glen L. "Notes on Fort St. Louis Excavation." Typescript. Texas Memorial Museum, The University of Texas, Austin.

Galve, Conde de, Viceroy. "Decreto," in "Testimonio de las Diligencias ejecutatadas para quitar las Boyas ó Valisas en el Lago de San Bernardo que llaman Bahía del Espíritu Santo." Archivo General de Indias, Audiencia de México, 1688-1690 (61-6-21), Dunn Transcripts. The University of Texas Archives, Austin.

Géry, Jean. Declarations ("Declaración," "Declaración del Prisionero," and "Segunda Declaración"). Archivo General de Indias, Audiencia de México,

1685-1688 (61-6-20), Dunn Transcripts. The University of Texas Archives, Austin.

Grollet, Jacques, with Jean L'Archevêque. Petitions. Archivo General de Indias, Audiencia de México, 1688-1690 (61-6-21), Dunn Transcripts. The University of Texas Archives, Austin.

Guzmán y Córdoba, Sebastián de. "Ynforme." Archivo General de Indias, Audiencia de México, 1678-1686 (61-6-20), Dunn Transcripts. The University of Texas Archives, Austin.

Iriarte, Pedro de, and Martín de Rivas. Letter. Archivo General de Indias, Audiencia de México, 1685-1688 (61-6-20), Dunn Transcripts. The University of Texas Archives, Austin.

Jordán de Reina, Juan. Diary ("Diario y derrotero del viaxe"). Archivo General de Indias, Audiencia de México, 1685-1688 (61-6-20), Dunn Transcripts. The University of Texas Archives, Austin.

Juntas. Reports to King (April 2 and June 18, 1686). Archivo General de Indias, Audiencia de México, 1685-1688 (61-6-20), Dunn Transcripts. The University of Texas Archives, Austin.

——. Reports ("Auto" and "Autos y diligencias"). Archivo General de Indias, Audiencia de México, 1685-1688, (61-6-20), Dunn Transcripts. The University of Texas Archives, Austin.

L'Archevêque, Jean, with Jacques Grollet. Petitions. Archivo General de Indias, Audiencia de México, 1688-1690 (61-6-21), Dunn Transcripts. The University of Texas Archives, Austin.

Ligaroa, Francisco, and Francisco de la Rocha. "Repuesta de oficiales reales." Archivo General de Indias, Audiencia de México, 1671-1685 (61-6-20), Dunn Transcripts. The University of Texas Archives, Austin.

Llanos, Francisco de. "Diario y derrota del Viaje que se hecho y Ejecutado a la Bahía de San Bernardo." Archivo General de Indias, Audiencia de México, 1688-1690 (61-6-21), Dunn Transcripts. The University of Texas Archives, Austin.

Marmolejo, Francisco Fernández de. Letter. Archivo General de Indias, Audiencia de México, 1685-1688 (61-6-20), Dunn Transcripts. The University of Texas Archives, Austin.

Mateos, Antonio. Letter. Archivo General de Indias, Audiencia de México, 1671-1685 (61-6-20). The University of Texas Archives, Austin.

Meunier, Pierre. Declaration. Archivo General de Indias, Audiencia de México, 1688-1690 (61-6-21), Dunn Transcripts. The University of Texas Archives, Austin.

Monclova, Conde de la, Viceroy. Letters. Archivo General de Indias, Audiencia de México, 1685-1688 and 1688-1690 (61-6-20), Dunn Transcripts. The University of Texas Archives, Austin.

Morales, Antonio de. Report of Junta ("Junta General"). Archivo General de Indias, Audiencia de México, 1678-1686 (61-6-20), Dunn Transcripts. The University of Texas Archives, Austin.

Munibe, Andrés de. Letters. Archivo General de Indias, Audiencia de México,

1678-1686 (61-6-20), Dunn Transcripts. The University of Texas Archives, Austin.

Munibe, Manuel. "Testimonio." Archivo General de Indias, Audiencia de México, 1678-1686 (61-6-20), Dunn Transcripts. The University of Texas Archives, Austin.

Navarro, Francisco de. Instructions. Archivo General de Indias, Audiencia de México, 1685-1688 (61-6-20), Dunn Transcripts. The University of Texas Archives, Austin.

——. Letters. Archivo General de Indias, Audiencia de México, 1685-1688 (61-6-20), Dunn Transcripts. The University of Texas Archives, Austin.

——. Reports ("Relación de las dos piraguas" and "Razón de lo que llevan las dos piraguas"). Archivo General de Indias, Audiencia de México, 1685-1688 (61-6-20), Dunn Transcripts. The University of Texas Archives, Austin.

Nicolás, Jorge. "Testimonio." Archivo General de Indias, Audiencia de México, 1678-1686 (61-6-20), Dunn Transcripts. The University of Texas Archives, Austin.

Novóa y Salgado, Benito de. "Parecer." Archivo General de Indias, Audiencia de México, 1688-1690 (61-6-21), Dunn Transcripts. The University of Texas Archives, Austin.

Otálora, Joseph de Murueta. Letters. Archivo General de Indias, Audiencia de México, 1678-1686 (61-6-20), Dunn Transcripts. The University of Texas Archives, Austin.

——. Report of Council. Archivo General de Indias, Audiencia de México, 1688-1690 (61-6-21), Dunn Transcripts. The University of Texas Archives, Austin.

Palacios, Gaspar de. Instructions ("Ynstrucción y Derrota"). Archivo General de Indias, Audiencia de México, 1678-1686 (61-6-20), Dunn Transcripts. The University of Texas Archives, Austin.

——. Letters. Archivo General de Indias, Audiencia de México, 1678-1686 (61-6-20), and 1685-1688 (61-6-20), Dunn Transcripts. The University of Texas Archives, Austin.

——. Report. Archivo General de Indias, Audiencia de México, 1685-1688 (61-6-20), Dunn Transcripts. The University of Texas Archives, Austin.

Pez, Andrés de. Letter. Archivo General de Indias, Audiencia de México, 1685-1688 (61-6-20), Dunn Transcripts. The University of Texas Archives, Austin.

——, and Juan Enríquez Barroto. "Paracer de Pez y Barroto." Archivo General de Indias, Audiencia de México, 1685-1688 (61-6-20), Dunn Transcripts. The University of Texas Archives, Austin.

——, and Martín de Rivas. Letter. Archivo General de Indias, Audiencia de México, 1688-1690 (61-6-20), Dunn Transcripts. The University of Texas Archives, Austin.

Quiroga y Losada, Diego de. "Auto sobre el mulato de Arguelles." Archivo General de Indias, Audiencia de México, 1685-1688 (61-6-20), Dunn Transcripts. The University of Texas Archives, Austin.

Ramón, Diego. Letter. Archivo Santa Cruz de Querétaro, K, Legajo 1, Number 7. Transcript courtesy The Bancroft Library, University of California, Berkeley.

Ramón, Domingo. Diary ("Derrotero para las Misiones de los Presidios Internos"). Archivo San Francisco el Grande, VIII. Photostat copy in The University of Texas Archives, Austin.

Rivas, Martín de. Letter. Archivo General de Indias, Audiencia de México, 1685-1688 (61-6-20), Dunn Transcripts. The University of Texas Archives, Austin.

——, and Pedro de Iriarte. Letter. Archivo General de Indias, Audiencia de México, 1685-1688 (61-6-20), Dunn Transcripts. The University of Texas Archives, Austin.

Rocha, Francisco de la, and Francisco de Ligaroa. "Repuesta de oficiales reales." Archivo General de Indias, Audiencia de México, 1671-1685 (61-6-20), Dunn Transcripts. The University of Texas Archives, Austin.

Ronquillo, Pedro de. "Copía de la Relación hecha al Rey Xpmo tocante a la Bahía del Espíritu Santo." Archivo General de Indias, Audiencia de México, 1685-1688 (61-6-20), Dunn Transcripts. The University of Texas Archives, Austin.

Saliases, Juan de. "Declaración." Archivo General de Indias, Audiencia de Guadalajara (New Mexico), 1683-1687 (67-4-11). Transcript, The University of Texas Archives, Austin.

Salinas Varona, Gregorio de. Declaration. Archivo General de Indias, Audiencia de México, 1688-1690 (61-6-21), Dunn Transcripts. The University of Texas Archives, Austin.

Seignelay, Marquis de. Letters ("Letters Translated from the French Language"). Archivo General de Indias, Audiencia de México, 1678-1686 (61-6-20), Dunn Transcripts. The University of Texas Archives, Austin.

Shelby, Charmion Clair. "International Rivalry in Northeastern New Spain, 1700-1725." Ph.D. dissertation, The University of Texas, Austin, 1935.

Thomas, Denis. "Declaración." Archivo General de Indias, Audiencia de México, 1678-1686 (61-6-20), Dunn Transcripts. The University of Texas Archives, Austin.

Vélez, Marqués de los. Report of Junta ("Junta de Guerra de las Yndias"). Archivo General de Indias, Audiencia de México, 1685-1688 (61-6-20), Dunn Transcripts. The University of Texas Archives, Austin.

Ventosa, Pedro Fernández de la. Letter. Archivo General de Indias, Audiencia de México, 1685-1688 (61-6-20), Dunn Transcripts. The University of Texas Archives, Austin.

Vera, Juan Felipe de. "Declaración." Archivo General de Indias, Audiencia de México, 1685-1688 (61-6-20), Dunn Transcripts. The University of Texas Archives, Austin.

Wilkinson, Ralph. Declarations (Havana, August 29, 1687; Veracruz, October 21, 1687; Mexico City, November 21, 1687). Archivo General de Indias, Audiencia de México, 1685-1688 (61-6-20), Dunn Transcripts. The University of Texas Archives, Austin.

Published Works

Alessio Robles, Vito. *Coahuila y Texas en la época colonial.* Mexico City: Editorial Cultura, 1938.

Arricivita, Juan Domingo. *Crónica seráfica y apostólica del Colegio de propaganda fide de la Santa Cruz de Querétaro en la Nueva España, segunda parte.* Mexico City: F. de Zuñiga y Ontiveros, 1792.

Ayer, Mrs. Edward E., trans. *See* Alonso de Benavides, *The Memorial of Fray Alonso de Benavides, 1630.*

Bancroft, Hubert Howe. *History of the North Mexican States and Texas.* Two volumes. San Francisco: A. L. Bancroft & Company, 1889.

Bandelier, Adolph. *The Gilded Man.* New York: D. Appleton and Company, 1893.

Bannon, John Francis, ed. *See* Herbert Eugene Bolton, *Bolton and the Spanish Borderlands.*

Benavides, Alonso de. *Benavides' Memorial of 1630.* Translated by Peter P. Forrestal, with historical introduction and notes by Cyprian J. Lynch. Washington, D.C.: Academy of American Franciscan History, 1954.

———.*The Memorial of Fray Alonso de Benavides, 1630.* Translated by Mrs. Edward E. Ayer; annotated by Frederick Webb Hodge and Charles Fletcher Lummis. Albuquerque: Horn and Wallace, Publishers, 1965.

Bolton, Herbert Eugene. *Bolton and the Spanish Borderlands.* Edited with an introduction by John Francis Bannon. Norman: University of Oklahoma Press, 1964.

———. "The Location of La Salle's Colony on the Gulf of Mexico." *Southwestern Historical Quarterly* 27, no. 3 (January, 1924): 171-189.

———. *The Spanish Borderlands: A Chronicle of Old Florida and the Southwest.* New Haven: Yale University Press, 1921.

———, ed. *Spanish Exploration in the Southwest, 1542-1706.* New York: Charles Scribner's Sons, 1908.

Boyd, Mark F. "The Expedition of Marcos Delgado from Apalachee to the Upper Creek Country in 1686." *Florida Historical Quarterly* 16, no. 1 (July, 1937): 2-32.

———,Hale G. Smith, and John W. Griffin. *Here They Once Stood: The Tragic End of the Apalachee Missions.* Gainesville: University of Florida Press, 1951.

Bugbee, Lester G. "The Real Saint-Denis." Texas State Historical Association, *The Quarterly* 1, no. 4 (April, 1898): 266-281.

Canedo, Lino Gómez ed. *Primeras exploraciones y poblamiento de Texas (1686-1694).* Monterrey: Instituto Tecnológico y de estudios superiores de Monterrey, 1968.

———, ed. *See* Fray Isidro Félix de Espinosa, *Crónica de los colegios de propaganda fide de la Nueva España.*

Carroll, H. Bailey, and Walter Prescott Webb, eds. *The Handbook of Texas.* Two volumes. Austin: The Texas State Historical Association, 1952.

Castañeda, Carlos Eduardo. *Our Catholic Heritage in Texas.* Seven volumes. Austin: Von Boeckmann-Jones Company, 1936-1950.

——, trans. *See* Juan Agustín Morfi, *History of Texas, 1673-1779*.

Cavelier, Jean. *The Journal of Jean Cavelier: The Account of a Survivor of La Salle's Texas Expedition, 1684-1688*. Translated and annotated by Jean Delanglez. Chicago: Institute of Jesuit History, 1938.

Clark, Robert Carlton. *The Beginnings of Texas, 1684-1718*. Bulletin no. 98, Humanistic Series no. 6. Austin: The University of Texas, 1907.

——. "Louis Juchereau de Saint Denis and the Re-establishment of the Tejas Missions." Texas State Historical Association, *The Quarterly* 6, no. 1 (July, 1902): 1-26.

Cochran, Estelle M. Fortier. *The Fortier Family and Allied Families*. N.p., 1963.

Delanglez, Jean, trans. *See* Jean Cavelier, *The Journal of Jean Cavelier*.

De León, Alonso, Juan Bautista Chapa, and Fernando Sánchez de Zamora. *Historia de Nuevo León, con noticias sobre Coahuila, Tamaulipas, Texas y Nuevo Mexico*. Monterrey: Biblioteca de Nuevo León, 1961.

Dunn, William Edward. *Spanish and French Rivalry in the Gulf Region of the United States, 1678-1702: The Beginnings of Texas and Pensacola*. Bulletin no. 1705, Studies in History no. 1. Austin: The University of Texas, 1917.

——. "The Spanish Search for La Salle's Colony on the Bay of Espiritu Santo, 1685-1689." *Southwestern Historical Quarterly* 19, no. 4 (April, 1916): 323-369.

Espinosa, Fray Isidro Félix de. *Crónica de los colegios de propaganda fide de la Nueva España*. New edition with notes and introduction by Lino G. Canedo. Madrid: Academy of American Franciscan History, 1964.

Esquemeling, John. *The Buccaneers of America*. New York: Dover Publications, Inc., 1967.

Fernández Duro, Cesareo. *Don Diego de Peñalosa y su descubrimiento del reino de Quivira: Informe presentado a la Real Academia de la Historia*. Madrid: Imprenta y Fundición de Manuel Tello, 1882.

Folmer, Henry. *Franco-Spanish Rivalry in North America, 1524-1763*. Glendale: Arthur H. Clark Company, 1953.

Forbes, Jack D. *Apache, Navaho, and Spaniard*. Norman: University of Oklahoma Press, 1960.

Forrestal, Peter P., trans. *See* Alonso de Benavides, *Benavides' Memorial of 1630*.

French, B. F. *Historical Collections of Louisiana and Florida, Including Translations of Original Manuscripts Relating to Their Discovery*. Second series, 1527-1702. New York: Albert Mason, 1875.

——. *Historical Collections of Louisiana and Florida, Including Translations of Original Manuscripts Relating to Their Discovery*. New series. New York: J. Sabin and Sons, 1869.

Garcilaso de la Vega. *The Florida of the Inca*. Translated and edited by John Grier Varner and Jeannette Johnson Varner. Austin: University of Texas Press, 1951.

Garrison, George P. *Texas: A Contest of Civilizations*. Boston: Houghton Mifflin Company, 1903.

Gil Munilla, Roberto. "Política española en el Golfo Mexicano: Expediciones motivados por la entrada del Caballero La Salle (1685-1707)," *Anuario de Estudios Americanos* (Seville), 12 (1955): 476-611.

Giraud, Marcel. *Histoire de la Louisiane Française.* Three volumes. Paris: Presses Universitaires de France, 1953.

Gómez Raposo, Luis. "Diario del descubrimiento que hizo el Capitán Don Andrés del Pez (Año de 1687)," *Colección de diarios y relaciones para la historia de los viajes y descubrimientos*, IV, 115-150. Madrid: Instituto Histórico de Marina, 1944.

Hackett, Charles Wilson, ed. *Historical Documents Relating to New Mexico, Nueva Vizcaya, and Approaches Thereto, to 1773.* Two volumes. Washington: Carnegie Institution, 1923, 1926.

———, ed. *See* José Antonio Pichardo, *Pichardo's Treatise on the Limits of Louisiana and Texas.*

Haring, C. H. *The Buccaneers in the West Indies in the XVII Century.* London: Methuen Company, Ltd., 1910.

Hatcher, Mattie Austin, trans. *The Expedition of Don Domingo Terán de los Ríos into Texas.* Preliminary Studies, vol. 2, no. 1. Austin: Texas Catholic Historical Society, 1932.

Institute of Texan Cultures. *The Indian Texans.* San Antonio: The University of Texas Institute of Texas Cultures, 1970.

Jones, Oakah L., Jr. *Pueblo Warriors and Spanish Conquest.* Norman: University of Oklahoma Press, 1966.

Joutel, Henri. *Joutel's Journal of La Salle's Last Voyage, 1684-7.* Edited with a biographical introduction by Henry Reed Stiles. Albany, New York: Joseph McDonough, 1906.

Le Clercq, Christian. *First Establishment of the Faith in New France.* Two volumes. Translated, with notes, by John Gilmary Shea. New York: John G. Shea, 1881 (first published in French, Paris: Amable Auroy, 1691, with royal privilege).

Leonard, Irving A. ed. and trans. *Spanish Approach to Pensacola, 1689-1693.* Albuquerque: The Quivira Society, 1939. Republished, New York: Arno Press, 1967.

———. "The Spanish Re-exploration of the Gulf Coast in 1686," *Mississippi Valley Historical Review* 22, no. 4 (March, 1936): 547-557.

McCann, Elizabeth. "Pénicaut and His Chronicle of Early Louisiana." *Mid-America* 23, no. 4 (October, 1941): 288-304.

McWilliams, Richebourg Gaillard. *Fleur de Lys and Calumet.* Baton Rouge: Louisiana State University Press, 1953.

Margry, Pierre, ed. *Découvertes et établissements des Français dans l'Ouest et dans le Sud de l'Amérique septentrionale.* Five volumes. Paris: Imprimiere de D. Jouaust, 1876-1886.

Miller, E. T. "The Connection of Peñalosa with the La Salle Expedition." Texas State Historical Association, *The Quarterly* 5, no. 2 (October, 1901): 97-112.

Morfi, Fray Juan Agustín. *History of Texas, 1673-1779.* Translated and annotated by Carlos E. Castañeda. Two volumes. Albuquerque: The Quivira Society, 1935.

Morison, Samuel Eliot. *The European Discovery of America: The Northern Voyages, A.D. 500-1600.* New York: Oxford University Press, 1971.

Navarrete, Martín Fernández de. *Colección de los viages y descubrimientos que hicieron por mar los Españoles desde fines del siglo XV, con various documentos inéditos concernientes á la historia de la marina castellana y de los establecimientos españoles en Indias.* Five volumes. Madrid, 1825-1837.

O'Connor, Kathryn Stoner. *The Presidio La Bahia del Espiritu Santo de Zuniga, 1721-1846.* Austin: Von Boeckmann-Jones Company, 1966.

O'Donnell, Walter J. *La Salle's Occupation of Texas.* Preliminary Studies, vol. 3, no. 2. Austin: Texas Catholic Historical Society, 1936.

Parkman, Francis. *La Salle and the Discovery of the Great West.* New York: The New American Library of World Literature, 1963.

Phares, Ross. *Cavalier in the Wilderness: The Story of the Explorer and Trader Louis Juchereau de St. Denis.* Baton Rouge: Louisiana State University Press, 1952.

Pichardo, José Antonio. *Pichardo's Treatise on the Limits of Louisiana and Texas.* Translated into English by Charles Wilson Hackett, Charmion Clair Shelby, and Mary Ruth Splawn; edited and annotated by Charles Wilson Hackett. Four volumes. Austin: University of Texas Press, 1931-1934.

Sonnichsen, C. L. *Pass of the North: Four Centuries on the Rio Grande.* El Paso: Texas Western Press, 1968.

Spain, Consejo Superior de Invistigaciones Científicos. *Colección de diarios y relaciones para la historia de los viajes y descubrimientos.* Fifty volumes. Madrid: Instituto Histórico de Marina, 1943-.

Stiles, Henry Reed, ed. *See* Henri Joutel, *Joutel's Journal of La Salle's Last Voyage, 1684-7.*

Tanguay, Cyprian. *Dictionnaire Généalogique des Familles Canadiennes depuis la Fondation de la Colonie Jusqu'à nos Jours.* Seven volumes. Quebec (I) and Montreal (II-VII): E. Senécal & Fils, 1871-1880.

Varner, John Grier, and Jeannette Johnson Varner, trans. *See* Garcilaso de la Vega, *The Florida of the Inca.*

Webb, Walter Prescott, and H. Bailey Carroll, eds. *The Handbook of Texas.* Two volumes. Austin: The Texas State Historical Association, 1952.

Weddle, Robert S. *San Juan Bautista: Gateway to Spanish Texas.* Austin: University of Texas Press, 1968.

———. *The San Sabá Mission: Spanish Pivot in Texas.* Austin: University of Texas Press, 1964.

Who Was Who in America. Historical Volume, 1607-1896, revised edition. Chicago: Marquis-Who's Who, 1967.

INDEX

Acosta, Gaspar de: 29-30, 32-33
Agreda, María de Jesús de: 205 n.
Aguayo, Marqués de San Miguel de: pursues land expedition, 53; seeks knowledge of northern region, 56; and first De León expedition, 57, 59, 64; report of, to viceroy, 91; gets news of white invaders, 166 n.-167 n.
Aguayo, Marqués de San Miguel de (second): 224
Aigron, Sieur d': and grounding of ship, 3, 99, 191
Aimable (supply vessel): on voyage to America, 2-3; wreck of, 3, 99, 197, 202, 223; remnants of, found by Spaniards, 98, 99 and n., 153, 190, 191; not observed by Gamarra and Pez, 111; Fort St. Louis built from timbers of, 209; in Meunier testimony, 217, 218 and n., 219
Aixaos (province): 17-18
Alabama: Spanish exploration in, xi, 80 and n.; Delgado and, 79, 87
Alabama Indians: 79 n., 83
Alabama River: 81, 82 n.
Alasapa Indians: 175
Alcano, Martín de (Fray): 45, 47
Alexander VI (Pope): 37, 188
Alonso (Indian): 60
Amichel: ix-x, 25
Anacacho Mountain: 134 n.
Antigua Veracruz: 31 n.
Antilles: 37
Antimuqua (province): 47
Antis, Juan: 11 n.
Apache Indians: 165
Apalache: in Echagaray proposal, 9 n,; in Pineda exploration, 25; and Espíritu Santo Bay, 25, 26; as starting point for search, 27, 29 and n.; and Corso shipwreck, 43, 44; Barroto-Romero expedi-

tion at, 47, 48, 67; and Delgado expedition, 75-76; Mateos from, 85; pirates and runaway slave at, 127; Torres expedition at, 239, 240; mentioned, 77, 244 n., 248. *See also* San Luis de Apalache, Presidio of
Apalache, Cape of: mentioned by Benavides, 17; on reconnaissance route, 30, 33; described by Gómez, 115 and n.
Apalache, Port of: 26
Apalachee Bay: ix, x
Apalachian Indian: 100
Apalachicola, Port of: 29 and n., 30-31
Apalachicola confederacy: 68
Apalachicola River: English trading activities on, 47; Barroto-Romero expedition passes, 48; Corso survivors on, 49; Delgado crosses, 78, 79, 80, 81
Apalachino Indians: 78, 82, 85
Ape (Hape) Indians: 177
Aqchay (Chocata village): 81
Aramburu, Joseph de: 226
Aranda y Avellaneda, Pedro de: 70, 86
Aransas Bay: 110
Archevêque. *See* L'Archevêque, Jean
Arguelles, Antonio: 70
Arguelles, Diego: 70
Arkansas Post: 211
Arkansas River: 252 n.
armada de barlovento (windward fleet): captures pirate vessel, 7; repair of, 28, 35, 95; Barroto officer in, 29; limited capabilities of, 88, 89; in maritime search, 91, 92, 93; Pez made admiral of, 237; Talons sail for Europe with, 253
armor, of Spaniards: 259
Arrecife de Alacrán: 116
Arriola, Andrés de: unable to lead search, 93; heads Pensacola enterprise, 241-247 *passim*